ON BORDERS

ON BORDERS

PERSPECTIVES ON INTERNATIONAL
MIGRATION IN SOUTHERN AFRICA

Edited by David A. McDonald

SOUTHERN AFRICAN MIGRATION PROJECT
ST. MARTIN'S PRESS
2000

© Southern African Migration Project 2000

First published in Southern Africa 2000 by
Southern African Migration Project
11 St. Lawrence Avenue, Kingston, Ontario, K7L 3N6, Canada
ISBN 1-874864-94-2

First published in North America 2000 by
St. Martin's Press
175 Fifth Avenue, New York NY 10010
ISBN 0-312-23268-3

Copy edited by Michail Rassool
Layout by Sandie Vahl
Typeset in Stone
Cover design by Graham Hankin

The map on the cover is entitled "Aethiopia inferior, vel exterior", drawn by Joan Blaeu in 1663, and is reproduced from "Africa: On Maps Dating from the Twelfth to the Eighteenth Century", Egon Klemp (ed.), Edition Leipzig, Leipzig, 1968.

All rights reserved. No part of this publication may be reproduced or transmitted, in any form or by any means, without prior permission from SAMP.

Reproduction by Mega Pre-Press, Cape Town
Bound and printed by Creda Press, Cape Town
Print consultants: Mega Print, Cape Town

Library of Congress Cataloging-in-Publication data applied for.

The Southern African Migration Project (SAMP) is a partnership between Queen's University, Idasa, Arpac, Sechaba Consultants and the Universities of Botswana, Namibia and Zimbabwe. SAMP is funded by the Canadian International Development Agency (CIDA).

Contents

List of tables and figures … viii
List of contributors … xii
Acknowledgements … xiii
Note on terminology … xiv

Introduction
Towards a better understanding of cross-border migration in Southern Africa
David A. McDonald … 1

Chapter One
Migrations past: An historical overview of cross-border movement in Southern Africa
Jonathan Crush … 12

Chapter Two
Lesotho and South Africa: Time for a new immigration compact
John Gay … 25

Chapter Three
Labour migration to South Africa: The lifeblood for southern Mozambique
Fion de Vletter … 46

Chapter Four
Who, what, when and why: Cross-border movement from Zimbabwe to South Africa
Lovemore Zinyama … 71

Chapter Five
Namibians on South Africa: Attitudes towards cross-border migration and immigration policy
Bruce Frayne and Wade Pendleton … 86

Chapter Six
Women on the move: Gender and cross-border migration to South Africa from Lesotho, Mozambique and Zimbabwe
Belinda Dodson … 119

Chapter Seven
What about the future? Long-term migration potential to South Africa from Lesotho, Mozambique and Zimbabwe
Donald M. Taylor and Kelly Barlow   151

Chapter Eight
The lives and times of African migrants and immigrants in post-apartheid South Africa
David A. McDonald, Lephophotho Mashike and Celia Golden   168

Chapter Nine
South African attitudes to immigrants and immigration
Robert Mattes, Donald M. Taylor, David A. McDonald, Abigail Poore and Wayne Richmond   196

Appendix A
Research methodology for the surveys in Lesotho, Mozambique, Zimbabwe and Namibia   219

Appendix B
Aggregate summary of results from surveys in Lesotho, Mozambique, Zimbabwe and Namibia   225

Appendix C
Aggregate summary of results from surveys of African migrants living in South Africa   267

Index   292

LIST OF TABLES AND FIGURES

Introduction
Figure 1:   Map of Southern African countries surveyed   4

Chapter One
Table 1.1:   Family history of migration to South Africa   13
Table 1.2:   Contract migration to the South African gold mines, 1920–1995   15
Table 1.3:   Miners' permanent residence applications for 1995 amnesty   16
Table 1.4:   Foreign-born Africans in South Africa, 1911–1985   18
Table 1.5:   Foreign-born African women in South Africa, 1960–1985   19
Table 1.6:   Country of birth of whites in South Africa, 1960–1991   20

Chapter Two
Table 2.1:   A profile of the sample population in Lesotho   27
Table 2.2:   Percentage of respondents who have visited South Africa at least once in their lives   28
Table 2.3:   Visits to South Africa in lifetime   28
Table 2.4:   Percentage of respondents who have worked in South Africa   29
Table 2.5:   Reasons for most recent visit to South Africa   30
Table 2.6:   Reasons for return to home country after most recent visit to South Africa   31
Table 2.7:   Attitudes towards borders   32
Table 2.8:   Attitudes towards rights of foreigners in South Africa   33
Table 2.9:   Willingness to allow Southern Africans into one's own country   34
Table 2.10:   Expected level of good treatment by South Africans   35
Table 2.11:   Long-term plans to stay in South Africa   36
Table 2.12:   Factors related to visits to South Africa   37
Table 2.13:   Reason for going to South Africa on last visit   38
Table 2.14:   Most preferred places to visit in South Africa   39
Table 2.15:   Work-related factors in visiting South Africa   40
Table 2.16:   Why respondent returned home from most recent trip to South Africa   41
Table 2.17:   Sources of knowledge of South Africa   42
Table 2.18:   Attitudes towards the border   43
Table 2.19:   Level of desire to live in South Africa temporarily   44

Chapter Three

Table 3.1:	Estimated wage labour by categories	49
Table 3.2:	A profile of the sample population in Mozambique	54
Table 3.3:	Demographic breakdown of Mozambican respondents who have been to South Africa	55
Table 3.4:	Reasons for visiting South Africa on most recent visit	57
Table 3.5:	Perceived impacts of migration on self, family, community, country	58
Table 3.6:	Most important concerns about friends and family going to South Africa	59
Table 3.7:	Decision-making factors in the migration process	61
Table 3.8:	Attitudes of Mozambicans towards borders	62
Table 3.9:	Attitudes of Mozambicans towards immigration laws	63
Table 3.10:	Attitudes of Mozambicans towards rights of non-citizens in South Africa	64
Table 3.11:	Desire and likelihood of moving to South Africa from Mozambique	65
Table 3.12:	Desire of Mozambicans to stay in South Africa permanently	67

Chapter Four

Table 4.1:	A profile of the sample population in Zimbabwe	77
Table 4.2:	Ages of respondents who have visited South Africa	78
Table 4.3:	Marital status of respondents who have visited South Africa	78
Table 4.4:	Highest educational level of respondents who have visited South Africa	79
Table 4.5:	Employment status of respondents who have visited South Africa	79
Table 4.6:	Frequency of visits to South Africa during the past five years	80
Table 4.7:	Average length of stay in South Africa during visits in the past five years	81
Table 4.8:	Mode of transport used during the most recent visit to South Africa	81
Table 4.9:	Purpose of most recent visit to South Africa during the past five years	83

Chapter Five

Table 5.1:	Sample areas and number of respondents for each area	89
Table 5.2:	A profile of the sample population in Namibia	90
Table 5.3:	Profile of visitors to South Africa	91
Table 5.4:	Length and frequency of visits to South Africa	93
Table 5.5:	Reasons for visiting and leaving South Africa	94
Table 5.6:	Methods of travel to South Africa on most recent visit	95
Table 5.7:	Factors in the migration decision-making process	96
Table 5.8:	Perceived impacts of migration on person/family/community/country	99
Table 5.9:	Desire and likelihood of moving to South Africa	100
Table 5.10:	Desire to stay in South Africa permanently	101

Table 5.11: Likelihood of short-term migration to South Africa from Namibia 103
Table 5.12: Likelihood of permanent migration to South Africa from Namibia 104
Table 5.13: Pride of citizenship and government approval ratings by respondents 105
Table 5.14: Attitudes towards borders 107
Table 5.15: Attitudes towards South African immigration laws 109
Table 5.16: Attitudes towards rights for non-citizens 110
Table 5.17: Attitudes towards political incorporation 112
Table 5.18: Summary of the trends in the Namibian data by demographic variable 113

Chapter Six
Table 6.1: Migration experience by gender 124
Table 6.2: Migration experience by marital status 125
Table 6.3: Migration experience by household status 126
Table 6.4: Migration experience by educational status 127
Table 6.5: Factors encouraging and discouraging migration to South Africa 128
Table 6.6: Desire and likelihood of migration to South Africa 130
Table 6.7: Frequency of visits and length of stay in South Africa 132
Table 6.8: Decision-making and migration 134
Table 6.9: Logistics of migration 134
Table 6.10: Reasons for visiting South Africa and returning home 136
Table 6.11: Job preferences and remittances 137
Table 6.12: Experiences with migration and impressions of South Africa 138
Table 6.13: Perceived impacts of migration 140

Chapter Seven
Table 7.1: A comparison of those who have been to South Africa and those who intend long-term migration to South Africa 152
Table 7.2: Respondents who wish to become permanent residents or citizens of South Africa 153
Table 7.3: Average age of those who intend migrating on a long-term basis 154
Table 7.4: Men and women who intend migrating compared with percentage who do not intend migrating 155
Table 7.5: Single respondents who intend migrating on a long-term basis 155
Table 7.6: Education and migration 156
Table 7.7: Respondents who claim they know how to get a job in SA 160
Table 7.8: Job preferences of potential migrants to South Africa 161
Table 7.9: The presence of friends and family in South Africa 164
Table 7.10: Making the decision and the ability to migrate to SA 165
Figure 7.1: Demographic stereotype of migrant 158
Figure 7.2: How respondents compare South Africa to their own country on six dimensions 160
Figure 7.3: Family encouragement to migrate to South Africa 164
Figure 7.4: The role of family and friends 166

Chapter Eight

Table 8.1:	Migrant communities selected for interviews	171
Table 8.2:	Country of citizenship of sample population	172
Table 8.3:	Gender breakdown of sample	172
Table 8.4:	Occupational categories of migrants in South Africa	173
Table 8.5:	Income per month (in rand)	174
Table 8.6:	Legal status of respondents	175
Table 8.7:	Migration histories of respondents (in selected countries of origin)	176
Table 8.8:	Migrant networks in South Africa (in selected countries of origin)	178
Table 8.9:	Perceived treatment in South Africa	179
Table 8.10:	Perceptions of South Africans' attitudes towards foreigners	181
Table 8.11:	Migrants as victims of crime	181
Table 8.12:	Levels of satisfaction in South Africa	182
Table 8.13:	Comparisons of South Africa and the home country	183
Table 8.14:	The primary reason cited for coming to South Africa on current visit	184
Table 8.15:	Perceived impacts of migration to South Africa on family, community, country	185
Table 8.16:	Attitudes of migrants towards the rights of non-citizens in South Africa	187
Table 8.17:	Attitudes towards immigration policy	189
Table 8.18:	Future plans of migrants	190
Figure 8.1:	Average length of stay in South Africa by country of origin (current visit)	179

Chapter Nine

Table 9.1:	South African attitudes to immigration	199
Table 9.2:	South African attitudes towards immigration in international perspective	201
Table 9.3:	Attitudes towards deportation	202
Table 9.4:	Attitudes towards amnesty	203
Table 9.5:	Attitudes towards rights for immigrants	204
Table 9.6:	Likelihood of taking action against foreigners	205
Table 9.7:	Perceived impacts of immigration	208
Table 9.8:	Perceived threats from immigration	209
Table 9.9:	Personal contact with non-citizens	210
Table 9.10:	Attitudes towards diversity	211
Table 9.11:	Attitudes towards integration of newcomers in South Africa	212
Figure 9.1:	Attitudes towards foreigners and other South Africans	207

List of Contributors

Kelly Barlow is a PhD candidate at McGill University in Montreal, Canada.

Jonathan Crush is the Director of the Southern African Migration Project (SAMP) and is Professor of Geography at Queen's University in Kingston, Canada.

Fion de Vletter is an economic consultant in Maputo, Mozambique.

Belinda Dodson is a former lecturer in the Department of Environmental and Geographical Sciences at the University of Cape Town, South Africa.

Bruce Frayne is a senior researcher at the Multidisciplinary Research Centre, Social Sciences Division, at the University of Namibia in Windhoek, Namibia.

John Gay is research associate at Sechaba Consultants in Maseru, Lesotho.

Celia Golden is a senior researcher at Labour Market Alternatives in Johannesburg, South Africa.

Lephophoto Mashike is a senior researcher at Labour Market Alternatives in Johannesburg, South Africa.

Robert Mattes is programme manager of the Public Opinion Service at the Institute for Democracy in South Africa (Idasa) in Cape Town, South Africa.

David A. McDonald is project manager of SAMP and Assistant Professor of Geography at Queen's University in Kingston, Canada.

Wade Pendleton is a senior researcher at the Multidisciplinary Research Centre, Social Sciences Division, at the University of Namibia in Windhoek, Namibia.

Abigail Poore is a PhD candidate at McGill University in Montreal, Canada.

Wayne Richmond is a Masters student at the University of Stellenbosch, South Africa.

Donald M. Taylor is Professor of Psychology at McGill University in Montreal, Canada.

Lovemore Zinyama is Professor of Geography at the University of Zimbabwe in Harare, Zimbabwe.

Acknowledgements

Although a considerable number of acknowledgements for this book are already made at the end of each chapter, there are additional words of thanks that need to be expressed. The first and most important are to the principal contributors to this book who made every effort to ensure that the research was methodologically sound and compatible across the various countries. Their commitment to the issues and their recognition of the very real consequences of the research for immigration policy and practice were a driving force behind the project, and informed all stages of the research. Such dedication to the subject matter was further reflected in the training and selection of research assistants who conducted the field work in a very professional and timely manner.

I would also like to thank my other colleagues at the Southern African Migration Project (SAMP), especially Jonathan Crush, Vincent Williams and Wilmot James who were available for advice and assistance at every stage of the research. Anne Mitchell of SAMP was invaluable in her prompt and accurate editing work and for the creation of the numerous tables and graphs in this book, and to her I owe a great debt of gratitude.

Research planning and assessment workshops were attended by a number of people other than the contributors to this book, and many of their inputs have been incorporated into the writing of this book. These additional individuals are: Luthando Myataza, Demetrios Papademetriou, Luis Covane, Lazarus Zanamwe, Monica Francis, Sally Peberdy and Thuso Green. It should also be noted that the bulk of the writing of the questionnaires for the research was done by Robert Mattes of Idasa's Public Opinion Service (POS). Additional training of research assistants was conducted by John Gay (in Namibia and South Africa) and by Robert Mattes (in Mozambique). Supplementary data analysis on the gender research in Chapter 6 was conducted by Victoria Esses and Tamara Armstrong of the University of Western Ontario and the aggregate data in the tables in Appendix C was compiled by Bruce Frayne. Megan Freer assisted with copy-editing and Michail Rassool did the final editing for publication.

I would also like to thank the office of the Vice-Principal of Research at Queen's University for their support for this project as well as the programme officers in the Southern Africa division at the Canadian International Development Agency (CIDA). Financial support for the research and the publication of this book was provided by CIDA through the Southern African Migration Project.

Finally, a word of thanks to the 6 901 interviewees who gave generously of their time for this research – most of whom will never see this book but, we hope, will benefit from the development of policies that may arise from it.

NOTE ON TERMINOLOGY

Migration terminology

In an effort to move away from the demeaning and criminalising terms "illegal immigrant" and "illegal alien", the term "undocumented migrant" will be used in this book to refer to those who are in a country other than their country-of-origin without official documentation. It should be noted, however, that "illegal immigrant" is the most commonly used (English) term in the region, and we have therefore used this terminology in our survey work to avoid confusion with interviewees who, in most cases, would not be familiar with the term "undocumented migrant".

Racial terminology

Although apartheid-era racial classifications are a social construct with no objective significance, the legacies of apartheid and the heavy correlation between race and class in South(ern) Africa are such that racial classifications remain an integral part of political analysis in the region. There are, however, many different versions of racial terminology and a brief explanation of the use of terms in this book is in order. Following the tradition of the democratic movement, "African", "coloured", "Asian" and "white" will be used to describe the four major apartheid racial categories in South Africa, with the most common use of upper and lower case letters being adopted. The term "black" is used to refer to Africans, coloureds and Asians as a whole, in recognition of their common oppression under apartheid.

Introduction

Towards a better understanding of cross-border migration in Southern Africa

by David A. McDonald

> *In the capital the concern was that the barbarian tribes of the north and west might at last be uniting. Officers of the general staff were sent on tours of the frontier. Some of the garrisons were strengthened. Traders who requested them were given military escorts. And officials of the Third Bureau of the Civil Guard were seen for the first time on the frontier, guardians of the State, specialists in the obscurer motions of sedition, devotees of truth, doctors of interrogation.*
> From J. M. Coetzee, Waiting for the Barbarians

Coetzee's image of "barbarians" massing on the frontier has a timeless and placeless quality to it that could represent any number of imperial epochs in history. From the Crusades of Christian Europe to the *swart gevaar* tactics of the apartheid state, the construction of a menacing, unwashed and unwanted "other" has long been used as a justification for acts of war and discrimination against groups of people.

In colonial and apartheid South Africa, the "barbarians" were kept at bay through a sophisticated and very brutal system of pass laws and immigration legislation which determined who had the right to enter the country and where people could move inside the country. These systems were never as successful as their architects had hoped, but they did serve to control most of the internal movement of black South Africans as well as the cross-border movement of Africans from other countries on the continent.

With the end of apartheid and the democratic election of a majority government in 1994, much of this has changed. There are no longer any restrictions on movement within the country and there has been a dramatic increase in cross-border traffic from other African countries into South Africa. The number of legal visitors from Southern African Development Community (SADC) countries alone has increased more than sevenfold since 1990 to more than three and a half million visitors per annum (Crush, 1997: 7) and visitors are arriving from all corners of the globe. South Africa has changed, and the quantitative and qualitative composition of migrant and immigrant activity is changing with it.

But there remain some very troubling concerns when it comes to cross-border migration in the region. For one, the apartheid-era immigration legislation, which is still in effect in South Africa, is arguably the most incongruous piece of legislation still on the books in the country. As the name implies, the Aliens Control Act of 1991 is rooted in the "control and expulsion" mentality of the apartheid era, with deeply racist and anti-semitic roots (Peberdy and Crush, 1998).

Equally disturbing is an increase in acts of violence in South Africa against Africans from other countries. The "necklacing" of two Mozambicans, the death of another Mozambican and two Senegalese chased by a mob at a train station near Johannesburg are extreme and, we hope, isolated cases of anti-foreigner sentiment in South Africa, but xenophobia is a widespread and growing concern in the country.

These anti-foreigner sentiments would appear to be aggravated by, perhaps even generated by, xenophobic coverage of immigration issues in the South African press. The print media in particular are full of stories about the "flood of illegal aliens" bringing crime and disease to the country and "stealing" South African jobs and resources. But it is not only the media that is to blame. Politicians, journalists, academics and members of the general public have made similarly troubling anti-foreigner statements and it is probably safe to say that xenophobic rhetoric has worsened in South Africa since the end of apartheid rather than improved. The Minister of Defence even threatened at one point to turn the electric fence along the Mozambican border to "lethal mode" to stem the flow of "illegals" from that country.[1]

The popular South African stereotype of (im)migrants from other African countries is one of uneducated and desperate people who are fleeing poverty and chaos in their own country to find work, peace and shelter in the "land of milk and honey". It is assumed that these migrants are entering the country "illegally" by crawling under fences or paying off corrupt border officials, and are entering by the millions. The image of "barbarians at the gate", it would seem, is far from eliminated from the South African mind.

Such perceptions contrast starkly with the reality of cross-border migration in Southern Africa described in this book. Based on extensive interviews with residents of Lesotho, Mozambique, Zimbabwe and Namibia as well as interviews with migrants of African origin living in South Africa, the chapters in this book depict a very different story of cross-border migration than the popular stereotypes. Far from being the kind of rootless and desperate criminals they are so often portrayed to be in the media, the residents of neighbouring countries who have been to South Africa, and those migrants who are now in South Africa, would appear to be relatively well-educated, responsible and law-abiding people. Moreover, most migrants visit South Africa for short-term, purpose-orientated reasons (not always related to work) and have very little interest in staying in the country permanently. There has been a significant increase in the amount of cross-border traffic between South Africa and other African countries, but the image of a flood of Africans amassed at the border simply does not bear itself out in the research.

This challenging of stereotypes comes at an important time in the immigration policy reform process in South Africa. The release of a Draft Green Paper on International Migration by the Department of Home Affairs in May 1997, a Refugee Bill in July 1998 and a White Paper on International Migration in March 1999 signals a significant shift in immigration policy thinking and there are pressures from a wide range of academics, NGOs and unions for change. There are also policy reforms in areas related to migration (eg mining, population and labour) that could have a direct impact on immigration legislation, and there are ongoing constitutional debates about the rights of non-citizens in South Africa (Klaaren, 1998).

These South African initiatives have been accompanied by the release of a *Draft Protocol on the Facilitation of Movement of Persons in the Southern African Development Community* by the SADC Secretariat in May 1998. This Protocol has met with mixed reaction in South Africa, but nevertheless signals a broader interest in the rationalisation and harmonisation of immigration policies in the region as a whole. It is essential, therefore, that policy-makers and other interested parties have the best possible information on which to make policy decisions. The lack of reliable information – or worse, the proliferation of misinformation – about cross-border activities in the region is a serious obstacle to rational legislative reform.

It is with this policy objective in mind that the Southern African Migration Project (SAMP) was established in 1996.[2] Part of SAMP's mandate was to establish a reliable and comparative assessment of attitudes towards and experiences with cross-border migration in the region. This book is a summary of research undertaken in this regard.

STRUCTURE OF THE BOOK

Chapter 1 presents a brief overview of the history and typology of cross-border migration in the region. Cross-border migration in Southern Africa has a long and complex history and it is essential to situate the current immigration policy reform process within an historical context.

This historical overview is followed by a country-by-country analysis of data that was collected in four source countries of migration to South Africa: Lesotho, Mozambique, Zimbabwe and Namibia (see chapters 2–5). The same survey was used in each country, and countries were selected using three basic criteria: their proximity to South Africa (all four have lengthy borders with South Africa [Figure 1]); their historical importance with respect to cross-border migration into South Africa (Lesotho and Mozambique being by far the two largest supplier states); and research affiliations in the participating countries. Surveys in

Lesotho, Mozambique and Zimbabwe were conducted simultaneously in 1997 and the survey in Namibia was conducted one year later. (The survey has also been conducted in Botswana but the results were not available at the time of writing and will be published separately.)

Figure 1

In total, there were 2 900 interviews conducted in the four countries (692 in Lesotho, 661 in Mozambique, 947 in Zimbabwe, and 600 in Namibia). The surveys in Lesotho and Zimbabwe were nationally representative while the survey in Mozambique was in the southern half of the country only. The survey in Namibia was based on a selection of key demographic and geographic regions. All four surveys were conducted on a sampling basis. These are the first surveys of their kind in each country and provide a wealth of information on attitudes towards and experiences with cross-border migration. The data also provides an invaluable source of comparative information. By being able to highlight differences and similarities between the countries surveyed when it comes to migration to South Africa, it is possible to both challenge the common stereotypes and identify bilateral particularities that may need to be acknowledged and addressed.

These country-by-country reports are followed by a detailed analysis of the data on a gender basis (chapter 6). While the individual country reports do highlight gender issues, the gendered history of cross-border migration in the region, and the significant increase in the cross-border movement of women in SADC countries in recent years, warrants a separate examination of the data on a gender basis.

Chapter 7 attempts to answer the question "What about the future?" Since the data from these countries inevitably represents attitudes towards migration at a particular point – attitudes which could change with political and/or economic disruptions – it is important to try to understand the longer-term relevance of the data (witness the political unrest in Zimbabwe and the military incursion in Lesotho by South African armed forces since the research was conducted). The chapter therefore tries to paint a picture of likely "out-migration" scenarios from Lesotho, Mozambique and Zimbabwe in the future based on data collected at a certain point in time.

We then turn to interviews conducted with 501 migrants from other African countries living in South Africa in mid-1998 (chapter 8). These interviews do not claim to be representative of the entire foreign population in South Africa, however. The actual number of non-citizens living in the country is simply unknown – and perhaps unknowable given the indeterminate numbers of undocumented migrants – and it is therefore impossible to know for sure what the quantitative and qualitative characteristics of the sample population would need to be. A "second-best" strategy of "snowball sampling" was therefore developed to provide an overview of key geographic and demographic representations of African migrants.

Despite these methodological limitations, the interviews described in chapter 8 do provide the largest set of interviews with foreign migrants living in South Africa to date. Importantly, the data also allows for comparisons with the interviews in Lesotho, Mozambique, Zimbabwe and Namibia and serve to reinforce the findings from that research. In other words, we have data on migration attitudes and experiences from residents of four neighbouring countries as well as data from migrants who are currently living in South Africa, and the two groups would appear to be saying the same things.

Chapter 9 rounds off the research with a discussion of a large, nationally representative survey of 3 500 South Africans on their attitudes towards migrants and immigration policy conducted in mid-1997. Once again the largest and most comprehensive survey of its kind ever undertaken, the interviews provide invaluable insight into the attitudes of South Africans towards one another and towards non-citizens. This analysis of attitudes towards "otherness" more generally helps to place South Africans' views of foreigners in context and allows for a more detailed discussion of xenophobia and other anti-immigrant sentiments.

The book concludes with three appendices. Appendix A is a detailed description of the methodologies employed in the surveys in Lesotho, Mozambique, Zimbabwe and Namibia. These methodological summaries are intended to lend further credibility to the research and also provide future researchers with background information on the strategies employed. Methodologies for the interviews with migrants living in South Africa and with South African citizens are discussed in those chapters.

Appendix B is an aggregate summary of the data from the interviews in Lesotho, Mozambique, Zimbabwe and Namibia. Aggregate results, in and of themselves, only provide a superficial presentation of the survey findings, of course, but the appendix does provide an overview of the main trends and allows for a comparison of aggregate data across the four countries. The appendix also provides a copy of the questionnaire used for the surveys.

Appendix C is a similar summary of the data from the interviews with migrants living in South Africa in Chapter 8. As with the interviews in Lesotho, Mozambique, Zimbabwe and Namibia, closed-ended response options were used in the survey instrument and only aggregate data is provided in the appendix (along with a copy of the questionnaire).

A NOTE ON METHODOLOGY

As noted above, research methodology is described in detail at various points in the book so we need not go into detail here. It is worth emphasising, however, that methodological rigour has been one of the touchstones of the research and researchers went to great lengths to ensure representivity, reliability and confidentiality in their interviews. This rigour is all the more important in a context of such concerns as weak (or non-existent) demographic data, confidentiality due to the legal status and past migration experiences of interviewees, remote interview points, limited communication facilities as well as the sheer number of languages and nationalities involved in the research.

But this methodological rigour is perhaps most important because of how it contrasts with the methodological inadequacies that have (mis)informed much of the recent work on cross-border migration in the region. One particularly problematic illustration of these methodological problems is found in a series of surveys conducted by the Human Sciences Research Council (HSRC) in South Africa in 1994 and 1995. In an attempt to find out how many non-citizens were living in South Africa, a random sample of South African citizens was asked the following questions: "Do any people who are not South African citizens live in the houses around this property? If so, how many?"[3] Incredibly, the numerical responses given by citizens were simply extrapolated by the researchers to give figures of 2.4 to 9.5 million non-South Africans living in the country. These figures have been reproduced *ad nauseam* by the South African press as "official estimates" of the number of non-citizens in the country ever since; they also found their way into the White Paper on International Migration.

Migration research in the region has also been plagued by sweeping generalisations about migrants and migration based on very small sample sizes of migrants (or even second-hand evidence and hearsay). Small samples are not inherently bad – indeed, case-studies and ethnographic work are essential to a deeper understanding of migration dynamics in the region – but to generalise these case studies to the entire population of migrants and migration activities is a serious problem. The myths that all Johannesburg-based Nigerians are drug smugglers and that every Mozambican is in South Africa "illegally" are just two illustrations of how poor research translates into popular stereotypes, with some tragic consequences.

This is not to suggest that the data in this book is free of methodological error. There are anomalies in our data (highlighted where applicable) and mistakes were made and lessons learned. Nor is this book the "final word" on cross-border migration in the region. Public opinion surveys using closed-ended, Likert-type questionnaires are useful insofar as they provide representative data with large, representative sample sizes that can be compared and analysed with relative ease, but they are not substitutes for detailed case and ethnographic studies. The data presented here should be seen as part of a much larger research agenda on the part of SAMP that covers a wide range of sectoral (eg agriculture, construction, housing), geographic (eg border zones) and topical research (eg Mozambican deportees, hawkers and traders). The data in this book is therefore intended to complement, rather than compete with, other methodologically sound migration research.

Having said that, the data in this book does provide a unique and incomparable source of information. With a total of 6 901 interviews with people from 29 African countries, in more than 20 languages, the surveys represent the most comprehensive set of migration-related data ever collected in Southern Africa. The questionnaires themselves consisted of approximately 200 questions (taking one to two hours to complete), which translates to 1.38 million responses in the combined data sets. Approximately 100 researchers and research assistants from a dozen countries worked on the research over a two-year period.

THE MAIN FINDINGS

Perspectives from the region and from migrants

The most important conclusion to be drawn from the interviews with residents of neighbouring countries and with migrants living in South Africa is that cross-border migration into South Africa from elsewhere on the continent is an eminently manageable process. Rather than the popular stereotype of an uncontrolled flood of migrants sneaking under fences and fording crocodile-infested rivers to get into the country, the overwhelming majority of those interviewed who have been to South Africa in the past as well as those who are currently in the country entered South Africa legally, through normal border posts, and with proper documentation. Moreover, most former and present migrants have above-average levels of education, are married with important responsibilities in their home country and are employed (or employable) in South Africa or at home.

The highly circular nature of cross-border migration was also apparent in the research. Most migrants have no desire to stay in South Africa permanently, and a large majority (including those who have never been to South Africa) prefer their home country to South Africa on a wide range of important criteria (eg peace, freedom, safety). Jobs and social services are deemed to be better in South Africa than they are at home by a majority of respondents, but jobs are not the only reason that people go to South Africa. Visiting friends and family, buying and selling goods, shopping, having access to good health care and going to school would appear to make up the bulk of the reasons for cross-border migration into South Africa. Most of these activities are short-term in nature and highlight the need to create a migration policy regime in South Africa that can manage these temporary and circular flows in a rational and humane manner rather than forcing people underground with unnecessarily restrictive immigration practices.

This is not to suggest that South Africa abandons border controls altogether. In fact, borders and immigration policy are taken very seriously by a majority of those interviewed. People in the countries surveyed as well as migrants currently in South Africa think that the South African government has every right to set limits on the number of people allowed into the country, as long as this is done in a humane and rational manner. Africans from outside the country do not expect South Africa to throw open its doors to whoever wants to enter, but they do want to see a just and transparent immigration policy that facilitates, rather than obstructs, short-term, purpose-orientated migration activities.

In the end, cross-border migration remains an integral part of the social, political and economic fabric of countries in Southern Africa. In Lesotho, for example, more than 80% of the resident population has been to South Africa at least once in their lives, with an average of 68 visits. Migration into South Africa is also becoming increasingly pan-African with migrants arriving from east, west and central Africa. Clearly, cross-border migration into South Africa from the rest of the continent is not going to disappear, no matter how draconian a policy regime is put in place. But the decision to migrate will not be an easy one. Superior work opportunities and better health and education facilities may well be draw cards, but these attractions would appear to be countered by other quality-of-life indices that would make decisions about cross-border migration into South Africa difficult at best.

South African attitudes towards immigrants and immigration

The first, and perhaps most surprising, result of the interviews with South African citizens on their attitudes towards migrants and immigration policy is that only 1% of respondents cited immigration as one of the three most important issues facing the country today. Despite increased reports of anti-immigrant sentiment and behaviour, and the high visibility of the issue in the press, surveys from 1994 to 1997 demonstrate that immigration is not a top priority for most South Africans. Also somewhat surprising, given the nature of press reports on attitudes towards immigrants, is the small but important cadre of South Africans who support a more liberalised immigration regime and accept immigrants and immigration. Although this group is clearly in the minority, the fact that such a minority does exist – and that all racial, economic, gender and ethnic groups are represented in it – suggests that there is at least some support for a more management- and service-orientated approach to immigration policy in the future.

But this potential for a new immigration regime in South Africa is countered by some disturbing trends, the most notable of which is that the majority of South Africans are resoundingly negative towards any immigration policy that might be welcoming to newcomers. Twenty-five percent of South Africans want a total ban on immigration and 45% support strict limits on the numbers of immigrants allowed in. Only 17% would support a more flexible policy tied to the availability of jobs and only 6% support a totally open policy of immigration. This is the highest level of opposition to immigration recorded by any country in the world where comparable questions have been asked.

While whites and blacks are equally opposed to immigration and immigrants, the specific reasons differ. For both groups, however, those who are most opposed to immigration and dislike immigrants display various forms of xenophobia. Those who oppose immigration are less inclined to accept diversity within South Africa, believe that immigrants weaken society and threaten the nation's health, and think that foreigners are unable to assimilate into the South African nation.

All South Africans appear to have the same stereotypical image of other Southern Africans, citing job loss, crime and disease as the negative consequences they fear from immigrants living in the country. Interestingly, though, only 4% of respondents reported that they actually interact with non-citizens from the region on a regular basis, suggesting that these stereotypes may be the product of second-hand (mis)information. Thus, it may be possible to counteract such stereotypes with a well-devised public education programme.

Policy-makers therefore face a major challenge in terms of fostering a climate that is more open to outsiders and their presence in the country. South Africans display a modest acceptance of diversity and have relatively favourable views of different racial and ethnic groups within the country (Africans more so than whites). But these favourable conditions for peaceful diversity are offset by very negative attitudes towards newcomers. What we have is an attitudinal profile that will not be easily overcome. South Africans are unlikely to be quickly persuaded to view non-citizens and immigrants more favourably simply by providing more realistic, positive and accurate information about what immigrants and migrants actually do or about their true impact on the country.

Nevertheless, creating a better public awareness about the actual experiences and intentions of foreign citizens living in South Africa (permanently and temporarily) is an expressed intention of the South African government, many NGOs and the Human Rights Commission. If South Africa is to address the problem of xenophobia in the country adequately and develop a more pragmatic approach to cross-border movements in the region, it is essential to have public support – or at least a softening of public opposition – for these policies to take root.

As noted above, the large majority of people who come to South Africa have no desire to stay in the country permanently. More importantly, migrants generally contribute to the social and economic fabric of the country and are responsible, relatively well-educated and law-abiding citizens of their own nation. Such information could help to ameliorate the anxiety that South Africans appear to have about the impacts of trying to accommodate culturally different and "unassimilable" people into the country.

Finally, public education should also concentrate on raising the curtain of ignorance that South Africans have about people from neighbouring countries, that great void in the public mind north of the Limpopo – not just information about what people from other African countries do while they are in South Africa but more and better information about Africa itself. What are its cultures like and how do its peoples live? Only this may eliminate the pervasive, yet fictional, popular notion that hordes of "barbarians" have already invaded the country, with millions more amassing on the borders.

We hope this research will contribute towards a better public understanding of cross-border migration in Southern Africa and help to build a more rational and humane immigration policy framework in South Africa itself.

REFERENCES

Crush, J, 1997, "Covert Operations: Clandestine migration, temporary work, and immigration policy in South Africa", SAMP Migration Policy Series, No. 1. Cape Town and Kingston: Southern African Migration Project.

Peberdy, S and Crush, J, 1998, "Rooted in racism: The origins of the Aliens Control Act", in J. Crush (ed), *Beyond control: Immigration and human rights in a democratic South Africa*. Cape Town: Idasa.

Klaaren, J, 1998, "Immigration and the South African Constitution", in J. Crush (ed), *Beyond control: Immigration and human rights in a democratic South Africa*. Cape Town: Idasa.

Minnaar, A and Hough, M, 1996, *Who goes there? Perspectives on migration and illegal aliens in Southern Africa*. Pretoria: Human Sciences Research Council.

ENDNOTES

1. Minister of Defence Joe Modise, as quoted in *The Star*, Johannesburg, 6 May 1997. Although Modise later retracted the statement, it is clear that he gave serious consideration to this option: "If we are not coping with the influx of illegal immigrants and our people are being threatened, there will come a time when we will switch on the fence to lethal mode."
2. Detailed information on the background of SAMP, its partners, publications and future activities can be found at www.queensu.ca/samp.
3. See Minaar and Hough, 1996, 259–62. The HSRC surveys were part of a quarterly omnibus survey conducted by one of the large survey companies in South Africa, and are reliable in terms of representivity. However, the fact that the migration questions were tacked on to surveys which had nothing to do with migration (and were most likely related to market research for consumer products) raises concerns about the context of the questions. It also begs the question whether respondents had adequate time to make the mental shift and think about the full implications of the questions.

Chapter One

Migrations past: An historical overview of cross-border movement in Southern Africa

by Jonathan Crush

Central to the moral panic over immigration which has gripped South Africa since 1994 is the notion that the country is being swamped by a "black tide" from the north (McDonald, et al, 1998). It cannot be denied that the numbers of non-citizens in the country at any one time has increased substantially since South Africa reconnected to the rest of the world, but it is highly misleading to assume that almost every non-citizen is actually an immigrant who wants to stay.

Unfortunately, South Africa's long history of cross-border migration seems to have faded from public view and myopia is everywhere evident, particularly in the more popular media with historical attention deficit disorder. Moreover, when a scholarly tract includes a chapter entitled "Illegals in South Africa: Historical overview", which assumes that cross-border migration did not begin until the first Mozambican crawled under the electrified fence in 1985, there is clearly a major problem of historical amnesia that needs to be addressed (Minnaar and Hough, 1996).

Cross-border migration between South Africa and its neighbours is nothing new. A significant proportion of the population of the surrounding countries has been to South Africa. As the surveys discussed in this book demonstrate, 42% of resident adults from Lesotho, Mozambique and Zimbabwe alone have gone to South Africa in the past, with a high of 81% in Lesotho and a low of 23% in Zimbabwe (Table 1.1). The more unexpected finding, perhaps, is that many of their parents and grandparents have also been. In fact, 50% of the respondents in these three countries have parents and 34% have grandparents who have *actually worked* in South Africa. If asked, many would undoubtedly have reported great-grandparents who had spent time in South Africa.

These findings are certainly not surprising to anyone with a basic knowledge of the history of cross-border migration in Southern Africa. In its modern form, migration to South Africa from the region dates back more than 150 years. Indeed,

TABLE 1.1: FAMILY HISTORY OF MIGRATION TO SOUTH AFRICA			
	Lesotho (%)	Mozambique (%)	Zimbabwe (%)
Visited South Africa personally	81	29	23
Parents worked in South Africa	83	53	24
Grandparents worked in South Africa	51	32	23
Source: SAMP Public Opinion Survey, 1997.			

long-distance migration for employment pre-dates the drawing of international borders by the colonial powers in the latter half of the nineteenth century.

Cross-border migration has taken various forms. At one end of the spectrum is the highly formalised and regulated contract system to the South African mines, which was put in place in the period between 1890 and 1920. At the other are various kinds of informal, unregulated or clandestine movements across borders. South Africa has been receiving and returning both kinds of migrants for decades.

This chapter provides a broad overview of the changing dimensions and spatial patterns of cross-border migration to South Africa from the region, from the discovery of diamonds in Kimberley in the mid-nineteenth century through to the early 1990s. The discussion is intended both to provide historical depth to the cross-sectional information emerging from the public opinion surveys reported in this book and to inject a much-needed historical perspective missing from contemporary debates about the character and impact of migration within South Africa.

The history of migration in Southern Africa is one of the most researched and well-documented academic fields in the region. Drawing on this literature, the chapter briefly examines four discreet streams of movement to South Africa from other SADC countries: contract mine migration, informal migration, white settler migration and refugee migration. It does not consider a host of other forms of short-duration cross-border movements with a similarly long historical pedigree: tourism, cross-border trading and shopping, visiting, migration for education, and so on.

CONTRACT MIGRATION

The history of mine migrancy and its role in the development of economic and racial oppression within South Africa has been well-documented (Wilson, 1972; Johnston, 1976; Lacey, 1981; Crush, Jeeves and Yudelman, 1992; James, 1992; Allen, 1992). So too have the negative health and social impacts of working on the mines for communities and countries of the Southern African region (First, 1983; Murray, 1981; Packard, 1989; Chirwa, 1992). These studies can easily be consulted by interested readers, who will notice a shift over the last 20 years from studies of the political economy of the migrant labour system towards studies of the actual experience of migration and minework by the migrants themselves (Moodie, 1994; Coplan, 1994). Contract migration to the South African diamond, gold and coal mines can be periodised into three major phases: (a) the formative phase, 1850–1920; (b) the expansionary phase, 1920–1970; and (c) the restructuring phase (1970–present).

Migrants from present-day Mozambique, Malawi, Lesotho and Zimbabwe came to work in the sugar cane fields of Natal and the diamond mines of Kimberley from the 1840s onwards, long before South Africa itself came into existence (Worger, 1987; Harries, 1994). They came primarily to earn money to buy guns to defend themselves against colonial encroachment and to buy agricultural implements to expand agriculture at home. The migrants came and went virtually as they pleased until pass laws and compounds were introduced to curtail and control their movements. Borders existed on colonial maps, not on the ground. Crossing borders was the least of their worries on the long and dangerous journey south.

With the discovery of gold in the 1880s, the Witwatersrand came into existence (Van Onselen, 1982). Within 20 years, Johannesburg had grown into a city of more than 200 000 people. Many were temporary residents from areas as far away as Central Africa. The mines had a voracious appetite for cheap, male labour and the rural areas of the subcontinent had begun to supply their demand. Colonial taxation, land dispossession and the destruction of peasant agriculture explain some of the movement. But migrants also had their own reasons for going – to earn money for *lobola*, to invest in agriculture back home, and to purchase consumer goods (Beinart, 1982; Crush, 1987; Eldredge, 1993; Harries, 1994).

During this formative phase, the mining companies competed fiercely with one another for labour and the wage bill began to rise (Jeeves, 1985). Collusion was the solution. After several abortive attempts, the mines established a centralised recruiting agency (called the NRC in South Africa and WNLA outside it, and, since 1977, TEBA). By 1920, the NRC/WNLA had eliminated all competition and become the only gate into the mining industry for migrants. Recruiting stations were established throughout the region and modern transport systems set up (road, rail, ferry and eventually air) for whisking migrants to the mines.

Neighbouring states did not want to lose the migrants permanently, so agreements were reached between governments to make sure that miners were recruited on fixed contracts and that they went home afterwards. Fearful that they might stay in South Africa if their families accompanied them, everyone agreed that only the migrants themselves could go.

In 1920, there were close to 80 000 Mozambicans on the gold mines alone (more than the total number of South Africans), and 10 000 Basotho (Table 1.2). During the expansionary phase that followed, the numbers of migrants on the mines grew rapidly as new regions were bundled into the system. Between 1920 and 1940 the number of foreign miners in South Africa doubled from 100 000 to 200 000. At the peak, in the early 1970s, the number rose close to 300 000. Some 80% of the mine workforce were foreign at that time.

Following a major health scandal, the mines were barred from recruiting north of $22°S$ from 1913 until the 1930s (Packard, 1989). But once these restrictions

| TABLE 1.2: CONTRACT MIGRATION TO THE SOUTH AFRICAN GOLD MINES, 1920–1995 ||||||||||||
Year	Ang.	Bots.	Les.	Mal.	Moz.	Swa.	Tan.	Zam.	Zim.	Other	Total
1920	0	2 112	10 439	354	77 921	3 449	0	12	179	5 484	99 950
1925	0	2 547	14 256	136	73 210	3 999	0	4	68	14	94 234
1930	0	3 151	22 306	0	77 828	4 345	183	0	44	5	99 355
1935	0	7 505	34 788	49	62 576	6 865	109	570	27	9	112 498
1940	698	14 427	52 044	8 037	74 693	7 152	0	2 725	8 112	70	168 058
1945	8 711	10 102	36 414	4 973	78 588	5 688	1 461	27	8 301	4 732	158 967
1950	9 767	12 390	34 467	7 831	86 246	6 619	5 495	3 102	2 073	4 826	172 816
1955	8 801	14 195	36 332	12 407	99 449	6 682	8 758	3 849	162	2 299	192 934
1960	12 364	21 404	48 842	21 934	101 733	6 623	14 025	5 292	747	844	233 808
1965	11 169	23 630	54 819	38 580	89 191	5 580	404	5 898	653	2 686	232 610
1970	4 125	20 461	63 988	78 492	93 203	6 269	0	0	3	972	265 143
1975	3 431	20 291	78 114	27 904	97 216	8 391	0	0	2 485	12	220 293
1980	5	17 763	96 309	13 569	39 539	8 090	0	0	5 770	1 404	182 449
1985	1	18 079	97 639	16 849	50 126	12 365	0	0	0	4	196 068
1990	0	15 720	108 780	72	50 104	17 816	0	0	2	0	192 044
1995	0	12 736	100 892	2	73 874	16 753	0	0	0	0	204 257

Note: Ang. = Angola, Bot. = Botswana, Les. = Lesotho, Mal. = Malawi, Moz. = Mozambique, Swa. = Swaziland, Tan. = Tanzania, Zam. = Zambia, Zim. = Zimbabwe.
Source: TEBA.

were lifted, they went on a major recruiting drive to the north. By the late 1960s, all of the states of the region were supplying migrants to the mines (Jeeves, 1985).

The largest supplier was Malawi (peaking at 120 000 in 1973), followed by Mozambique, Lesotho, Botswana and Swaziland. Even Zambians, Angolans and Tanzanians came in their thousands before their newly independent governments told them not to. The only country where the numbers were small was Zimbabwe, which had its own mining industry and employment opportunities.

The contract migration system was consistently expansionist for most of its history. Few rural areas of the subcontinent were inaccessible to the sophisticated recruiting apparatus of the South African mining industry (Crush, Jeeves and Yudelman, 1992). Although the migrant flow from particular zones fluctuated over time, few rural areas were untouched. Some, such as Lesotho and southern Mozambique, became highly integrated into, and deeply marked by, the system (Murray, 1981; First, 1983).

Since 1970, the system of contract migration to the mines has been reshaped. Change in unionisation, health and safety, and the compound system have been considerable (Crush, Jeeves and Yudelman, 1992; Crush and James, 1995). But contract migrancy has shown remarkable persistence.

The 1970s and 1980s witnessed a major shake-up in patterns of migration to the mines. South Africans, traditionally hesitant to work there, came in greater numbers pushing the foreign component of the workforce down to 40% by

1980. Zimbabwe joined Tanzania, Zambia and Angola by withdrawing altogether. Malawi was thrown out after a dispute over HIV testing. But migrants continued to come from the traditional sources of Mozambique, Lesotho, Swaziland and Botswana.

In the late 1980s and early 1990s the mines suffered massive retrenchments. The companies laid off three South Africans to every one foreign miner. In proportional terms, the mine workforce is now more than 50% foreign once again. Mozambique in particular seems to be as popular as ever as a source region (De Vletter, 1998).

Since the late 1970s, when it became apparent that there were more migrants wanting jobs than there were jobs available, migrants have become "career miners". They work continuously on the mines, returning home for annual leave. Basotho miners are close enough to make short visits home on weekends off. Most Mozambican miners still go home only once a year. The mine workforce has also aged significantly in the last decade, with few opportunities for new workers to join the workforce (De Vletter, 1998; Sechaba Consultants, 1996).

Many assumed that migration and minework were so despised that miners would move permanently to South Africa with their families if they had half a chance. This was the thinking behind the 1995 amnesty which offered permanent residence in South Africa to those who had worked in the country for more than 10 years. To everyone's surprise, only half of the eligible miners actually applied (Table 1.3) (Crush and Williams, 1999).

Two new studies from SAMP explain the lukewarm response to this amnesty (Sechaba Consultants, 1996; De Vletter, 1998). Those who refused have resources and attachments at home. Those who accepted did so for strategic reasons such as taxation benefits, hire purchase and access to other employment. Few want to stay permanently in South Africa and almost none wish to become South African citizens. Foreign miners seem to want to remain migrants, as long as South Africa will have them. The mines say they need them, and so far the South African government has bought the argument (as did governments before them).

TABLE 1.3: MINERS' PERMANENT RESIDENT APPLICATIONS FOR 1995 AMNESTY				
	Employed in SA Mines	Eligible for 1995 Amnesty	Applied for 1995 Amnesty	Percentage that applied
Botswana	12 429	9 580	3 886	40.1
Lesotho	96 105	61 886	34 017	55.0
Malawi	0	0	350	n/a
Mozambique	74 380	23 806	9 159	38.5
Swaziland	16 243	9 210	4 092	44.4
Total	199 157	104 483	51 504	49.3

Note: Officially there are no Malawians on the mines. Interestingly, 350 applied for the amnesty.

INFORMAL MIGRATION

Minework is physically and psychologically debilitating. Many migrants do not fit the physiological bill and many more prefer to avoid the mines altogether. This is nothing new. When the mines experienced periodic labour shortage "crises", as in the first decade of the twentieth century, it was usually because migrants could find work in other sectors (Jeeves, 1985).

For much of the twentieth century, clandestine migration referred not to the "illegal" crossing of borders *per se* but to the process of going to South Africa without documentation (travelling passes in the early days, identity documents and passports more recently). However, since governments were generally more interested in monitoring the movement than controlling it, passes were relatively easy to get. There were no border posts and people crossed wherever they wanted.

Outside the contract system, the journey south for migrants was for many years a fairly hazardous undertaking (Jeeves, 1985). Migrants had to pay for their own transport or travel on foot, often stopping to work en route to their final destination. One pioneering study documents the stop-go route taken by Malawian, Zambian and Zimbabwean migrants on their way to the Witwatersrand (Van Onselen, 1976). An elaborate word-of-mouth information network told migrants where to look for work and whom to avoid.

Most migrants headed for the towns and cities and found work in construction, services and secondary industry. There they were subject, like black South Africans, to pass laws and constant police harassment. Many who were arrested were shipped off to work on the farms under apartheid's notorious prison labour system. But the farmers were desperate for labourers. They even organised private recruiting companies and intercepted migrants at the borders, dragooning them into farmwork. South Africa's rich agricultural farmland in Mpumalanga and KwaZulu-Natal was developed with the labour of migrants from the east and north (Jeeves and Crush, 1997). As early as the 1920s, the Bethel area became synonymous with the atrocious conditions meted out to foreign migrants (Murray, 1997: 75-93). The sordid reputation of the area persisted for decades.

The numbers of informal migrants are impossible to gauge with any accuracy since record-keeping was so poor. One rough measure is the South African census which recorded the birthplace of every person in the country (Table 1.4). The census figures show a gradual increase in the numbers of foreign-born Africans living in South Africa as the twentieth century progressed. In the jump between 1936 and 1951 the era of South Africa's post-war industrial expansion is particularly noticeable. Those captured by the census were in large measure migrants, not permanent immigrants. Even those who remained in South Africa for many years eventually went home.

The history of informal cross-border migration in Southern Africa also reveals a certain panic attached to one particular group of migrants – women. Women migrants from the region, like their South African counterparts, were always marginalised and pushed to the back of the queue in local labour markets (Bozzoli, 1991; Berger, 1992). The only paid work that many could get was domestic service in white homes. Many others turned to professions that at least

TABLE 1.4: FOREIGN-BORN AFRICANS IN SOUTH AFRICA, 1911–1985								
	1911	1921	1936	1946	1951	1970	1980	1985
Angola			28	6 716	6 322	3 859	589	392
Botswana	5 020	11 959	4 048	38 559	51 017	49 469	33 366	26 015
Lesotho	75 132	111 733	163 838	199 327	219 065	157 499	172 879	135 563
Malawi	4 573	22 122	17 657	61 005	63 655	110 777	36 087	28 712
Mozambique	114 976	110 245	98 031	141 417	161 240	142 512	64 813	63 561
Namibia	2 230	2 926	1 879	4 990	4 129	2 518	10 342	9 210
Swaziland	21 662	29 177	31 092	33 738	42 914	29 167	31 981	30 722
Tanzania			118	2 937	7 127	288	145	887
Zambia	2 158		12 189	13 515	13 544	2 194	1 495	926
Zimbabwe	2 526		2 167	32 034	32 697	13 392	20 552	7 019
Other	930	5 146	2 730	22 569	4 282	4 369	4 234	14 003
Total	229 207	279 819	333 777	556 807	605 992	516 044	376 483	317 010
Source: South African Census Reports, 1911–1985.								

ensured them a livelihood – informal trading, liquor production and prostitution. All were "illegal" and placed women in constant conflict with the law (Crush and Ambler, 1993). From very early in the century, therefore, black women in town were depicted as moral polluters (Eales, 1991). Their mere presence in town seemed to signify the disintegration of rural society.

These images were, of course, highly misleading. In the supplier areas, colonial governments, chiefs and male elders conspired to keep women in the rural areas (Walker, 1991). This "patriarchal coalition" checked women's migration though some escaped its chains. Studies of women migrants from Lesotho, Swaziland and Botswana show that as the decades passed, more and more women spent time in South Africa (Miles, 1991; Cockerton, 1995). Initially, they accompanied spouses and partners. Later, they went on their own as young, single women. The numbers involved were never overwhelming (Table 1.5). The 1960 South African census, for example, captured only 48 000 African women from the Southern African region.

After 1948, and particularly after 1960 (with the political independence of black Africa), the apartheid government spied a new *swaart gevaar* (black peril) from the north. Migrants, once welcomed for economic reasons, were now seen as a political threat. Border posts were established between South Africa and Botswana, Lesotho and Swaziland (the "BLS" countries) for the first time in the early 1960s. In 1960, the apartheid state appointed the Froneman Commission of Inquiry into Foreign Bantu. Froneman recommended that foreign Africans should no longer be allowed into the country. The recommendations were so politically explosive that the report was never released to the public.

As the government attempted to roll back internal black urbanisation, many non-South African migrants were caught up in the dragnet. The oppressive

TABLE 1.5: FOREIGN-BORN AFRICAN WOMEN IN SOUTH AFRICA 1960–1985				
	1960	1970	1980	1985
Angola	4	82	96	152
Botswana	5 259	7 387	3 974	4 591
Lesotho	33 387	32 568	20 978	16 642
Malawi	564	969	1 159	898
Namibia	179	401	1 742	2 571
Swaziland	7 646	10 834	10 423	9 405
Tanzania	12	63	24	419
Zambia	1 152	875	744	578
Zimbabwe	137	96	108	111
Other	344	412	3 921	1 293
Total	48 684	53 687	43 169	36 660

Source: South African Census, 1960–1985.

conditions and human rights violations of the late apartheid years made South Africa an increasingly unpleasant place to go. Employers (except the mines) were pressured by the Department of Bantu Administration to stop employing non-South African migrants (Posel, 1991). Under these pressures, the numbers of foreign-born Africans seems to have stabilised and then fallen in the 1960s and 1970s (Tables 1.4 and 1.5).

In the 1960s all foreign women coming to South Africa were ordered to carry passes (Wells, 1993). This, taken with increased harassment by the police, made life very uncomfortable for migrant women. Many returned home for good during this period of heightened oppression and the numbers of foreign-born African women shrank thereafter. The numbers began to rise again in the 1980s when informal sector activity was unbanned in South African cities. Women traders and informal sector operators, skilled through years of trading in their own countries, were quick to exploit the opportunities of the new South African market. Most women who come to South Africa from neighbouring countries these days still come to buy and sell and to trade (see Chapter 6).

WHITE FLIGHT

One of the great imponderables of the history of migration in Southern Africa is whether more people from the region would have made South Africa their permanent home if they had been allowed to. It is generally assumed that the reason black people continued to migrate, rather than immigrate, to South Africa was that they had no choice. The policies of the day ensured that they remained migrants. Others would argue that the impact of the policies has been exaggerated that even if immigration had been allowed, most would have continued to migrate.

Certainly, black people from the region could never aspire to be legal immigrants under apartheid. Legislation specified that all immigrants had to be "assimilable" by the white population (Peberdy and Crush, 1998). This restriction was on the statute books right up until 1986. Thereafter, there was a brief hiatus when skilled black people could emigrate to the "independent" bantustans. Policy since 1994 has made it more difficult again.

Unsurprisingly, the apartheid government's hostile attitude to potential black immigrants contrasts sharply with the attitude taken towards whites from the region. White settlers had always crossed freely backwards and forwards between South Africa and the neighbouring states, most of whom had settler populations. The racist underpinnings of South African immigration policy became particularly transparent in the 1970s and 1980s when whites threatened by political independence in neighbouring states were welcomed with open arms in South Africa.

The drift south of whites from the region began in Zambia, Kenya and Malawi in the 1960s with political independence from Britain. The white flight accelerated dramatically when Angola and Mozambique won their independence in the mid-1970s. The number of Portuguese in South Africa who had been born in Portugal, Angola or Mozambique increased from 4 539 in 1960 to 45 727 in 1980 (Table 1.6). The haven of white South Africa was even more attractive to whites who *"bakkied"* south from newly independent Zimbabwe in the 1980s. The Rhodesian-born population of South Africa rose from fewer than 10 000 in 1960 to more than 90 000 in the early 1990s. All the new arrivals were immediately given permanent residence and allowed to stay. Their black counterparts had never had the option.

TABLE 1.6: COUNTRY OF BIRTH OF WHITES IN SOUTH AFRICA, 1960–1991				
	1960	1980	1985	1991
Angola	32	2 700	2 682	2 788
Kenya	1 202	6 825	6 410	6 025
Mozambique	1 030	8 187	7 405	7 221
Portugal	3 477	34 840	34 472	31 870
Zambia	3 198	18 893	19 988	21 242
Zimbabwe	9 393	51 987	89 476	91 228
Total	18 332	123 432	160 433	160 374

Source: South African Census, 1960–1991.

REFUGEES

In the 1980s, South African destabilisation wrought havoc on the landscape and peoples of Mozambique. The South African-sponsored civil war had a calamitous impact on Mozambique and as a result Southern Africa faced its very first mass refugee migration. Surrounding countries such as Malawi, Zimbabwe and Swaziland took the refugees in while South Africa did its utmost to keep them out, electrifying the Mozambican border and arresting and deporting asylum seekers.

The South African government's callous failure to provide protection to refugees by virtue of its own policies represented apartheid at its most cynical. Nevertheless, the government found it impossible to keep out desperate people and by 1990 an estimated 350 000 refugees had crossed the border. Rights and privileges normally accorded to refugees under international conventions were denied to these Mozambicans, however, as South Africa had never signed these protocols. But as long as these Mozambicans remained in border villages they were not harassed. If they left those areas they were arrested and deported as "illegal aliens".

In 1994, a voluntary refugee repatriation programme was put into operation by the United Nations High Commissioner for Refugees (UNHCR) and the International Organisation for Migration (IOM). Only 67 000 refugees went home, however, and the new South African government was left with a major policy dilemma: What should be done with the Mozambicans who remained? Some of the refugees have been able to acquire permanent residence in South Africa through the SADC amnesty programme of 1996, and there are ongoing initiatives by the South African government to offer amnesty to a majority of the remaining refugees, even though the situation remains unresolved and problematic (Crush and Williams, 1999).

CONCLUSION

South Africans have had to contend, since 1994, with a deluge of misinformation and several competing visions of the implications of migration and immigration for their country. The natural tendency is to assume the worst and to pull up the drawbridge.

Post-1994 public policy on migration and immigration in South Africa has been based on two main sources of information. The first are the extravagant claims and simplistic imagery of xenophobia in the popular press. Migrants rarely "enter" or "come" to South Africa; rather, they "flood", "deluge" and "swarm".

The other is the appeal to "science". Rarely does an opportunity go by without the South African Minister of Home Affairs making reference to the "scientific basis" of his policies. He refers here to studies commissioned from the Human Sciences Research Council (HSRC) in the mid-1990s (eg Minnaar and Hough, 1996). The studies are not only suspect methodologically, but advance a policy position consistent with garnering more resources for border controls and policing.

Migrations past are of little interest to this agenda. This chapter, on the contrary, drives home the point that cross-border migration in the Southern African region is *nothing new*, that borders have always been exceedingly porous. The truth is that if people really want to come they will find a way to do so. In South Africa there will always be vested interests in people coming into the country (eg as cheap labour) who will therefore lobby for and facilitate their entry.

One of the least surprising findings of the surveys referred to in this book is how, overwhelmingly, Southern Africans who go to, or wish to go to, South Africa continue to be (and see themselves as) migrants not immigrants. Logically there was no reason why 1994 should have brought an epochal change in long-standing patterns and modes of migrant behaviour.

Why should or would temporary migrants instantaneously become permanent immigrants? A recent study by the Centre for Development and Enterprise claims that "there is nothing so permanent as a temporary migrant" (1997: 9). This kind of anti-immigrant sentiment garnered from the rhetoric of "Fortress Europe" has little relevance to Southern Africa. What is remarkable in this part of the world, perhaps, is that there seems to be nothing so temporary as an "illegal immigrant".

The findings reported in this chapter, and this book, cut across the logic of xenophobia and pseudo-science. They therefore, by definition, run counter to the drift of current South African policy. That is the reason they are unlikely to be welcomed and all the more reason why they should not be ignored.

ACKNOWLEDGEMENTS

The historical research reported in this chapter was funded by the Social Sciences and Humanities Research Council of Canada (SSHRC). Funding for data collection and analysis was provided by the Canadian International Development Agency (CIDA). I am particularly grateful to Genevieve Crush for her help with the tables.

REFERENCES

Allen, V, 1992, *The history of black mineworkers in South Africa*. Keighley: Moor Press.
Beinart, W, 1982, *The political economy of Pondoland, 1860–1930*. Cambridge: Cambridge University Press.
Berger, I, 1992, *Threads of solidarity: Women in South African industry, 1900–1980*. Bloomington: Indiana University Press.
Bozzoli, B, 1991, *Women of Phokeng: Consciousness, life strategy and migrancy in South Africa, 1900–1983*. Portsmouth, New Hampshire: Heinemann.
Centre for Development and Enterprise, 1997, "People on the move: Lessons from international migration policies". Johannesburg: CDE.
Chirwa, W, 1992, *Theba is power: Rural labour, migrancy and fishing in Malawi, 1890s–1985*, PhD thesis. Kingston, Ontario: Queen's University.
Cockerton, C, 1995, *Running away from the land of the desert: Women's migration from colonial Botswana to South Africa, c.1895–1966*, PhD thesis. Kingston, Ontario: Queen's University.
Coplan, D, 1994, *In the time of cannibals: The word music of South Africa's Basotho migrants*. Chicago: University of Chicago Press.

Crush, J, 1987, *The struggle for Swazi labour, 1890–1920*. Montreal, Quebec and Kingston, Ontario: McGill–Queen's University Press.

Crush, J and Ambler, C (eds), 1993, *Liquor and labour in Southern Africa*. Athens: Ohio University Press.

Crush, J and James, W, 1995, *Crossing boundaries: Mine migrancy in a democratic South Africa*. Cape Town and Ottawa: Idasa/IDRC.

Crush, J, Jeeves, A and Yudelman, D, 1992, *South Africa's labor empire: A history of black migrancy to the gold mines*. Boulder: Westview Press.

Crush, J and Williams, V, 1999, *The new South Africans? Immigration amnesties and their aftermath*. Cape Town: Southern African Migration Project.

De Vletter, F, 1998, "Sons of Mozambique: Mozambican miners and post-apartheid South Africa", SAMP Migration Policy Series No. 8. Cape Town and Kingston: Southern African Migration Project.

Eales, K, 1991, "Gender politics and the administration of African women in Johannesburg, 1903–1939", MA thesis. Johannesburg: University of Witwatersrand.

Eldredge, E, 1993, *A South African kingdom: The pursuit of scarcity in nineteenth-century Lesotho*. Cambridge: Cambridge University Press.

First, R, 1983, *Black gold: The Mozambican miner, proletarian and peasant*. Brighton: St Martin's Press.

Harries, P, 1994, *Work, culture and identity: Migrant labourers in Mozambique and South Africa, c.1860–1910*. Portsmouth, NH: Heinemann.

James, W, 1992, *Our precious metal: African labour in South Africa's gold industry, 1970–1990*. Cape Town: David Philip Publishers.

Jeeves, A, 1985, *Migrant labour in South Africa's mining economy: The struggle for the gold mines' labour supply, 1890–1920*. Montreal, Quebec and Kingston, Ontario: McGill-Queen's University Press.

Jeeves, A and Crush, J (eds), 1997, *White farms, black labour: The state and agrarian change in Southern Africa, 1910–1950*. Portsmouth, NH: Heinemann.

Johnstone, R, 1976, *Class, race and gold: A study of class relations and racial discrimination in South Africa*. London: Routledge and Kegan Paul.

Lacey, M, 1981, *Working for Brook: The origins of a coercive labor system in South Africa*. Johannesburg: Raven Press.

McDonald, D, Gay, J, Zinyama, L, Mattes, R and De Vletter, F, 1998, "Challenging xenophobia: Myths and realities about cross-border migration in Southern Africa", SAMP Migration Policy Series No. 7. Cape Town and Kingston: Southern African Migration Project.

Miles, M, 1991, "Missing women: A study of female Swazi migration to the Witwatersrand, 1920–1970", MA thesis. Kingston, Ontario: Queen's University.

Minnaar, A and Hough, M, 1996, *Who goes there? Perspectives on migration and illegal aliens in Southern Africa*. Pretoria: HSRC.

Moodie, D, 1994, *Going for gold: Men, mines and migration*. Berkeley: University of California Press.

Murray, C, 1981, *Families divided: The impact of migrant labour in Lesotho*. Cambridge: Cambridge University Press.

Murray, M, 1997, "Factories in the fields: Capitalist farming in the Bethel District, c.1910*1950", in Jeeves, A and Crush, J (eds), *White farms, black labour: The state and agrarian change in Southern Africa, 1910–1950*. Portsmouth, NH: Heinemann.

Packard, R, 1989, *White plague, black labour: Tuberculosis and the political economy of health and disease in South Africa*. Berkeley: University of California Press.

Peberdy, S, and Crush, J, 1998, "Rooted in racism: The origins of the Aliens Control Act", in *Beyond control: Immigration and human rights in a democratic South Africa*. Cape Town: SAMP/Idasa.

Posel, D, 1991, *Making of apartheid, 1945–1961: Conflict and compromise*. Oxford: Clarendon Press.

Sechaba Consultants, 1996, "Riding the tiger: Lesotho miners and permanent residence in South Africa", SAMP Migration Policy Series No. 2. Cape Town and Kingston: Southern African Migration Project.

Van Onselen, C, 1976, *Chibaro: African mine labour in Southern Rhodesia, 1900–1933*. London: Pluto Press.

Van Onselen, C, 1982, *New Babylon, New Nineveh: Studies in the social and economic history of the Witwatersrand, 1886–1914*. London: Longman.

Walker, C (ed), 1991, *Women and gender in Southern Africa to 1945*. Cape Town: David Philip Publishers.

Wells, J, 1993, *We now demand: The history of women's resistance to pass laws in South Africa*. Johannesburg: Witwatersrand University Press.

Wilson, F, 1972, *Labour in the South African gold mines, 1911–1969*. Cambridge: Cambridge University Press.

Worger, W, 1987, *South Africa's city of diamonds: Mine workers and monopoly capitalism in Kimberley, 1867–1895*. New Haven: Yale University Press.

Chapter Two

Lesotho and South Africa: Time for a new immigration compact

by John Gay

If Lesotho and South Africa were truly distinct and separate, it would be natural to speak of migration or immigration from Lesotho into South Africa. Such terms suggest images that apply better to the movement of people from Mozambique or Zimbabwe into South Africa. Kruger Park, Swaziland and the flood plain of the Pongola River are natural barriers to Mozambicans entering South Africa, and the linguistic and cultural affinities across the border are limited. Similarly, Zimbabweans north of the Limpopo River are mainly of Shona and Ndebele origin without great many relatives to the south. Thus, for Mozambique and Zimbabwe, migration and immigration are the appropriate terms. Mexicans entering the United States or Burmese entering Bangladesh offer a comparable situation. Lesotho, on the other hand, is different for many reasons.

One reason is the construction of colonial borders. When Afrikaner settlers trekked up from Cape Town in the late 1830s, the territory of Lesotho, according to the 1843 Napier Boundary, was at least 50% larger than the present 30 355 square kilometres (Gill, 1993: 90). The additional 15 000 square kilometres were taken away from the Basotho by the Boers who were to establish the Orange Free State through warfare, theft and diplomacy. Most Basotho have never forgotten that what is now the Free State province in South Africa was once claimed by their ancestors.

The so-called "conquered territories" run from Bethulie near the Gariep Dam in the south-west to roughly Marquard and Winburg in the north, and are largely, although not totally, Sesotho-speaking. Nor is the old Napier Boundary the limit of where Sesotho is spoken. Much of the Eastern Cape from Matatiele to Aliwal-North, and much of the Free State from Bloemfontein north to Orkney and east to Harrismith and Vrede, is Sesotho territory. Rough estimates are that there are about three million Sesotho speakers in South Africa as opposed to two million in Lesotho.

Linguistically and culturally a case can be made that Lesotho should be considered the place where Sesotho is spoken and where Basotho live. From this perspective, the present nation-state of Lesotho is an artificial sub-region within what some consider should be, and in some sense is, a "Greater Lesotho". Nevertheless, Lesotho is a nation-state with defined boundaries, a member of the United Nations, a sovereign country. But in the larger sense that informs this chapter, Lesotho is a culture and a society arbitrarily cut off from itself by boundaries it did not make and did not want. What's more, the queue of Basotho who wait patiently every day for border guards to take a cursory look at their passports realise in the very weariness of that wait that they are still an integral part of that divided nation.

More concrete evidence of this "uniqueness" is to be found in the survey of public attitudes towards cross-border migration on which this chapter is based. This survey of 692 Basotho in 1997 provides the first nationally representative data on attitudes towards migration in Lesotho and provides detailed information on places visited in South Africa, frequency of trips, employment patterns, reasons for leaving or returning, attitudes towards South Africa and South African immigration policy, and expectations of treatment in South Africa. More importantly, the data allow for a direct comparison with the results from the same survey conducted concurrently in Mozambique and Zimbabwe (the survey was subsequently conducted in Namibia, but the results were not available at the time of writing). Who the Basotho are and what makes their situation unique with respect to migration to South Africa comes out most clearly by contrasting them with others.

After a brief description of research methodology, the chapter compares the survey data from Lesotho with that from the other two countries. This comparative assessment is followed by an analysis of how Basotho differ among themselves on issues of cross-border migration. The chapter concludes with a discussion on future directions, possible policy implications around closer co-operation between South Africa and Lesotho, arising from the research findings.

A NOTE ON METHOD

These survey findings represent a nation-wide sample of Basotho. The locations of households included in the sample were based on the population distributions given by recent national censuses. The individual to be chosen from a given household was selected at random from all members 16 years and older. In Lesotho a cut-off age of 65 years was used, while in the other two countries there was no upper age limit. Research assistants in Lesotho alternated between choosing males and females in successive households, while no such restriction was in place in Mozambique or Zimbabwe. These inter-country differences are not believed to have brought about any serious distortion in comparing results.

It is important to recognise that this survey was conducted before the September 1998 violence and subsequent "peacekeeping" operation by soldiers from South Africa and Botswana in Lesotho. It is likely that many of the opinion-based questions would have been answered differently following this unrest. This chapter is thus based entirely on data recorded in 1997. The policy implications drawn at the end of this report have also been based on the situation prior to the military intervention, since it is not clear at this point (so soon after the conflict) what new immigration-related policies may have to emerge between Lesotho and South Africa.

The sampling strategy and field methodology employed are described in greater detail in Appendix A. The questionnaire and aggregate summary of the results of the survey are provided in Appendix B. A profile of the sample population in Lesotho is provided in Table 2.1.

COMPARING LESOTHO WITH MOZAMBIQUE AND ZIMBABWE

Frequency of visits

One of the most marked differences among Lesotho, Mozambique and Zimbabwe when it comes to their relationship with South Africa is the sheer number of people who have visited South Africa from Lesotho and the long history of this movement. As Table 2.2 on the next page illustrates, travel to South Africa has been a way of life for an overwhelming majority of Basotho for at least three generations.

The frequency of visiting South Africa is also much higher for Basotho than for citizens of the other two countries. The mean number of visits of the Basotho who have visited South Africa in their lifetime is a very high 68, while the mean number for the Mozambicans and Zimbabweans who have visited South Africa is only six. Table 2.3 gives the number of visits in a lifetime for all three countries.

The patterns for Mozambique and Zimbabwe are quite similar, and very different from the pattern for Lesotho, where more than a third of Basotho interviewees who had visited South

TABLE 2.1: A PROFILE OF THE SAMPLE POPULATION IN LESOTHO	
Number of interviews	692
Gender (%)	
Male	51
Female	49
Race (%)	
African	99
White	–
Coloured	–
Age (%)	
15–24	26
25–44	48
45–64	25
65+	2
Urban or rural (%)	
Urban	59
Rural	41
Marital status (%)	
Married	64
Separated/divorced/abandoned	5
Widowed	9
Unmarried	22
Household status (%)	
Household head	47
Spouse	26
Child	21
Other family	3
Other	3

Note: Figures in tables may not add to 100% due to rounding. A hyphen (-) signifies a value of greater than zero but less than 0.5%.

TABLE 2.2: PERCENTAGE OF RESPONDENTS WHO HAVE VISITED SOUTH AFRICA AT LEAST ONCE IN THEIR LIVES

	Lesotho	Mozambique	Zimbabwe
Has personally visited South Africa	81	29	23
Parents visited South Africa	83	54	24
Grandparents visited South Africa	72	38	25

Note: N = 2 300.

TABLE 2.3: VISITS TO SOUTH AFRICA IN LIFETIME

Percentage who made:	Lesotho	Mozambique	Zimbabwe
1–5 visits	25	71	79
6–10 visits	12	19	10
11–30 visits	18	9	6
31–50 visits	10	2	4
More than 50 visits	36	0	0

Note: N = 971.

Africa had been there more than 50 times. Some even claimed to have made more than 1 000 visits in their lifetime, quite realistic in view of the fact that they shop or attend school or go to work there on a daily basis.

Ease of travel

Basotho find it easier to travel to South Africa than citizens of Mozambique or Zimbabwe do. Firstly, 87% of the Basotho interviewees hold passports, while only 29% of Mozambicans and 30% of Zimbabweans have passports. Secondly, travel from Lesotho to South Africa is generally easier in terms of available and affordable transport than from Mozambique or Zimbabwe, and for most Basotho the border is much closer.

Moreover, while in all three countries the presence of friends or family members was important in the decision to visit South Africa, the proportion of Basotho who had such friends or family in South Africa before they left (74%) was significantly higher than that of Mozambicans (61%) or Zimbabweans (64%). Finally, 73% of Basotho know where they would stay if they went to South Africa, while 61% of Mozambicans and only 45% of Zimbabweans said they would know where to stay. In short, experience counts and enables Basotho to know South Africa and South Africans. Travel to South Africa is travel to a place they are familiar with, a place with friends and relatives to visit.

Language is also a factor here. When asked where they were most likely to go when they visited South Africa, 76% of Basotho identified towns or cities which are predominantly Sesotho- or Setswana-speaking (Welkom in the Free State being the most commonly mentioned). An additional 14% said they go to communities within Gauteng (which itself has a large Sesotho-speaking population), and the remaining 10% said they would go to other parts of South Africa. When the interviewee was asked where he or she had stayed on their last visit to South Africa, 71% stated a Sesotho- or Setswana-speaking community, 11% Gauteng and 18% some other location. When the interviewee was asked where he or she would prefer to live, 68% suggested a Sesotho- or Setswana-speaking community, 14% Gauteng and 18% some other location.

Clearly, Basotho prefer to live in an area where their own language is spoken. This possibility is much less likely for persons entering South Africa from Mozambique or Zimbabwe, but it is always possible in the Free State or Gauteng to find Sesotho speakers. In fact, in much of the area, Sesotho is the preferred language over either English or Afrikaans. It makes life much easier in shops in Bloemfontein or Welkom to negotiate in Sesotho. Even many whites in these areas are conversant in Sesotho. Setswana, moreover, is mutually intelligible with Sesotho, since both (along with Sepedi in Mpumalanga and Selozi in the Caprivi Strip and in south-western Zambia) are dialects of one common Sotho language.

Employment in South Africa

When it comes to employment, Lesotho once again presents a different picture from the other two countries. As is evident from Table 2.4, almost a third of all Basotho citizens have worked at some point in their lives in South Africa, the overwhelming majority of whom work(ed) in the mines. Basotho who work, or have worked, in South Africa also remain in their jobs longer than persons from the other two countries do. The mean length of stay of Basotho workers is 143 months, while Mozambicans stay a mean of 47 months and Zimbabweans only 28 months. Broadly, this means an average employment of 12 years for the Basotho who answered this question, but only four years for Mozambicans and two for Zimbabweans. Of course, the total length of employment will be higher than this figure, because most of those who were interviewed are in mid-career and can be expected to continue in their jobs until either retirement or retrenchment. The median lengths of time for the three countries are 84 months for Basotho, 24 months for Mozambicans and 12 months for Zimbabweans.

Basotho who are employed in South Africa are also more likely to send money home to their families (89%) than Mozambicans (66%) or Zimbabweans

TABLE 2.4: PERCENTAGE OF RESPONDENTS WHO HAVE WORKED IN SOUTH AFRICA			
	Lesotho	Mozambique	Zimbabwe
Worked in SA	32	8	19
Worked in mines in SA	22	10	1
Note: N = 2 300.			

(70%). This indicates a closer relationship of Basotho with their home country than migrant workers from the other two countries. There is no significant difference, however, between the amounts sent home and an average of R320 per month being sent. Mozambicans sent slightly more and Zimbabweans slightly less, but not significantly so. The reason is very likely that family needs are the same in all three countries, so that if the migrant worker is faithful to the family the money must be enough to support those left behind.

Why Basotho visit South Africa

The high percentage of Basotho who have worked in South Africa at some point in their lives notwithstanding, it is also clear that work is only one part of the cross-border movement equation. As Table 2.5 illustrates, a much smaller percentage of Basotho went to South Africa on their last visit to work or look for work than their Zimbabwean and Mozambican counterparts. Fully one third of Basotho went to South Africa to visit friends and family on their last visit (compared to about one-tenth of Zimbabweans and Mozambicans). Shopping – possibly for some a euphemism for buying and selling goods – is the second most frequent reason given, with studying, holidays and medical treatment also cited as important primary reasons for going to South Africa.

Zimbabweans and Mozambicans, on the other hand, are less likely to go South Africa for shopping, family affairs or other personal matters (with the notable exception of "shopping" for Zimbabweans – again, possibly for purposes of buying and selling goods). Mozambicans have a similar pattern to that of Basotho – going to work or seeking work. Roughly the same overall proportion of interviewees from Mozambique and Lesotho who have been to South Africa last went there to

TABLE 2.5: REASONS FOR MOST RECENT VISIT TO SOUTH AFRICA			
Percentage whose reasons were:	Lesotho	Mozambique	Zimbabwe
Looking for work	8	22	14
Going to work	17	45	15
Buying and selling goods	3	2	21
Studying	1	1	2
Shopping	19	4	21
Business	2	2	8
Visiting family or friends	34	12	13
Holiday/tourism	2	5	3
Medical treatment	6	4	2
Other	8	2	3

Note: N = 971.

seek work, and only slightly fewer from Mozambique went because they had a job. Zimbabweans and Basotho have a very similar pattern of crossing the border for business, which mostly means buying and selling goods.

Those who reported having gone to South Africa have a different set of reasons for returning home according to their country of origin. The most common reason cited for Basotho and Zimbabweans returning home is simply that their visit had ended. The most common reason cited by Mozambicans is that they no longer had work. It is also much more common for Mozambicans to have been deported than citizens of Lesotho or Zimbabwe (see Table 2.6).

TABLE 2.6: REASONS FOR RETURN TO HOME COUNTRY AFTER MOST RECENT VISIT TO SOUTH AFRICA			
Percentage whose reasons were:	Lesotho	Mozambique	Zimbabwe
Returned after holiday or visit ended	35	15	26
Wanted to come back home	15	22	25
Family reasons	8	9	7
Sick/injured	5	3	1
Contract ended	2	18	9
Retired from job	2	3	3
Lost job or retrenched	11	10	2
Found job at home	1	1	1
Travel documents expired	4	2	5
Expelled or deported from SA	1	11	4
Studies ended	–	0	1
Goods sold out	–	2	9
Other	18	5	9
Note: N = 971.			

Attitudes towards South Africa

The impression created thus far is that Basotho behave as if South Africa (or at least the neighbouring Sesotho-speaking parts of South Africa) is an extension of their home. This behavioural pattern is also reflected in the expressed opinions that Basotho have of South Africa. Many of the questions in the survey assessed people's attitudes towards South Africa and the differences between South Africa and their home country. These questions show a generally positive attitude on the part of Basotho towards their giant neighbouring country, more so than their Mozambican or Zimbabwean counterparts.

Table 2.7 explores the question of borders between countries, particularly the border between the home country and South Africa. From the number of

respondents who answered "yes" to the first three questions, it is obvious that most Basotho see borders as unnecessary and artificial. A sizeable minority of Mozambicans and Zimbabweans feel the same way but the percentages are significantly different, no doubt influenced by the fact that these two countries have several international borders while Lesotho is completely surrounded by South Africa.

The response to the fourth question in Table 2.7 (on whether people differ across borders) may seem a paradox given the responses to the first three questions, but it can be explained by noting that Basotho have much more contact with South Africa than citizens of the other countries. Eighty-one percent of Basotho have visited South Africa and base their knowledge of South Africa on personal experience while Mozambicans and Zimbabweans rely much more on second-hand stories from friends and relatives and the media for their information about South Africa. Basotho, therefore, are arguably more sensitive to the important social, cultural and economic differences between the countries.

The most striking fact to emerge from Table 2.7 is that 41% of Basotho believe that Lesotho and South Africa should merge into one country.[1] Ever since Basutoland was brought under the direct rule of the Cape in South Africa in 1879, this has been a matter of contentious debate. The Gun War was fought over the issue, a war which the Basotho won, leading to Britain once again taking direct control over the colony in 1884. Furthermore, in 1910, when the Union of South Africa was formed, incorporation into the new nation was resisted by the Basotho. The Freedom Charter of 1955 asserted that Basutoland should be free to join the new South Africa if it wished. At no stage during this history, however, was Lesotho willing to lose its sovereign independence, mainly because it would not submit itself to the indignities of apartheid.

With the birth of a new democracy in South Africa in 1994 the situation changed and the sovereignty debate has been resurrected. Not only has the

TABLE 2.7: ATTITUDES TOWARDS BORDERS			
Percentage who agreed that:	Lesotho	Mozambique	Zimbabwe
It is a basic human right for people to be able to cross from one country into another without obstacles	82	53	65
It is ridiculous that people from this country cannot freely go to another country, all because of some artificial border	78	40	43
It is very important for [respondent's country] to have a border that clearly differentiates it from other countries	45	74	76
People who live on different sides of borders between two countries are very different from one another	70	47	44
South Africa and [respondent's country] should join together under one government	41	7	9
Note: N = 2 300.			

National Union of Mineworkers, with its more than 100 000 Basotho members, argued for incorporation, but in 1996 the Congress of South African Trade Unions "took a secret decision to work towards the unification of both Lesotho and Swaziland with South Africa by extra-parliamentary means" (Boot, 1998: 5). This 1997 survey suggests that Basotho are more ready for this eventuality than has been previously believed. Very few of the citizens from Mozambique and Zimbabwe, on the other hand, feel that their country and South Africa should merge.

The military intervention of troops from South Africa and Botswana in September 1998 would appear to have generated strong anti-South African sentiment among Basotho, and it is likely that public sentiment favouring incorporation would have dropped after that. But given the long-standing social, economic, geographic and cultural integration of the two countries, it is unlikely that the debate over incorporation will disappear altogether.

Rights of foreigners

In a further set of questions, people were asked their opinion about what rights they feel the South African government should give to foreigners living in South Africa (see Table 2.8). The results from Mozambique and Zimbabwe are very similar, but Lesotho is different in two important respects.

Firstly, the number of Basotho who agreed or strongly agreed with the questions about rights for foreigners was extremely high (more than 90% in many cases), and significantly higher than the other two countries. These responses suggest that Basotho feel strongly that foreigners deserve many of the same rights as South Africans. By "foreigners" it should not be assumed that Basotho are simply referring to special rights for themselves, however. More than two-thirds of

TABLE 2.8: ATTITUDES TOWARDS RIGHTS OF FOREIGNERS IN SOUTH AFRICA			
The SA government should offer people from other African countries who are in SA:	Percentage who "agree" or "strongly agreed"		
	Lesotho	Mozambique	Zimbabwe
Same rights as South Africans	87	70	64
Same chance for a job	95	81	73
Same access to medicine	98	87	85
Same access to housing	90	76	76
Same access to education	97	83	80
Right to vote	66	17	30
Right of permanent residence	81	30	42
Right to become a citizen	82	24	42
Amnesty for all illegal aliens	70	48	46
Note: N = 2 300.			

Basotho responded "no" when asked if people from Lesotho should get special treatment in South Africa.

Secondly, although a large majority of Mozambicans and Zimbabweans also gave positive responses to the first five questions in Table 2.8, only a minority gave positive responses to the last four questions. In other words, Mozambicans and Zimbabweans expect the same economic rights as South Africans but they do not necessarily expect the same political rights. Basotho, on the other hand, want both economic and political rights in South Africa, highlighting once again their stronger sense of attachment to South Africa.

Importantly, a majority of Basotho is willing to return the favour of rights in their country to South Africans, as are citizens of Mozambique and Zimbabwe, as shown in Table 2.9. The fact that a majority of Basotho are willing to let "anyone into this country who wants to enter" (as opposed to a small minority from Mozambique and Zimbabwe) highlights their openness to South Africans in particular.

The big exception in the case of Lesotho (and Zimbabwe) is farming. Only Mozambicans would welcome citizens of other countries to come as farmers. Both Zimbabwe and Lesotho are short of farmland, while Mozambique still apparently has a surplus. In the case of Lesotho, the fear of South African occupation of farmland also has deep historical roots, since most Basotho still assert their rights to land in the Free State which was taken from them in the mid-nineteenth century.

TABLE 2.9: WILLINGNESS TO ALLOW SOUTHERN AFRICANS INTO ONE'S OWN COUNTRY			
How about people from other countries coming here to [respondent's country]? Do you agree or disagree with the following statements, or haven't you heard enough yet to have an opinion? The government of [respondent's country] should:	Percentage who "agreed" or "strongly disagreed"		
	Lesotho	Mozambique	Zimbabwe
Allow people from other Southern African countries to come and sell goods in this country	69	79	75
Encourage people from South Africa to invest here	75	88	77
Encourage people from South Africa to come and farm crops and/or livestock here	23	67	28
Let anyone into this country who wants to enter	61	12	16
Note: N = 2 300.			

Expectations in South Africa

One of the more surprising results of the survey was the overwhelming majority of Basotho who said they expect good or very good treatment when they go to South Africa – even from police and border officials (two groups notorious for harassing foreign Africans). South Africa offers a warm welcome to Basotho, according to those who were interviewed. Table 2.10 compares the percentages of those who expect to be received positively by various South African groups, and illustrates the significant differences between the three countries.

Table 2.10 confirms the impression that Basotho feel at home in South Africa – in many ways. The only group from which Mozambicans and Zimbabweans expect as good treatment in South Africa as the Basotho is their fellow citizens. Otherwise they have serious suspicions and fears as to how they will be received when they enter South Africa.

TABLE 2.10: EXPECTED LEVEL OF GOOD TREATMENT BY SOUTH AFRICANS			
If you were to go and live in SA, would you expect good or bad treatment from:	Percentage who responded "good" or "very good"		
	Lesotho	Mozambique	Zimbabwe
White South Africans	79	38	32
Black South Africans	90	50	45
South African trade unions	93	43	38
South African employers	89	58	59
South African government officials	90	38	48
South African police	91	32	41
Fellow citizens in South Africa	95	93	85
Other Southern Africans	84	63	55
Note: N = 2 300.			

Degree of permanence

And finally, there are important differences between citizens of Lesotho and those of Mozambique and Zimbabwe when it comes to how long people expect to stay in South Africa, as shown in Table 2.11.

Although the majority of respondents in all three countries desire to live temporarily in South Africa (as opposed to permanently) there is an important difference between "wishing" to do something and being "likely" to do it. In other words, what one would like to do and what one realistically thinks one can do are often very different. Accordingly, in Table 2.11 the differences between lines one and two, and then between three and four drop significantly for Mozambique and Zimbabwe. In Lesotho, on the other hand, the percentages actually rise slightly. Basotho, far more than Mozambicans or Zimbabweans, not only wish permanent residence and citizenship in South Africa, they are seemingly more likely to pursue it. A significant number of Basotho even have the desire to retire or be buried in South Africa. Mozambicans and Zimbabweans show very little interest in these last options, which reflects their strong identification with their home country.

TABLE 2.11: LONG-TERM PLANS TO STAY IN SOUTH AFRICA			
	Percentage who "agreed" or "strongly agreed"		
	Lesotho	Mozambique	Zimbabwe
Wishes to live temporarily in South Africa	51	60	51
Likely to live temporarily in South Africa	60	43	42
Wishes to live permanently in South African	24	35	20
Likely to live permanently in South African	25	15	13
Wishes for South African permanent residence	35	15	12
Wishes for South African citizenship	36	8	14
Wishes to retire in South Africa	29	4	7
Wishes to be buried in South Africa	19	1	4
Note: N = 2 300.			

HOW DO BASOTHO DIFFER AMONG THEMSELVES?

The preceding section points to a consensus around issues of migration among Basotho, which differs substantially from the views and activities of citizens of Mozambique and Zimbabwe. That consensus, however, should not hide the very significant differences among Basotho themselves on the issues at hand. This section examines the attitudes and practices of basic sub-groups of the population of Lesotho.

Not surprisingly, age, status in the household, gender, education and social class give rise to the most important differences in attitude to South Africa, with level of work, income and residence following in significance. The following tables take up the key issues that were raised in the previous section and list the most important distinctions among groups.

Where attitudes or practices mentioned in the first section do not appear in the following tables, it is because there are no significant differences between the various subgroups of Basotho on these questions. For example, roughly equal proportions of all Basotho groups agree that foreigners in South Africa should all have the same access to employment, medical care, housing and education, as well as the same rights to vote have permanent residence, become a citizen and receive amnesty if "illegally" in South Africa.

Visits to South Africa

Table 2.12 lists the most important distinctions concerning visits to South Africa and related topics.

As is evident from the table, there is a strong tendency for older people, males, household heads and employed persons to have visited South Africa, and

TABLE 2.12: FACTORS RELATED TO VISITS TO SOUTH AFRICA				
	Has visited SA at least once (%)	Has a Lesotho passport	Has visited SA > 30 visits	Had friends in SA before last visit
15–24 years old	61	75	23	81
25–44 years old	85	91	45	73
> 44 years old	94	93	59	71
Male	86	89	55	68
Female	76	85	33	81
Household head	90	93	58	68
Other member	74	82	30	80
Employed	87	91	54	72
Unemployed	68	81	24	78

Note: N = 692.

to have made more than 30 visits in their lifetime. Likewise, older people and household heads are more likely to have Lesotho passports. On the other hand, there is no significant difference between the proportion of males and females that have passports.

These comparisons aside, a passport is an essential item in Lesotho. Eventually almost everyone will get one, although the data show that the proportion increases with age. Lesotho issues two types of passports – the local passport (valid only with neighbouring countries) and the international passport (used world-wide). The number of people with international passports was relatively small, and obtaining an international passport requires the signature of the Minister of Home Affairs. The local passport, on the other hand, is available to any Mosotho with minimum bureaucratic formality. The passport system, however, is in the process of being changed.

In terms of the logistics of travel, we have already seen that a high proportion of Basotho have friends or relatives in South Africa, but young women and those who are not a head of household are most likely to have a network of friends to receive them when they visit. The fact that older men are less likely to have these connections may simply be an indication that age, gender and household status afford them the confidence to travel. Nevertheless, it must be remembered that in the majority of cases Basotho also travelled to where they had friends or relatives.

Why visit South Africa?

There are strong differences among the various sub-groups of Basotho who were interviewed on why they last visited South Africa. Table 2.13 provides a breakdown of the responses given by age, gender, education, household and

On Borders

TABLE 2.13: REASON FOR GOING TO SOUTH AFRICA ON LAST VISIT							
	To look for work	To work	Business	Study	Shopping	Family matters	Other
15–24 years old	7	2	3	3	11	28	46
25–44 years old	7	13	6	2	20	31	21
> 44 years old	3	29	4	1	12	37	14
Male	10	24	6	1	13	26	20
Female	2	4	4	2	17	38	33
< = Primary school education	8	19	4	1	12	29	26
> Primary school education	3	6	6	2	20	36	27
Household head	7	26	5	2	14	26	20
Other member	5	3	4	2	16	36	34
Employed	8	21	6	1	16	30	18
Unemployed	4	2	2	3	14	35	40

Note: N = 561.

employment status, with each column giving figures for the percentage of the sub-groups that cited a particular reason for why they went.

The age distribution is particularly significant. Not surprisingly, many younger persons are seeking work, while those who already have work in South Africa are in the higher age group. These figures correspond to data from The Employment Bureau of Africa (TEBA), which reports that very few novices from Lesotho are being taken on to the mines (not more than 2 000 in the course of a year). Although the overall number of miners from Lesotho is decreasing by perhaps 3 000 a year, mostly because of retirement, Basotho mineworkers are experienced and valued workers, and the mines are reluctant to let them go. The average age of Basotho miners is therefore increasing.

Women are far less likely than men to go to South Africa to work or even to look for work. There is a serious bias against employing women in South Africa, even though it has long been shown that Basotho women are generally better educated than men. One reason for this bias is that the main source of employment for Basotho is the mines, which hire almost exclusively men.

Family matters are a reason for a high proportion of the older age group to travel to South Africa. Females are also more likely than males to travel for family affairs, as are persons other than the household head or unemployed persons (groups that are likely to overlap). This conclusion is supported by the fact that household heads, far more often than other household members, go to South Africa for work or to seek work. Shopping is done almost equally by all groups and is one of the main reasons why people cross the border into South Africa.

People with primary school education or lower are more likely to travel to

South Africa to work or seek work than those with secondary or higher education. This is so because better-educated men tend to find jobs at home in Lesotho, while mining jobs are often held by men with a lower level of education.

Where to go in South Africa

Closely related to the question of why a person goes to South Africa is the question of where he or she would prefer to go. This is strongly influenced by age and family status. Table 2.14 lists the percentages stating the most preferred areas by sub-population.

Older people and household heads (there is, of course, much overlap between these two groups) prefer to visit areas where their own language is spoken. Younger persons and those without responsibility for the household are more adventurous, willing to visit such places as Gauteng and more remote parts of South Africa. It is true that Gauteng has a great many Sesotho speakers, but it nonetheless must be classed as a collection of mixed-language communities. The differences notwithstanding, these data reinforce the argument made earlier that the majority of Basotho, even the youngest, prefer to travel to an area that would be included in the "greater" Lesotho, as defined at the beginning of this chapter. For them such travel can be considered travel within their "nation".

TABLE 2.14: MOST PREFERRED PLACES TO VISIT IN SOUTH AFRICA			
	Sesotho/Tswana Area	Gauteng	Other
Age 15–24 (%)	54	17	29
Age 25–44 (%)	70	15	16
Age > 44 (%)	82	10	8
Household head (%)	75	14	11
Other member (%)	63	15	23
Note: N = 692.			

Work in South Africa

Employment is one of the major reasons for visiting South Africa, even though it is far from the only reason, as noted earlier. Table 2.15 shows the principal work-related factors, which differ significantly, by population sub-group.

The most important point to highlight here is the fact that work in South Africa is clearly becoming harder to find. Only 7% of the youngest group have been able to find work in South Africa, while 27% of the middle-age group have done so, and a staggering 65% of the oldest group have at one time or another worked in South Africa. No doubt these figures are influenced by the length of time a person has been on the job market, but given the difficulties that younger

TABLE 2.15: WORK-RELATED FACTORS IN VISITING SOUTH AFRICA				
	Has worked in SA (%)	Has worked on mines in SA (%)	Sends money home from SA (%)	Knows how to get work in SA (%)
15–24 years old	7	2	7	28
25–44 years old	27	19	28	39
> 44 years old	65	47	65	45
Male	51	43	55	45
Female	12	0	11	30
< = Primary school education	44	29	48	37
> Primary school education	15	10	18	39
Household head	55	41	56	46
Other member	11	5	12	30
Employed	46	32	46	45
Unemployed	7	3	8	24

Note: N = 692.

people experience in finding work there would appear to be a significant change in employment trends.

Women have an even harder time finding work, or even looking for work, in South Africa. In the past, women used to regularly find informal/undocumented work on farms, brewing beer or doing domestic work in South Africa, but this is less common now. Although access to South Africa is easier, and thus women can find their way into South Africa without legal hassle, fewer women are finding work because competition for these low-level jobs has grown substantially.

There is, however, still a demand for seasonal labour on farms near the Lesotho border, particularly when the time arrives for picking asparagus or fruit, and women are finding work in this sector. There is also still a demand in South Africa for skilled women. Nurses, teachers, doctors, secretaries and social workers are very much in demand, and although the numbers are relatively small the result is an ongoing brain drain of skilled Basotho to South Africa.

The final column of Table 2.15 is something of an anomaly, however, in that it indicates an optimism about finding work in South Africa that is not borne out by the data. A very surprising 28% of young people say they know how to get work in South Africa, which contradicts the actual 7% who have such work. Similarly 30% of women say they know how to find work, whereas only 12% have actually done so. Even 24% of the unemployed are optimistic about their chances.

Reasons for returning home

Many people have at some point in their lives worked in South Africa or visited there for some other reason, but have by this time returned home. It is important to explore the reasons people give for returning to Lesotho. Table 2.16 lists the principal reasons for coming home after having visited South Africa and signifies the differences between the various Basotho sub-groups (with figures in brackets once again meaning that there is no significant difference statistically). It must be kept in mind that most of the people who answered this question did not in fact return from work, but returned for a wide variety of other reasons.

"Personal reasons" and being "sent home" (through expiry of passport or discovery of "illegal entry") provide almost the same percentage for every sub-group, but the other reasons show significant differences between the groups. Family matters draw those back home who are older, have primary school education or less, are household heads and are employed. It is the last of these characteristics which is most likely the key factor. It has already been shown that persons who are older, with less education and household heads are most likely to be employed in South Africa. Many of these people will have to leave their workplaces to return home to deal with family problems, such as funerals, weddings or illness. Most of these will then return to their work if they can.

Returning home for personal reasons is a residual category in the sense that it is most common for those who are not working in South Africa. Such people go across the border for shopping purposes, to seek medical care or visit family and friends, and return when they have accomplished their short-term mission. On the other hand, even the employed persons and the household heads do return home from time to time for personal reasons. The border is not as formidable an obstacle in Lesotho's case as it is with other countries. In the case of mining, work schedules now are such that workers can return home at the end of two weeks or at worst at the end of a month for a weekend off. In short, Basotho leave South Africa on their own initiative (rather than being forced out) and would appear to come and go on a very regular basis.

TABLE 2.16: WHY RESPONDENTS RETURNED HOME FROM MOST RECENT TRIP TO SOUTH AFRICA (%)							
	End of visit	Personal reasons	Family reasons	End of job/work	On leave	Sent home	Other
15–24 years old	53	28	4	10	0	6	0
25–44 years old	41	27	8	16	3	6	0
> 44 years old	22	30	16	25	4	2	1
Male	25	28	8	30	5	5	0
Female	52	29	11	5	1	5	0
< = Primary school	28	29	12	22	4	5	0
> Primary	52	27	6	11	1	4	0
Household head	23	28	12	27	5	5	0
Other member	53	28	6	7	0	5	1
Employed	29	29	11	23	4	4	0
Unemployed	58	25	5	5	0	7	0
Note: N = 561.							

Knowledge of South Africa

People's understanding of South Africa, in terms of their sources of information, also differs significantly among Basotho. Table 2.17 lists the principal means of knowing about South Africa and the distinctions among the various sub-groups.

As can be expected from previous results, older persons, males, household heads and employed persons largely know South Africa through personal experience. For younger persons, females, other members of households and unemployed persons, secondary sources make up the bulk of their information. But very few people in any of the categories said they "don't know about South Africa", illustrating once again the familiarity that most Basotho have with the country.

TABLE 2.17: SOURCES OF KNOWLEDGE OF SOUTH AFRICA (%)				
	Personal experience	Other people	Media or school	Don't know about SA
15–24 years old	22	18	53	7
25–44 years old	50	19	25	6
> 44 years old	71	10	15	4
Male	59	13	22	6
Female	37	19	37	7
Household head	65	13	17	5
Other member	33	19	41	7
Employed	58	13	25	4
Unemployed	32	22	38	8
Note: N = 692.				

Attitudes towards the border

The next issue to be raised concerns attitudes towards the border separating Lesotho and South Africa. Table 2.18 looks at several aspects of the border situation, and lists attitudes of Basotho towards the problems that are encountered there, particularly as these attitudes differ among the different sub-groups.

Although the data in Table 2.18 does not display the same kinds of disparities as previous tables, certain suggestive facts emerge. Firstly, those with less education are less willing to acknowledge the importance of borders and are more likely to ask for special privileges for Lesotho. On the other hand, the unemployed who also feel that Lesotho should have special status are more likely to think that borders are important.

The desire to cross the border freely increases with age, doubtless because these people are more likely to work in South Africa. Equally, older persons and employed persons know better how to travel to South Africa safely.

Lesotho and South Africa: Time for a new immigration compact

TABLE 2.18: ATTITUDES TOWARDS THE BORDER (PERCENTAGE SAYING "YES")				
	Borders are important	People should be able to cross freely	Lesotho should have special privileges	Knows how to travel safely
15–24 years old	49	77	34	62
25–44 years old	42	81	32	79
> 44 years old	41	89	36	80
< = Primary school education	40	85	37	75
> Primary school education	53	78	28	75
Employed	41	79	29	86
Unemployed	52	84	40	63
Note: N = 692.				

Attitudes to the relationship between Lesotho and South Africa are not clearly differentiated by population sub-group, however. The only clear relation between sub-group and attitude is in the decreasing desire for Lesotho to join with South Africa decreasing with the level of education. Altogether 52% of functionally illiterate Basotho would like Lesotho and South Africa to merge, 45% of those with primary education, 33% with secondary and only 29% of those with higher education wish the countries to join.

Living and working in South Africa

The final set of attitudes to be considered concerns the desire to live and work in South Africa, whether temporarily or permanently. There are few differences among groups on desire or expectation to live there permanently. Of the unmarried and no longer married 33% think it likely or very likely that they would live in South Africa permanently, while only 21% of married persons consider it to be a serious possibility, suggesting that married persons are less likely to consider a permanent move. Similarly, only 33% of household heads and their spouses would like to have South African citizenship, whereas 46% of other household members (more likely to be unmarried) have that desire. Also significant is that such a high proportion of Basotho generally wish for South African citizenship, in contrast to the relatively small number who would like to live there permanently, highlighting once again the desire for a more radical form of sovereignty association than that expressed by Mozambicans and Zimbabweans.

Also significant are the differences between sub-groups on their desire to live in South Africa for a short period. Table 2.19 lists the level of desire by population sub-groups. Young people and males generally are more likely to want to live in South Africa for a short period than older people and females. Likewise household members other than the head and the spouse, who are inevitably more settled, are more interested in living temporarily in South Africa. But it must not be forgotten that temporary means temporary. These people eventually want to return to Lesotho. Presumably, the majority of the young men who go across to seek their fortune plan to return to Lesotho to marry and settle down.

TABLE 2.19: LEVEL OF DESIRE TO LIVE IN SOUTH AFRICA TEMPORARILY (%)				
	Not at all	Not much	To some extent	To a great extent
15–24 years old	29	12	41	18
25–44 years old	39	12	35	14
> 44 years old	49	6	30	15
Male	33	10	38	19
Female	45	10	33	12
Household head	41	10	35	14
Spouse	50	7	32	11
Other member	25	14	40	22
Note: N = 692.				

POSSIBILITIES FOR CLOSER CO-OPERATION

The analysis of the survey clearly displays the uniqueness of Lesotho in the Southern African region. It is part of South Africa in a way that Mozambique and Zimbabwe may never be. People move back and forth across the border for work, shopping, family matters and personal needs. Much of South Africa is, to the Basotho, simply an extension of their own country.

The key policy implication of this finding is that a new and special immigration compact should be worked out between Lesotho and South Africa. A number of proposals have been made, ranging from complete incorporation to limited economic integration. These are summarised in Sechaba Consultants' 1995 report on Lesotho (Gay et al, 1995: 187–190), and include reclaiming the so-called "conquered territories" in a larger Lesotho, integrating Lesotho into a larger federation of Southern African states, allowing Lesotho to remain as it is, and adopting a relationship similar to that between Ireland and the United Kingdom (Cobbe, 1992).

Basotho surveyed expressed an interest in two main options for closer, more integrated co-operation between Lesotho and South Africa. Many still wish to see the first option, namely, a restored Greater Lesotho. But this is an unlikely possibility and is not taken seriously by planners, even though the rhetoric still can be heard in political speeches within Lesotho.

Many, but not a majority, of those who were interviewed would like the second option of some sort of merger with South Africa. It would prove difficult to achieve, given the political realities of the region, especially the jobs of Lesotho's chiefs, politicians and civil servants. As noted before, the military incursion by South Africa in Lesotho in late 1998 will no doubt also have had some impact on these sentiments.

The third option, maintaining the status quo, is perhaps the most likely in the short run, but perhaps also the least satisfactory. The border remains a nuisance to many people, blocking them from their natural interaction with South Africa and their family, friends and fellow Basotho who live there, as well as the workplaces they have depended on for so many years.

The fourth option fits the data best at this point. It would involve opening the border to free travel in both directions. It would allow Basotho to own land and seek jobs in South Africa, without losing their citizenship. Lesotho's government would continue to be responsible for social services within its own borders, but Basotho would have the chance to improve their material conditions within South Africa. Short of total integration with South Africa, this model seems to have the best chance of satisfying the desires of the people who gave their time and energies to these interviews, and to match their actual behaviour as workseekers in, visitors to, but not ultimately citizens of South Africa.

REFERENCES

Boot, W, 1998, "Lesotho on edge as poll is disputed", *Mail & Guardian*, 29 May to 4 June.

Cobbe, J, 1992, *Lesotho and the New South Africa: Economic trends and possible futures*. Seattle, Washington: African Studies Association.

Gay, J, Gill, D, and Hall, D, 1995, *Lesotho's long journey: Hard choices at the crossroads*. Maseru: Sechaba Consultants.

Gill, S, J, 1993, *A short history of Lesotho from the late Stone Age until the 1993 elections*. Morija: Museum and Archives.

ENDNOTES

1   Of the 41% who wish Lesotho and South Africa to join together, 45% would lik,e to see Lesotho become a new province within South Africa, 12% would like it to become part of the Free State and 39% would like to see it as part of Lesotho.

Chapter Three

Labour migration to South Africa: The lifeblood for southern Mozambique

by Fion de Vletter

Mozambique stands out as a special and enigmatic case within the southern African migration schematic. The principal exporter of contracted labour to South African mines and farms for almost a century, Mozambique has a long-standing history of migration to South Africa. Differentiated by language, culture and colonial legacy from other major migrant source-countries, like Lesotho and Zimbabwe, Mozambique has the added distinction of having been marginalised from South Africa socially, politically and, to a large extent, economically. As a result, contract migrant labour, limited trade and the port services of Maputo remain the major links with South Africa.

But the relative importance of contract migration from Mozambique to South Africa has diminished in the last 25 tumultuous years, being subject to some of the most dramatic series of political and economic upheavals in modern history. Migration patterns have become more complex (albeit diminished) than the old formal flows of relatively privileged miners, accompanied as they are by movement of refugees fleeing the ravages of war, seeking survival in a more peaceful environment and/or forced by economic circumstances to find alternatives to limited domestic opportunities. The sharp dichotomy between the two countries led some migrants to earn relative "fortunes" (uneducated miners often earning more than government ministers) while, at the other extreme, many Mozambicans, for the sake of survival, were willing to endure penury from what was effectively bonded labour with employers exploiting their plight.

In more recent years, especially since peace in 1992, Mozambique has undergone a dramatic reversal in economic policy and investment patterns with a GNP growth rate surpassed by few, if any, countries in Africa. Although too early to detect the impact these economic changes may have had on migration patterns, the comparative economic instability of South Africa is likely to have reduced the disparities between the two countries and the incentives to leave. The end of formal apartheid in South Africa, with its accompanying economic opportunities for non-whites, has made migration factors for Mozambicans even more complex.

It is in this context of dramatic change that the Southern African Migration Project (SAMP) conducted its migration survey in southern Mozambique in mid-1997. Conducted simultaneously with national surveys in Lesotho and Zimbabwe, the results provide the most comprehensive set of data on cross-border migration attitudes and experiences in Mozambique to date, and allow, for the first time since contract migration began, direct comparisons between some key migrant-supplying states through a common questionnaire.

This chapter will highlight the main features of the Mozambican survey, emphasising some of the main differences in attitudes, perceptions and future plans that distinguish Mozambique from Lesotho and Zimbabwe. The survey has since been implemented in Namibia, but the results were not available at the time of writing.

The chapter begins with an overview of the history and demography of Mozambique plus a brief typology of major categories of migration from the country to help put the survey results in perspective. This overview is followed by a brief discussion of research methodology and provides a demographic breakdown of the sample population. The remainder of the chapter discusses survey results and offers some policy-related conclusions.

OVERVIEW OF MOZAMBIQUE

The economy

Events over the past few years and significant shifts in economic trends have led to a dramatic turnaround in Mozambique's economy. It is important to understand the nature of these changes in order to put migration into better perspective. If an attitude survey of this nature were undertaken a few years ago during the war and economic depression, it could conceivably have rendered quite different results.

At the time of independence, Mozambique witnessed a mass exodus (90%) of Portuguese settlers who had occupied virtually all skilled, and even lower-skilled, positions. By 1973, the year before independence, the manufacturing sector was the sixth largest in sub-Saharan Africa. The new Frelimo government, with minimal skills and managerial capacity, set itself the ambitious goal of socialist development and equality for all. This meant nationalisation of many strategic or abandoned enterprises, a focus on big heavy-industry projects and large state farms. Although impressive advances were made in the provision of basic health and education services, the combination of economic mismanagement and a civil war with South African-backed *Renamo* led to economic collapse.

In 1994, Mozambique joined the World Bank and International Monetary Fund (IMF), and implemented a self-designed structural adjustment programme. Growth followed but was accompanied by high inflation, severe drops in the foreign exchange values of the *metical,* and increasing poverty. The situation was aggravated by the legacy of a very destructive war and one of the worst droughts of the twentieth century.

But with the end of the drought, and with stabilisation brought about by peace and relatively fair elections, the economic situation began to improve. Inflation was reduced from 54.1% in 1995 to 16.6% in 1996 and to 5.6% in 1997. The exchange rate stabilised, depreciating only 5.3% from the end of 1995 (compared with more than 60% the year before) and remained virtually unchanged in 1997.

Using 1990 as a base year, analyses show that over the five-year period 1990–94, Mozambique experienced the highest average annual growth rate of any sub-Saharan African country (just ahead of Lesotho) (Gray, 1996). Growth in 1996 was 7.4% and in 1997 around 7%. Exports for 1996 increased by 30% over 1995, reaching US$226 million. Principal exports were shrimp (27.2%), cotton (8.7%) and cashew nuts (6.3%). Imports for 1997 amounted to approximately US$855 million, about 40% of which came from South Africa.

The National Accounts statistics for 1994 were estimated at US$1.816 billion or a per capita GDP of US$107. Recent calculations suggest that by including the contribution from activities that are neither registered nor recorded, the informal sector accounts for 43.7% of total marketed production and that the GDP is underestimated by about 70% (Ardeni, 1997).

Mozambique, after Sierra Leone, is the most aid-dependent country in the world, having received, over the period 1987-95, more than US$8 billion of support in grants, credit and debt relief. Mozambique tops the IMF's list of eight countries with "unsustainable" debts, with a foreign debt probably exceeding US$5.5 billion. Debt repayments are expected to reach US$300 million per annum in 1999 (Hanlon, 1995). Dominated by foreign investors, authorised investment increased to US$445 million in 1996, 24.7% higher than in the previous year. In 1997, with the prospect of the US$1 billion aluminium refinery, total investment could top US$2.5 billion.

Minimum wages are currently less than US$30 per month and have tended to fall – in dollar terms – to about half of what they were at the outset of the stabilisation programme. In the private sector, average industrial wages have been maintained at about US$39 per month. In 1993 and again in 1995, the urban population manifested its displeasure about the rising cost of living with riots, firstly in reaction to price increases in transport and then rice.

More than three-quarters of the population are rural-based and largely dependent on subsistence agriculture. The active labour force is currently estimated to be about 8 million of which only about 17% are officially in wage employment. Table 3.1 provides very rough approximations of how wage labour is likely to be distributed between sectors. The figure for external migrant workers may well be much higher.

Since the early 1980s, the number of formally employed workers has dropped considerably, initially because of economic stagnation and war. Since 1987,

TABLE 3.1: ESTIMATED WAGE LABOUR BY CATEGORIES	
Private sector formal employment	
Non-agriculture	460 000
Agriculture	40 000
Public service	100 000
Domestic service	150 000
Non-household agricultural enterprises	250 000
Non-agricultural/informal	250 000
Migrant workers	500 000
Note: These estimates assumed a population base of 18m. Wage employment is assumed to be 17%. The categories are very rough estimates made by the author.	

significant retrenchment of workers (estimated at about 100 000) took place through enterprise restructuring and privatisation. Although up to another 30 000 workers may lose their jobs through privatisation, the recent surge and likely continued increase in foreign investment implies that demand for formal wage labour should soon increase significantly.

A stagnant formal economy and a war-torn rural economy meant that economic survival occurred through two principal channels, the informal sector (mainly urban) or external employment (mainly clandestine) in surrounding countries. The urban informal sector has been by far the fastest growing economic sector, absorbing basically equal numbers of men and women.

The southern provinces – with the exception of the Limpopo valley, in particular around Chokwe – are agriculturally less productive than the more northern provinces. Whether agricultural production is low because of the long-term effects of migration, as in the case of Lesotho, or because the region is agriculturally less suitable, is not clear. It is probably a combination of both.

Demography

The population of Mozambique in mid-1995 was estimated at 17.3 million residing in 3.2 million households. More than three-quarters (77.4%) of households are rural, using 97% of cultivated land while producing less than a third of total GDP. Preliminary results of the 1997 national census put the population at 15.7 million, considerably less than the 18 million projected.

The population is characterised by high levels of mortality and fertility, high population growth and a young age structure. An estimated 60% of the population live in absolute poverty (Green, 1989). Just prior to peace, there were about 4.5 million displaced persons within the country and 1.5 million refugees outside the country. Health indicators are among the worst in the world. From 1990 to 1995, the infant mortality ratio was estimated at 148 per 1 000 live births. From 30% to 40% of rural health facilities were destroyed during the war. Only about 30% of the population had relatively convenient access to health services, 22% to safe water and 20% to sanitation (UNFPA, 1995).

Adult literacy is very low at 33% (45% for males and 21% for females) up from 10% at independence. An estimated 42% of the schools were destroyed during the war and currently about half the school-age children are not in school. Only about one-third of children entering primary school are able to complete their primary education. The transition rate of children from primary to secondary level is low and the secondary school rate enrolment rate is only 7% (UNFPA, 1995).

Land is generally not scarce in Mozambique but its distribution is quite skewed. It is estimated that, for the average household, about 1.5 ha would be needed to meet subsistence needs, though this would vary greatly by region. In the southern provinces, it is estimated that 40% of the households cultivate less than 1 ha (20% for the northern provinces) and that the proportion of female-headed households with less than 1 ha is twice that of male-headed households. About one-third occupy areas larger than 2 ha, accounting for 70% of cultivated land (UNESCO/ILO, 1997). It is likely that labour shortages, caused mainly by migration, account for many of the households cultivating such small parcels. It is estimated that less than a third (29%) of rural households sell food crops.

And finally, recent demographic survey data has found that 36% of households in southern Mozambique are female-headed versus 15% in the north, reflecting much higher levels of external migration in the southern provinces. Spot surveys by the NGO World Relief found that as many as two-thirds of households in the south were female-headed.

MIGRATION TYPOLOGIES

The term "migration" is used in this chapter primarily to depict short- to long-term departure for the purposes of seeking an income-generating activity. It excludes social visits, trips for personal shopping as well as commercial purchases. The following is a typology of the major streams of migration from Mozambique to South Africa and is intended as an additional context to the survey results.

Miners

There are currently some 85 000 Mozambican mine workers in service in South Africa. It has generally been assumed that Mozambican mine workers are almost exclusively rural-based, but recent studies show that considerable numbers come from urban areas (De Vletter, 1998). Though the best known of migrant categories, and often assumed to be the most numerous, it is possible that they represent a minority of the Mozambican migrants in South Africa.

Mozambican miners are not a favoured group among their South African peers, being generally seen as largely illiterate, subservient and willing to accept poor working conditions. There is also a perception that Mozambicans are disinclined to join unions and often work as scab labour. In a 1996 SAMP study,

Mozambican miners often mentioned that they felt discriminated against in South Africa (De Vletter, 1998). Mozambicans, perhaps for many of the same reasons that they are disliked by their peers, are popular with employers, and numbers recruited on the mines have risen fairly steadily since independence despite decreased recruitment from all other sources. If current trends are maintained, Mozambicans could soon outnumber Basotho miners.

With the introduction of stabilisation policies on the mines in the 1980s, miners effectively became career workers. With an average age of about 40 and a mean of 15 contracts (De Vletter, 1998), miners return home to Mozambique regularly, helping to explain why in the current survey "miner" was the most common type of work mentioned by respondents who had worked in South Africa.

Agricultural workers

Farm workers have usually been seen as the second most important category of migrant Mozambicans in South Africa, the result of long-standing competition between the mines and farms for Mozambican labour. In contrast to the miners, Mozambican farm workers (concentrated in the adjoining South African provinces of Mpumalanga and KwaZulu-Natal) are generally regarded by South Africans as "illegal" and, for many years, epitomised the image of foreign "aliens" willing to undercut local labour by working for wages considerably lower than what would normally be regarded a decent living wage. Some unions are more sympathetic and feel that the Mozambicans are often exploited by employers who capitalise on their "illegal" status. Farm work is regarded by Mozambicans as one of the lowest forms of employment and most subject to abuse. Labour representatives and human rights activists cite regular instances of exploitation by farm owners in South Africa, the most common of which is turning in undocumented migrants to authorities just before payday.

In addition to colluding with police, there is evidence that farmers have made deals with local officials "selling" Mozambican migrants to employers effectively as bonded labour, as employers are given immunity from prosecution by receiving "legal" documents. Workers are dissuaded from leaving the farms because their papers are kept by their employers (Crush, 1997).

"Illegal legals"

Until recently, very little information has been available about Mozambicans who migrate to South Africa and effectively assimilate as South Africans through the unauthorised acquisition of South African identity documents. There is strong evidence from both the current survey as well as recent work done by Stephen Lubkemann in Machaze district in southern Manica Province that this form of migration from Mozambique may be widespread, perhaps even involving numbers in the tens or hundreds of thousands.[1] Lubkemann's findings suggest that a type of district level "homeboy" network is in place to help new arrivals acquire the necessary documentation that effectively ensure permanent residence without formal process.

Undocumented migrant workers

There is a popular perception in South Africa that hundreds of thousands of "illegal" Mozambican migrants are crawling under electrified fences and traversing game parks populated with man-eating beasts in desperate search of work and/or social services in South Africa. Those who enter the country legally are assumed to overstay their visas, and once in the country it is assumed that all Mozambicans want to stay in South Africa forever.

No one knows for sure the exact extent of undocumented migration from Mozambique, but widely-cited estimates by politicians, academics and the popular press in South Africa are most likely wildly exaggerated (McDonald et al, 1998). South African embassy staff in Mozambique, for example, have stated that they believe there are approximately 8 million Mozambicans in South Africa – almost one half of the Mozambican population.[2] Outrageous and unfounded estimates aside, clandestine migration from Mozambique is clearly a growing phenomenon. Official deportations of undocumented Mozambicans from South Africa give some indication of this growth, having increased from 42 330 in 1990 (79% of all deportees) to 146 285 in 1997 (83% of all deportees) (Covane et al, 1998). Many of these deportees are repeat cases involved in a process of "revolving door" deportations.

South African immigration officials have recently suggested that undocumented migrants from other African countries who are apprehended in South Africa simply claim to be from Mozambique because it will be easier and closer to get back into South Africa from Mozambique (South African Press Agency, 05/01/1998). These important caveats notwithstanding, there is a consistent and substantial upward trend in the absolute number of Mozambican deportees. Surprisingly, however, data provided by Crush (1997: 19) show that only 4 457 Mozambicans overstayed their South African visas in the four-month period from January to April 1996 (compared to 48 334 Basotho and 24 179 Zimbabweans).

Refugees

Despite the return of a vast majority of the approximately 6 million Mozambican refugees who fled the civil war in the country, it is estimated that about 320 000 of these refugees still remain in South Africa. In 1994 the UNHCR/IOM succeeded in repatriating only 67 000 out of an estimated refugee population of 350 000. The reasons for this low rate of return are still unclear, although it has been suggested by some that many refugees did not want to return to Mozambique because they still feared that it was too risky to return. Other observers have argued that the motive to stay is more economically related.

Mozambican refugees are very tightly controlled in South Africa and have not historically been accorded rights normally attributed to refugees by international convention, resulting in a lack of access to identity papers and travel documents. These practices should come to an end now that the new Refugee Act in South Africa has been passed (in late 1998), but before then refugees were only protected from arrest and deportation if they remained in designated areas (Crush, 1997).

A NOTE ON METHOD

Contrary to the parallel surveys in Lesotho and Zimbabwe, which were nationally representative, the survey in Mozambique only covered the southern half of the country, specifically the three southernmost provinces of Maputo, Gaza and Inhambane. This decision was made primarily for logistical and budgetary reasons, but also because the southern half of Mozambique has traditionally been the principal supplier of labour to the mines and farms of South Africa and would appear to supply the bulk of clandestine migrants as well. These provinces have a population of approximately 6.5 million (38% of the population).

In total, 661 people were interviewed using random sampling procedures (sampling strategy and field methodology are described in greater detail in Appendix A; the questionnaire and aggregate summary of the results of the survey are provided in Appendix B). It should be stressed, however, that the respondents interviewed should in no way be seen as proxy for the many thousands of Mozambicans who were living in, working in, or simply visiting South Africa at the time of the survey. The survey was a study of the resident population of southern Mozambique plus those migrants who were transitionally home either on holiday or for some or other reason. The survey should therefore not be used to quantify or explain existing migration patterns, but provide instead a very useful instrument for gauging potential migration activities and assessing some past migration experiences.

It is also important to note that there were considerably more males than females interviewed (61% versus 39%), partly because females were often working in the fields during the time of the interview, and that sometimes, for cultural reasons, the male head of household insisted on answering instead of his spouse. With respect to location, just more than half of the respondents were from urban and peri-urban areas (51%) with the remainder living in rural villages (42%), rural towns (6%) or rural shack settlements (2%). Almost a quarter (23%) spoke mainly Portuguese at home (mostly in urban areas) while the rest spoke one of the principal African languages of the south (eg Shangaan or Tsonga). A more detailed profile of the sample population is provided in Table 3.2 on the next page.

SURVEY RESULTS

Who has been to South Africa?

In terms of past experience of migration, the survey illustrates just how pervasive migration from Mozambique to South Africa has been for the past three generations. A third of respondents claimed that at least one of their grandparents had worked in South Africa in the past, while more than half (53%) stated that at least one of their parents had worked in South Africa. While only 29% of respondents said they had been to South Africa themselves (versus 81% of Basotho and 23% of Zimbabweans), it must be remembered that these figures do not take into account absentee Mozambicans.

Of greatest significance is that 72% of the respondents stated that at least one member of their family was currently living or working in South Africa versus 60% in Lesotho and only 32% in Zimbabwe. A further two-thirds of respondents had friends in South Africa (versus 56% of Basotho and 42% of Zimbabweans) and slightly more than half (51%) said that most or almost all of the members of their communities were in South Africa (versus 47% of Basotho and 8% of Zimbabweans).

A demographic breakdown of respondents who said they had been to South Africa in the past also reveals some interesting results. Far from being the kind of rootless, uneducated criminals that they are so often portrayed to be in the South African media, the bulk of resident Mozambicans who have been to South Africa in the past are relatively well-educated with employment and other important responsibilities at home. Almost three-quarters of those who have been to South Africa are married or co-habiting, two-thirds are heads of household, 87% own their own homes, 49% have full- or part-time work in

TABLE 3.2: A PROFILE OF THE SAMPLE POPULATION IN MOZAMBIQUE	
Number of interviews	661
Gender (%)	
Male	61
Female	39
Race (%)	
African	95
White	–
Coloured	4
Asian	–
Age category (%)	
15–24	32
25–44	46
45–64	16
65+	5
Urban or rural (%)	
Urban	51
Rural	49
Marital status (%)	
Unmarried	36
Widowed	5
Separated/divorced/abandoned	4
Married/co-habitating	55
Household status (%)	
Household head	40
Spouse	17
Child	32
Other family	9
Other	2

Note: Figures may not add to 100% due to rounding. A dash (–) signifies a value of greater than zero but less than 0.5%.

Mozambique and 38% have at least some high school education (Table 3.3). Once again, these respondents cannot be taken as proxy for the current migrant population of Mozambicans in South Africa, but the results do challenge the stereotypes.

It should also be noted that men far outnumber women in terms of those who say they have been to South Africa in the past (88% of those who have been to South Africa were men). While this is not entirely surprising given the gender history of contract migration in the region, the figures are far more imbalanced than either Lesotho or Zimbabwe, where only 54% and 61% – respectively – of the respondents who said they had been to South Africa were men.

Modes of entry into South Africa

As noted above, for many the term "Mozambican migrant" evokes the image of clandestine entry. The results of the survey, however, suggest that the majority of respondents who have been to South Africa in the past entered the country through conventional methods. Forty-three percent went to South Africa by road, using car, bus or minibus, and 38% went by train. Only 14% said they arrived on foot, and it is likely that many of these were actually referring to the practice of taking a bus or minibus to the border post and then going through customs on foot to get on another bus on the South African side.

It would also appear that the vast majority (75%) was able to obtain a passport before going to South Africa and 73% obtained a visa or entry permit. Almost two-thirds (62%) had a

TABLE 3.3: DEMOGRAPHIC BREAKDOWN OF MOZAMBICAN RESPONDENTS WHO HAVE BEEN TO SOUTH AFRICA	
Male (%)	88
Female (%)	12
Urban (%)	44
Rural (%)	56
Average age (in years)	41
Marital status (%)	
Married	74
Unmarried	19
Widowed	4
Separated/divorced/abandoned	3
Household status (%)	
Household head	66
Spouse	9
Child	18
Other	8
Home ownership (%)	
Own	87
Rent or share	13
Level of employment activity (%)	
Full-time	32
Part-time	17
Looking for work	29
Inactive	22
Level of education (%)	
No schooling	18
Some primary school	30
Primary school completed	14
Some high school	24
High school completed	10
Post-grad and further	4
Note: N = 189.	

place to stay before they went. Just over half (51%) knew of a place where there were people who could take care of them when they first arrived, suggesting that contacts through a type of "homeboy" network is common. Most respondents either knew how to get the relevant documentation or knew how to find out about it while 60% claimed to know the safest way to get to South Africa.

Despite the pervasive image of Mozambicans being expert and experienced "fence hoppers", only 4% said it was "very likely" that they would know how to stay in South Africa without being returned by police. Similarly, only 4% said it was "very likely" that they would know how to get through the border without being caught by the police. As a result, 59% of respondents said that "not being sure if [they] could get into South Africa legally" would be a real deterrent for them going.

Work experience

The results of the research are perhaps most noteworthy in relation to the motives that respondents gave for visiting South Africa in the past. With the caveat that these results are not necessarily suitable for drawing empirical conclusions about current migration patterns, they do show overwhelmingly that movement to South Africa by Mozambicans has been, and is likely to continue to be, economically motivated.

Of the 29% of Mozambican respondents who had been to South Africa in the past, 71% went for income-generating purposes: ie to work (45%); to find work (22%); to buy and sell goods (2%); or for business (2%). Others went principally to see family or relatives (12%) or for some other reasons, such as medical treatment, holiday or schooling. By comparison, the Basotho and Zimbabwean resident population who had visited South Africa had mainly been to visit family and friends or to shop (Table 3.4). Of those who said they worked in South Africa on their last visit, 40% said that they had been miners (versus 63% of Basotho and 9% of Zimbabweans), with bricklayers, mechanics, business owners and farm work as the other main categories. Average monthly earnings were R724.

Perceptions of whether Mozambicans compete for or complement job opportunities in South Africa were also very interesting. Whereas more than half of the Basotho (52%) and 46% of the Zimbabweans interviewed felt that their workers take jobs away from South Africans, few (18%) Mozambicans feel that this is the case with their nationals. Furthermore, a surprisingly small number of Mozambicans (11%) felt that Mozambicans lose jobs to South Africans, compared to 53% of Basotho and 31% of Zimbabweans. In terms of job availability, there was an overwhelming consensus across all three countries that the availability of decent jobs was better or much better in South Africa.

The possibility that Mozambican labour in South Africa may be playing a complementary role rather than substituting for South African labour is very significant and could possibly enhance Mozambique's bargaining position for negotiating a new labour agreement with South Africa. It has, for example, been demonstrated that many Mozambicans have qualifications that remain scarce in

TABLE 3.4: REASONS FOR VISITING SOUTH AFRICA ON MOST RECENT VISIT (%)			
What was the purpose of your most recent visit?	Mozambique	Lesotho	Zimbabwe
To look for work	22	8	14
To work	45	17	15
Buy and sell goods	2	3	21
School	1	1	2
Shopping	4	19	21
Business	2	2	8
Visit family or friends	12	34	13
Holiday, tourism	5	2	3
Medical treatment	4	6	2
Other	2	8	3
Note: N = 192.			

South Africa, especially on the mines (De Vletter, 1987). This may also be the case for other sectors requiring mechanical and building skills. More problematically, it is also known that Mozambicans, because of their comparatively disadvantaged position, have been willing to accept jobs that many South African workers have refused. This is not to suggest that Mozambicans should gladly accept dangerous or unhealthy work, but rather that immigration policy-makers acknowledge different wage incentives and develop appropriate labour legislation standards.

Given the bad press and anecdotes that prevail about bad employer treatment of Mozambicans, it seems surprising that almost half (49%) of the Mozambicans who had been to South Africa in the past felt that treatment by employers was better in South Africa than Mozambique – a sad indictment of what labour conditions must be like at home. Nevertheless, when all respondents were asked about the type of treatment they could expect from South African employers if they were to go to the country in future to find work, only 7% expected "very good" treatment (as opposed to 36% of Basotho and 9% of Zimbabweans), suggesting that Mozambicans are sceptical about labour conditions in South Africa as well.

Views on migration

Another surprising result is that, despite all of the negative press and academic coverage of migration from Mozambique to South Africa, Mozambicans on the whole were very positive about the impact migration has had on them personally (68% positive or very positive), their family (69% positive or very positive), community (60% positive or very positive) and country (58% positive or very positive). Moreover, Mozambicans were considerably more positive than their Basotho or Zimbabwean counterparts (see Table 3.5). Respondents who had actually been to South Africa demonstrated even higher levels of positiveness, with 83% indicating that they had had positive or very positive experiences.

When asked about the main concerns or worries that people had with respect to someone "close" going to South Africa, one-third of the Mozambican

TABLE 3.5: PERCEIVED IMPACTS OF MIGRATION ON SELF, FAMILY, COMMUNITY, COUNTRY (%)			
	Mozambique	Lesotho	Zimbabwe
Many people from this country are going to SA to stay or work. Has this had any impact on you personally?			
Very positive/positive	68	52	48
No impact	20	12	46
Very negative/negative	8	35	5
Don't know	3	2	2
Many people from this country are going to SA to stay or work. Has this had any impact on your family?			
Very positive/positive	69	47	46
No impact	17	13	46
Very negative/negative	17	33	6
Don't know	4	7	3
Many people from this country are going to SA to stay or work. Has this had any impact on your community?			
Very positive/positive	60	50	50
No impact	15	4	25
Very negative/negative	13	33	7
Don't know	11	12	19
Many people from this country are going to SA to stay or work. Has this had any impact on [your country]?			
Very positive/positive	58	46	47
No impact	7	3	14
Very negative/negative	19	40	15
Don't know	15	10	24
Note: N = 2 300.			

respondents said that they would be afraid that person would never come back, which is their greatest single concern (by contrast, with only 13% of Zimbabweans and 7% of Basotho). This result underscores the growing importance of non-contract types of migration from Mozambique – perhaps even an indication of the aforementioned "illegal/legal" category – and suggests that a more permanent kind of emigration may be developing. Table 3.6 provides a breakdown of the "most important" concerns that respondents from the three countries gave.

Falling victim to a crime was the second greatest concern of Mozambicans (mentioned by 23% of the sample), but Mozambicans would appear to be less worried than their Basotho and Zimbabwean counterparts in this respect. While just more than half (51%) of Mozambicans think it is likely that Mozambicans would become a "victim of crime" if they went to South Africa, these figures are considerably lower than the results in Lesotho (82%) and Zimbabwe (81%). Mozambicans are also less likely to think that people from their country would "become involved in crime" as perpetrators, with only 27% of Mozambicans saying this would be likely, as opposed to 61% of Basotho and 59% of Zimbabweans.

Mozambicans also felt less strongly than their counterparts about disease. Only 10% felt that Mozambicans "carry diseases to South Africa", versus 26% of Basotho and 52% of Zimbabweans (no doubt reflecting a heightened awareness on the part of Zimbabweans in particular of the high incidence of AIDS in that country). Similarly, much smaller numbers of Mozambicans (34%) felt that their country's migrants "get diseases in South Africa" (versus 86% of Basotho and 69% of Zimbabweans). These figures reflect a poor understanding on the part of

TABLE 3.6: MOST IMPORTANT CONCERNS ABOUT FRIENDS AND FAMILY GOING TO SOUTH AFRICA (%)			
If someone close to you went to SA, what would be your main concern?	Mozambique	Lesotho	Zimbabwe
Become involved in an affair	4	3	2
Get injured	9	63	20
Become a victim of crime	23	8	24
Become involved in crime	9	2	5
Get a disease	6	4	14
Have a second family	7	3	3
Never come back	33	8	13
Lose own language and culture	2	–	1
Lose religious or moral values	1	–	–
Nothing would worry me	0	3	3
Get killed there	0	0	8
Other	7	5	5
Note: N = 2 300.			

Mozambicans of the well-documented and tragically high levels of transmission of sexually transmitted diseases (STDs) through migrant workers in the region, and highlight the need for better and urgent public education on the issue in Mozambique.

Finally, it is interesting to note that while almost two-thirds (63%) of Basotho respondents said they would be worried about somebody "getting injured" in South Africa – no doubt a reflection of the relatively high proportion of miners from that country – only 9% of Mozambicans gave this as a response.

General attitudes towards South Africa

When asked about their general impressions of South Africa, the vast majority of respondents in all three countries had favourable to very favourable impressions. But when asked to evaluate their expected treatment in South Africa there were some notable differences across the three countries, with Mozambicans and Zimbabweans being much less likely to expect good treatment while in the country than Basotho.

While approximately a third of Basotho consistently said they would expect "very good" treatment from both white and black South African citizens, the South African police, trade unions, employers, and customs and immigration officials, only about 5% of Mozambican and Zimbabweans answered in this way (with only 2% of Mozambicans saying they would expect "very good" treatment from custom and immigration officials). These differences stem, no doubt, from the very close linguistic, cultural and historical ties that Lesotho has had with South Africa and reflect the relative ease with which Basotho integrate into South African society (see Chapter 2).

There was more consensus among the three countries when it came to questions asking respondents to compare their home country to South Africa on a variety of fronts. As noted earlier, a large majority of respondents felt that access to decent jobs was much better in South Africa. Similarly, most respondents felt that access to health care and decent education was better in South Africa. Importantly, however, respondents from all three countries were also in broad agreement that access to basic necessities like clean water, housing and land were much better at home. Respondents also felt that less tangible, but critically important, factors like peace, crime and safety of self and family were much better at home. This last point is particularly noteworthy in the context of Mozambique where 20 years of brutal civil war have put a premium on peace.

These conflicting opinions about South Africa are also reflected in the responses to questions about what factors would influence a respondent's decision about whether or not to go to South Africa (Table 3.7). Jobs and social services remain key factors in drawing people from the region to South Africa, but these "pull" factors are countered by some very strong feelings about access to land and lower rates of crime and violence at home. It is difficult to say how these competing factors play off one another in the decision-making process,

TABLE 3.7: DECISION-MAKING FACTORS IN THE MIGRATION PROCESS (%)			
Of the things we have just discussed that would cause you to go to SA, which is the most important to you?	Mozambique	Lesotho	Zimbabwe
Land	1	–	2
Water and food	2	1	1
Houses	0	–	1
Jobs	40	50	35
Trade	4	–	8
Overall living conditions	14	–	5
Safety of self and family	1	–	–
Crime	1	0	–
Peace	–	0	–
Education, schools	7	9	2
Health care	14	10	3
Place to raise family	–	0	–
Disease, HIV/AIDS	1	0	0
Freedom	0	–	1
Getting necessary travel documents	1	–	1
Shopping	9	17	26
Nothing	0	0	8
Other	5	8	7
Of the things we have discussed that would cause you to stay in [your country], which is the most important to you?			
Land	17	40	14
Water and food	4	3	3
Houses	6	6	2
Jobs	3	2	1
Trade	–	–	–
Overall living conditions	5	7	5
Safety of self and family	13	1	12
Crime	4	5	6
Peace	17	10	23
Education, schools	1	1	2
Health care	–	–	1
Place to raise family	5	1	5
Disease, HIV/AIDS	–	1	1
Freedom	3	10	6
Getting necessary travel documents	6	–	1
Shopping	–	–	—
I grew up in [this country]	0	2	11
Other	14	8	9
Note: N = 2 300.			

and the weights attributed to them will vary from person to person. It is clear, however, that the migration decision-making process is not an easy one for Mozambicans or their Basotho and Zimbabwean counterparts and the decision to live or work in South Africa will not be taken lightly – a conclusion that most South Africans would probably find very surprising.

Attitudes towards borders and immigration policy

When it comes to attitudes towards borders and immigration policy the responses from the Mozambique survey are likely to be just as surprising for most South Africans. Although a majority of the Mozambicans interviewed would like to see a relaxation of border controls with South Africa, only 49% consider it a "basic human right" to be able to move from one country to another (versus 81% of Basotho and 63% of Zimbabweans) and 67% feel it is important to have a border "that clearly differentiates Mozambique from other countries". As Table 3.8 makes clear, most Mozambicans would like to see policies in place which make it easier to move from one country to another, and many question the legitimacy of borders that were created during the colonial era, but they do not advocate a radical dismantling of current border systems.

Even more important is the fact that a majority of respondents felt that the South African government should be able to restrict the number of (im)migrants allowed into the country and that they should also have the right to deport people who are there "illegally", are "not contributing to the well-being of the country" or have "committed serious criminal offences". As Table 3.9 illustrates, respondents would like to

TABLE 3.8: ATTITUDES OF MOZAMBICANS TOWARDS BORDERS (%)	
It is a basic human right for people to be able to cross from one country into another without obstacles	
Agree	49
Neither agree nor disagree	6
Disagree	37
Don't know	6
It is ridiculous that people from this country cannot freely go to another country, all because of some artificial border	
Agree	38
Neither agree nor disagree	14
Disagree	42
Don't know	6
People who live on different sides of borders between two countries are very different from one another	
Agree	43
Neither agree nor disagree	15
Disagree	33
Don't know	8
It is very important for [Mozambicans] to have a border that clearly differentiates it from other countries	
Agree	66
Neither agree nor disagree	8
Disagree	16
Don't know	10

Note: N = 661.

see the South African government define these restrictions and categories in a humane and rational manner, but do not reject the idea of selective (im)migration, nor do they necessarily expect the government of South Africa to grant amnesty to every non-South African currently living in the country. Nor do the majority expect preferential or privileged treatment for people from

TABLE 3.9: ATTITUDES OF MOZAMBICANS TOWARDS IMMIGRATION LAWS (%)	
How about people from other countries going to SA? Which one of the following do you think the SA government should do?	
Let anyone into SA who wants to enter	13
Let people into SA as long as there are jobs available	67
Place strict limits on the number of foreigners who can enter SA	15
Prohibit all people entering into SA from other countries	1
Don't know	4
How about people from other Southern African countries who are presently in SA? Which one of the following do you think the SA government should do?	
Send them all back to their own countries	2
Send back only those who are not contributing to the economic well-being/livelihood of SA	27
Send back only those who have committed serious criminal offences	57
Send back only those who are here without the permission of the SA government	8
The government should not send back any people to their own countries	3
Don't know	2
The SA government should offer amnesty to all foreigners now living illegally inside the country	
Disagree	31
Neither agree nor disagree	17
Agree	44
Haven't heard enough about it/don't know	9
Do you think that people from [Mozambique] should receive special immigration treatment (compared to people from all other countries)	
Disagree	29
Neither agree nor disagree	16
Agree	47
Haven't heard enough about it/ don't know	1
Note: N = 2 300.	

Mozambique, despite their history of cross-border relations and proximity to South Africa.

Equally interesting is that Mozambicans do not necessarily expect to have all the same rights and privileges as South African citizens. Although a majority of respondents feel that non-citizens should have the same access to jobs and basic services like education, health care and housing as South African citizens, they were much more hesitant when it came to questions of a more political nature: the right to vote, the right to become permanent residents or citizens of the country, and the right to request amnesty for non-nationals (see Table 3.10). In other words, Mozambicans want the same basic human rights and the same economic opportunities as South African citizens, but they do not necessarily expect (or want) the political rights of citizenship.

FUTURE MIGRATION INTENTIONS

In an attempt to try to gauge future migration trends from Mozambique to South Africa, respondents were asked a series of questions about their desire to migrate in the near future, the likelihood of migrating and for how long they would migrate (ie, temporarily versus permanently). The responses highlight some important temporal differences as well as some strong inconsistencies between "want" and "will".

With respect to the degree of permanence of migration, Mozambicans are more inclined to say they would prefer to live or work in South Africa on a short-term basis (up to two years)

TABLE 3.10: ATTITUDES OF MOZAMBICANS TOWARDS RIGHTS OF NON-CITIZENS IN SOUTH AFRICA (%)

The SA government should offer people from other African countries who are in SA:	
The same chance at a job as South Africans	
Agree	79
Neither agree nor disagree	5
Disagree	14
Haven't heard enough about it/don't know	3
The same access to medical services as South Africans	
Agree	84
Neither agree nor disagree	3
Disagree	10
Haven't heard enough about it/don't know	3
The same access to a house as South Africans	
Agree	73
Neither agree nor disagree	10
Disagree	13
Haven't heard enough about it/don't know	3
The same access to education as South Africans	
Agree	79
Neither agree nor disagree	5
Disagree	12
Haven't heard enough about it/don't know	4
The right to vote in SA elections	
Agree	15
Neither agree nor disagree	10
Disagree	65
Haven't heard enough about it/don't know	9
The right to become a permanent resident of SA	
Agree	28
Neither agree nor disagree	18
Disagree	48
Haven't heard enough about it/don't know	5
The right to become a citizen of SA	
Agree	23
Neither agree nor disagree	18
Disagree	54
Haven't heard enough about it/don't know	5

Note: N = 661.

rather than on a permanent basis. But even these figures are quite low, with only 15% of respondents saying they "want" to go to South Africa "to a great extent" (Table 3.11), once again challenging the popular perception in South Africa that everyone in the region wants to live or work in South Africa.

The numbers drop further when it comes to the likelihood of migration, with only 3% of Mozambicans saying it is "very likely" that they would leave for South Africa permanently in the foreseeable future and only 6% saying it was "very likely" they would migrate even for a short period. These differences between "want" and "will" are all the more interesting in Mozambique given that a majority of respondents, considerably more than in either Lesotho or Zimbabwe, said they had the personal freedom to leave the country: almost half (48%) stated that their family would tend to encourage them to go to South Africa (versus 44% of Basotho and 40% of Zimbabweans); more than half (54%) said that they themselves would make the final decision about migration (versus 46% of Basotho and 39% of Zimbabweans);[3] and 76% stated that they would be able to go to South Africa if they wanted to (versus 64% of Basotho and 68% of Zimbabweans). Mozambicans were also much less concerned than their Basotho or Zimbabwean counterparts about leaving assets behind if they went to South Africa (only 27% of Mozambicans versus 60% of Basotho and 40% of Zimbabweans) and were less concerned with the prospect of leaving family behind

TABLE 3.11: DESIRE AND LIKELIHOOD OF MOVING TO SOUTH AFRICA FROM MOZAMBIQUE (%)	
To what extent do you want to leave Mozambique to go and live in SA permanently?	
A great extent	14
Some extent	18
Not much	14
Not at all	46
Don't know	7
To what extent do you want to leave Mozambique to go and live in SA for a short period (up to 2 years)?	
A great extent	15
Some extent	42
Not much	19
Not at all	19
Don't know	5
How likely or unlikely is it that you would ever actually leave Mozambique to go and live permanently in SA in the foreseeable future?	
Very likely	3
Likely	10
Neither likely nor unlikely	12
Unlikely	36
Very unlikely	33
Don't know	5
How likely or unlikely is it that you would ever actually leave Mozambique to go and live for a short period in SA in the foreseeable future?	
Very likely	6
Likely	34
Neither likely nor unlikely	20
Unlikely	20
Very unlikely	15
Don't know	6
Note: N = 661.	

in Mozambique (35% of Mozambicans versus 71% of Basotho and 57% of Zimbabweans). The possibility of not having friends or a place to stay, cost of travel, the absence of a job, obtaining necessary travel documents, the possibility of being illegally in South Africa and even the prospect of being caught were all regarded as being much less important than in either Lesotho or Zimbabwe.

But this apparently greater personal freedom to migrate is likely to be offset by some important constraining factors. Mozambicans, due in large part to the country's long political turmoil, are much less likely to have identity documents and are therefore more likely to face problems in getting travel documents than Basotho or Zimbabweans. The survey showed that only 29% of the total Mozambican sample held a passport, for example, versus 87% of the Basotho sample. Rural-based Mozambicans are especially unlikely to hold passports.

South Africa is also much more "foreign" to Mozambicans than it is to Basotho and Zimbabweans, with language and culture being a major psychological barrier to entry. And the costs of travel, visas and being in transit in Maputo are all serious obstacles compared to Lesotho in particular. On monetary terms alone, it is not surprising to see such discrepancy between desire and likelihood in migration.

One last obstacle to realising a desire to migrate is the prospect of engaging in decent income-generating activity while in South Africa. In contrast to the 50% of Basotho who claim to know where they could get a job in the country, or claim to at least know where to find one, only 33% of Mozambicans had this kind of information.

In terms of how long they would stay if they were to go to South Africa, 58% of Mozambican respondents said they preferred to stay for more than six months, but only 4% said they would stay indefinitely. This preference for temporary movement is also found in a series of questions asking respondents how serious they would be about staying in South Africa on a more permanent basis, with the number of positive responses decreasing dramatically with the "degree of permanence".

Starting with a rather modest 14% of Mozambicans who said they would like to become a "permanent citizen" of South Africa, only 7% said they would like to become a "citizen" of the country, 4% said they would like to live in South Africa when they "retire", and a mere 1% said they would like to be "buried" there (as opposed to 17% of Basotho [see Table 3.12]). Perhaps the concerns that many Mozambican respondents had about friends and family going to South Africa and "never coming home" are not as serious as they might think. The fact that 92% of respondents said that they would return home to visit friends and family during their hypothetical sojourn in South Africa, and that 87% said they would send money home (mostly to parents or spouse), is further evidence of a likely continuation of circular migration from Mozambique.

POLICY IMPLICATIONS AND CONCLUSIONS

Contrary to popular impressions that most Mozambicans want to go to South Africa and stay there permanently, a large majority of respondents made it clear that they are ambiguous at best about whether to migrate and would most likely only stay in South Africa on a temporary basis. These are only stated intentions, of course, and dramatic changes in the social, political and economic future of the region could alter these plans considerably, but it is safe to say that the stereotypes about migration intentions from Mozambique are simply not borne out in the research.

The reality for South Africa in relation to Mozambique is that the vast majority of those who have entered South Africa in the past have done so legally, at least for entry purposes. Caution is needed when interpreting entry data, however, given the high proportion of Mozambicans who are deported from the country and the apparent phenomenon of "illegal legals". Whatever the case may be, Mozambicans are crossing the South African border in the hundreds of thousands. Many are detained and returned. A large proportion of those deported simply return. This futile merry-go-round of entry, detention, deportation and re-entry causes unnecessary misery, and costs the South Africa government hundreds of millions of rands.

TABLE 3.12: DESIRE OF MOZAMBICANS TO STAY IN SOUTH AFRICA PERMANENTLY (%)	
Would you want to become a permanent resident of SA?	
Yes	14
No	83
Don't know	3
Would you want to become a citizen of SA?	
Yes	7
No	90
Don't know	3
Would you like to live in SA when you retire?	
Yes	4
No	95
Don't know	–
Would you like to be buried in SA?	
Yes	1
No	96
Don't know	3
Note: N = 661.	

In the eyes of many South Africans, such an expensive system of control is justified because it is generally assumed that undocumented migrants from one of the poorest countries in the world will naturally wish to take up permanent residence where economic opportunities and standards of living are among the highest in Africa. As noted, these fears appear to be unfounded. The vast majority of Mozambicans would appear to see South Africa as a source of employment or income-generating activity for a determinate period. Those Mozambicans who will not or cannot obtain proper documentation to enter South Africa find their way there anyway, using elaborate and effective networks that depend on corrupt officials belonging to the control system meant to keep them out. Strict regulations, costly border patrols and deportations are only likely to have stemmed a marginal number of economic migrants.

One particularly interesting finding from the research was the perception that Mozambican migrants complemented South African labour needs. Contrary to the Basotho and Zimbabweans interviewed, Mozambicans did not feel that they substituted for South African workers, nor did they feel that South

Africans were threatening to fill work opportunities normally taken up by the Mozambicans. This is an issue which appears to merit further study as it suggests that a situation not unlike that of Germany with Turkish migrants, or of the United States with Mexicans, may exist with Mozambicans who are willing to undertake certain forms of work shunned by the South African workforce. Another aspect of the perception of complementarity is that many Mozambicans, especially on the mines and in sectors requiring construction and mechanical skills, are comparatively better skilled than their South African counterparts (De Vletter, 1987).

Complacency on this issue would be dangerous. Whether the Mozambican perception about complementarity is right or wrong, the killing of three non-citizens (including a Mozambican) by South Africans, who were probably resentful about perceived impacts on job availability and employment conditions, suggests that many South Africans may see the Mozambican presence in the country quite differently.

Recent economic and political developments such as the promotion of the "Maputo Corridor" will ensure a much greater degree of integration with South Africa. The consequences will likely be greater ease of access to movement across the border with a growth in cross-border movement patterns more akin to those of Lesotho (ie more shopping and visiting of relatives).

Though Mozambique is not a member of the Southern African Customs Union, there are currently serious initiatives to open up trade and reduce tariff barriers. Furthermore, as large South African investments take place, such as the US$1 billion Mozal aluminium refinery, there will be a need for South African labour to come to Mozambique. It is likely, therefore, that pressure will build in South Africa for a softening of borders between the two countries for both capital and labour, already an explicit wish of the premier of Mpumulanga.

South African fears of a mass invasion of Mozambican work-seekers should be further allayed by the fact that a combination of economic factors is reducing the relative disparity between the two countries. As the rand depreciates and the South African economy slows down, Mozambique's current economic growth, large injections of foreign investment, a stabilising currency and lowered inflation will possibly make South Africa a less appealing alternative to domestic employment. Furthermore, the consolidation of peace and internal stability, accompanied by improved infrastructures, will further reduce the perceived quality of life differences.

The current policy by South Africa to control immigration, though largely ineffective in stemming the inflow of Mozambican work-seekers, has also encouraged labour exploitation on the part of South African employers. Although this survey did not address the issue directly, there is much evidence that points towards widespread abuse of undocumented Mozambican migrants, with employers regularly exploiting their employees' vulnerability by paying extremely low wages or, worse still, by not paying them at all and turning them over to police or immigration officials for deportation prior to payday. Deported Mozambicans commonly claim that they are denied the opportunity to collect their belongings before deportation, a reason for many to return to South Africa (Covane *et al*, 1998).

The exploitation of Mozambican labour has been the subject of increasing concern of both Mozambican officials and of the press and more recently by the trade unions. It is unlikely, however, that serious progress will be made on these issues until South African immigration officials and legislators acknowledge the need to accommodate temporary migration from Mozambique in a more humane and rational manner and address the fears and concerns of South African citizens about the role of Mozambican migrants in the social, political and economic fabric of the country.

Surveys such as this should help to convince the South African government of both the need for a new approach to dealing with migration from Mozambique and for a pro-active public education campaign on the realities of migration potentials in the future.

REFERENCES

Ardeni, P, 1997, "The informal economy of Mozambique: An introductory study", paper for Informal Sector and Economic Policy Conference, Bamako, Mali, March.

Covane, L, Macaringue, Julio and Crush, J, 1998, "The revolving door", *Crossings*, 2(2). Cape Town: Southern African Migration Project.

Crush, J, 1997, "Covert operations: Clandestine migration, temporary work and immigration policy in South Africa", *SAMP Migration Policy Series*, No. 1. Cape Town: Southern African Migration Project.

De Vletter, F, 1987, "Foreign labour on the South African gold mines: New insights on an old problem", *International Labour Review*, Vol. 126, No.2.

De Vletter, F, 1998. "Sons of Mozambique: Mozambican miners in post-apartheid South Africa", *SAMP Migration Policy Series*, No. 8. Cape Town: Southern African Migration Project.

Gray, C, 1996, "Growth of sub-Saharan African economies in response to structural adjustment", unpublished paper prepared for the United States Agency for International Development (USAID).

Green, R, H, 1989, *Poverty in Mozambique*. Maputo: Ministry of Finance.

Hanlon, J, 1995, *Peace without profits: How the IMF blocks rebuilding in Mozambique*. London: James Currey.

McDonald, D, Gay, J, Zinyama, L, Mattes, R and De Vletter, F, 1998, "Challenging xenophobia: Myths and realities about cross-border migration in Southern Africa", *SAMP Migration Policy Series*, No. 7. Cape Town: Southern African Migration Project.

United Nations Educational, Scientific and Cultural Organisation (UNESCO)/ International Labour Organisation (ILO), 1997, *Country review for Mozambique*. Maputo: ACC Task Force on Employment and Sustainable Livelihoods.

United Nations Family Planning Association (UNFPA), 1995, "Mozambique: Programme review and strategy development report", No 47.

ENDNOTES

1. Stephen Lubkemann is a PhD candidate in anthropology at Brown University in the United States. These findings are based on his ongoing field work in Manica Province and are preliminary at this point in time.
2. Taken from personal and confidential communication with various members of the diplomatic corps in Mozambique.
3. This point may be influenced by the larger number of male respondents in the Mozambican sample.

Chapter Four

Who, what, when and why: Cross-border movement from Zimbabwe to South Africa[1]

by Lovemore Zinyama

The past decade has seen growing numbers of Zimbabweans going to South Africa, Botswana and, to a lesser extent, Mozambique and Zambia, some to engage in small-scale trading and others in search of employment. The types, patterns, causes and impacts of the various forms of regional cross-border migration are complex and little understood. For instance, little is known as yet about who travels outside the country, why and how often. This chapter seeks to address some of these questions based on the results of a nation-wide survey of a large, randomly selected population of Zimbabweans in 1997.

This chapter begins by outlining the current harsh economic conditions affecting many in Zimbabwe and the range of strategies which people, especially in lower-income households, use to cope with these difficulties. A brief description of methodology is then followed by a presentation of data, with a focus on those respondents who have been to South Africa in the past. While the number of people who have travelled to South Africa in the past is relatively small (23%) compared to the total sample size, it is shown that, among those who have, trade is a primary reason. It then goes on to discuss differences in cross-border activity by gender among those who have previously travelled to South Africa, addressing questions such as who travelled (in terms of age, marital status, education, etc), frequency of travel, length of stay in South Africa, modes of transport used, and why they went there.

The results presented here are set in the context of the ongoing process of developing a new (im)migration policy regime in South Africa. It is suggested that a better understanding of the nature of cross-border movement between the two countries would assist in the adoption of a more enlightened policy in South Africa than is currently envisaged in the atmosphere of xenophobia that has prevailed for the past few years.[2]

COPING WITH ECONOMIC HARDSHIPS IN ZIMBABWE

Cross-border migration between Zimbabwe and South Africa has historically been an exclusively male activity. This was partly because it was deemed too far and too risky for women in pre-independence Zimbabwe to travel to South Africa on their own, and partly because migration was strictly regulated by the requirements of the South African mines for labour from north of the Limpopo River (Zinyama, 1990: 748-67). But during the past decade, political and economic conditions have changed considerably in both countries. In South Africa, the pariah apartheid state is no more and the country is now a full member of the Southern African Development Community (SADC) and of the Commonwealth, both of which seek to promote the free movement of their nationals between member states (Southern African Development Community, 1996). In Zimbabwe, economic conditions have deteriorated so much that people, especially those from lower- and middle-income households, are finding it necessary to adopt a wide range of strategies for coping with these hardships. As a result, women can no longer remain recipients of their husbands' wages while staying at home and are having to go out to look for work in the formal and informal domestic sectors, while others travel to South Africa and elsewhere in an effort to support their families.

Economic growth since the mid-1980s has been slow and erratic in Zimbabwe, with high and growing levels of unemployment. Apparently under pressure for balance-of-payment support from the World Bank and the International Monetary Fund (IMF), the government reluctantly abandoned the socialist policies it had pursued since independence in 1980 and 1991 started implementing liberalisation policy reforms under the Economic Structural Adjustment Programme (ESAP) (Government of Zimbabwe, 1991). Under the reform programme, the government undertook to reduce public expenditure by, among other things, removing subsidies on basic foodstuffs, reducing budgetary allocations, even to essential social services such as education and health care, and downsizing the public service. According to the ESAP policy document, the objectives of the programme were to ensure higher medium- and long-term economic growth, to reduce poverty and improve living conditions especially for the poorest groups, and to address the problems of burgeoning unemployment (Government of Zimbabwe, 1991).

Today, almost 10 years after the start of ESAP, unemployment continues to worsen unabated and has in fact been compounded by retrenchments in both the public and private sectors; both local and foreign investment have not been as forthcoming as initially envisaged; many large firms have closed down and there is strong evidence of de-industrialisation, due to increased competition from imports; and price inflation has spiralled. More than 50 000 people are said to have been retrenched by private sector companies alone with the approval of the Ministry of Public Service, Labour and Social Welfare during the period 1991–97 (*The Standard*, 3–9 May, 1998). It is also known that many other firms were retrenching labour without reporting to the ministry. During the same period, the government cut the number of public service employees by over 23 000

(Government of Zimbabwe, 1998). In a country of about 12.5 million, where less than one million people are in formal employment, these reductions represent significant losses in family incomes. Not surprisingly, the umbrella Zimbabwe Congress of Trade Unions (ZCTU) reported that its membership had dropped from 1.5 million in 1992 to less than one million (*The Standard* 3–9 May, 1998).

According to most commentators, Zimbabweans are worse off today than they were at independence in 1980. Available evidence suggests that the economic reform programme has brought little but economic hardship, not only for the poorest groups, but also to middle-income households, in both rural and urban areas (Gibbon, 1995; MacGarry, 1994; Tevera, 1995). Instead of delivering on the economic benefits that it promised, ESAP as a medicine has, to paraphrase Tevera (1995), almost killed the patient. For instance, the country has seen the considerable advances made in social service delivery during the 1980s eroded as the government has implemented cost recovery measures in such sectors as education and health care even for the poor. From a position of offering free primary education for all children and free health care for the poorest during the 1980s, the re-introduction of high user charges has led to a denial of access to these services for many households in both rural and urban areas. For the growing army of these vulnerable groups, the deterioration in their economic situation has been compounded by the recurrent droughts that have hit the country, and indeed the whole of Southern Africa, since the early 1980s.

The people of Zimbabwe, particularly the lower-income groups, have devised a variety of strategies for coping with these economic hardships. In urban areas, the most apparent of these coping strategies is the massive expansion of informal sector activities such as petty commodity trading and manufacturing, and the provision of services such as public commuter transport. Cultivation on any available undeveloped piece of urban public land is now widespread as both low- and middle-income households seek to supplement their food supplies and family incomes (Mudimu, 1996: 179–94; Smith and Tevera, 1997: 25–38). Many in formal employment now commonly resort to "moonlighting" in order to supplement their wages. Homeowners let out "rooms" or put up additional structures on their properties to accommodate rent-paying lodgers. The latter phenomenon has become widespread in all urban centres, affecting not only low-income residential areas but also middle-income suburbs.

Another coping strategy involves cross-border travel for informal trade in neighbouring countries. Since the mid-1980s, large numbers of Zimbabweans have been going to Botswana and South Africa with various types of items, notably crotchetware, for sale in those countries. This cross-border trade has increasingly become dominated by women seeking to supplement their family incomes to clothe and educate their children (Cheater and Gaidzanwa, 1996: 189–200). The money obtained while in South Africa is used to purchase goods for importing back to Zimbabwe and subsequent resale of those known to be in short supply at home. In fact, during the 1980s before the relaxation of foreign currency controls by the government as part of the economic reform programme, these cross-border traders are known to have been key players in supplying commerce and industry with scarce requirements, such as spare motor vehicle parts for electrical appliances and small items of machinery.

More recently, female Zimbabwean cross-border traders have been going to Mozambique, Zambia and even as far as Tanzania to purchase and bring home for resale second-hand clothing, some of it reportedly brought into those countries by European charitable organisations for distribution to the needy. While some people choose to engage only in circulatory cross-border trading, others have chosen to migrate for varying periods of time to seek employment in South Africa or Botswana. This migration includes both the poorly educated, without skills, as well as highly qualified professional people.

A recent International Labour Organisation (ILO) study by Fultz and Pieris (1998), quoting the Zimbabwe High Commission in Pretoria, gave an estimate of 60 000 migrants working in South Africa in professional positions, such as teachers, university academics, doctors, nurses, engineers and accountants. On the other hand, some of the unskilled migrants can only hope to get jobs as exploited and underpaid domestic workers and farm labourers in the Northern Province of South Africa. They will cross the border legally, if they have valid passports, entry visas and work permits; or they may enter South Africa without valid entry documents. Likewise, they will return home to their families at Christmas and New Year, either legally or "illegally". Such cross-border migration is thought to be common especially in the southern and western districts of the country, close to the border with South Africa and Botswana.

While the governments of Zambia and Mozambique have not publicly expressed concern about the movement of people from Zimbabwe and have not taken any action to curtail such movements where these are legal, this has not been the case with South Africa or, to a lesser extent, Botswana. In South Africa, the years since the end of apartheid in 1994 have seen growing xenophobia in the local press and among the general public directed at foreign nationals, particularly those from Mozambique and Zimbabwe. This xenophobia has often culminated in physical violence against foreigners – themselves and/or their property (see Chapter 9).

Common stereotypes are that these foreigners are coming in vast numbers, both legally and "illegally", and that they are a threat to the economic prosperity and security of the country (Buthelezi, 1997; Institute for Futures Research, 1996). Zimbabweans and others are seen as taking away jobs from South Africans, thereby adding to the unemployment of South African nationals and, by accepting lower wages, depressing remuneration levels for local labour (Crush, 1997). This stereotyping extends to trade in the informal sector where foreigners are accused of taking away business from South African hawkers and vendors through increased competition. Foreigners, particularly undocumented migrants, have also been accused of gun-running and drug trafficking, and being responsible for the increased level of violent crime in South Africa. They are accused of placing a burden on South Africa's health and educational services because those in their own countries have been allowed to collapse by their own national governments.

Another common stereotype in South Africa is that foreign nationals are coming to the country because of political repression, civil unrest and economic chaos in their home countries (Institute for Futures Research, 1996), or because they want to enjoy the benefits of the most enlightened and democratic constitution in Africa. In the words of the former Deputy Minister of Home Affairs, Penuell Maduna, "hunger and fear are driving forces that are much stronger than even the most sophisticated aliens control measures...South Africa has become the country of survival for many people from countries within Africa, and also from other parts of the world" (Maduna, 1995: 7). According to the South African Minister of Home Affairs, Mangosuthu Buthelezi (1997), not only do foreign men take South African women and engage in marriages of convenience, but they also bring in diseases, notably STDs and HIV. These varied assertions about foreigners in South Africa have been well documented by, for example, the South African Institute of Race Relations (1997) and Centre for Policy Studies (De Villiers and Reitzes, 1995).

Estimates of the number of undocumented foreigners in South Africa are variously put at between 500 000 and 8 million. According to the South African High Commission in Harare, about 75 000 Zimbabweans were believed to be staying "illegally" in South Africa after the expiry of their temporary residence permits during 1997, while an additional unknown number had entered and remained there without legal documentation. The South African government deported or repatriated 14 651 and 21 673 Zimbabweans during 1996 and 1997, respectively. The Zimbabwean High Commission in Pretoria estimates that some 400 000 Zimbabweans, including both legal and undocumented migrants, may be working as domestics, farm labourers and in the construction industry (Fultz and Pieris, 1998), sectors known to employ large numbers of foreign workers.

In order to counter the inflow of foreigners, the South African government has been urged to impose stringent controls on their entry into the country, particularly the less-educated and unskilled, and only selectively allow entry to those with skills and capital for investment in the country (Buthelezi, 1997; South African Institute of Race Relations, 1997; *The Citizen*, 12 February, 1996). "Undocumented migrants (either because they will have entered the country unlawfully in the first instance or because they have overstayed the time stipulated in their original entry permits) should be rounded up and deported." This public perception of foreigners as parasites appears to have substantial support among senior politicians and officials within the Department of Home Affairs, in the police and in other arms of government responsible for implementing the country's immigration policies and border control. But it remains unclear how true these fears are that Zimbabweans, together with other foreigners, are queuing to enter South Africa in large numbers and causing considerable harm to that country's prosperity and security. We therefore need to get a clear sense of the numbers of Zimbabweans who are entering South Africa, their reasons for going there, how long they remain there and what their long-term intentions are regarding permanent settlement in that country.

Unfortunately, objective assessment of these issues in South Africa has been clouded by press hysteria that the country is about to be overrun by an army of "illegal aliens" who are waiting across the border in Mozambique, Zimbabwe and other countries north of the Limpopo River, or who are already in the country (South African Institute of Race Relations, 1997). This paranoia is illustrated by the tightening of immigration control regulations by the South African High Commission in Harare on Zimbabwean passport holders since October 1996, supposedly to curtail the numbers of people who were staying beyond the expiry date of their entry visas. Applicants for entry visas into South Africa would now be required to produce proof of confirmed and paid hotel accommodation or a letter of invitation from a business associate, friend or relative legally resident in South Africa. The letter would include detailed information on that person, including his or her national identity number, physical address in South Africa and the length of the intended visit. Zimbabwean visitors are also required to provide acceptable proof that they are able to sustain themselves while in South Africa (eg through bank statements or traveller's cheques), produce a letter from their employers to confirm that they are gainfully employed in Zimbabwe and will return immediately on completing their business and – for unemployed persons – proof of marriage in Zimbabwe or an affidavit from a spouse.

The last requirement is particularly harsh and discriminatory against female travellers, especially single women who are trying to support their families through cross-border informal trading. (It is also of interest to note that immigration from Europe and North America into the Cape Town area in recent years has not been seen as a problem by South African officials.) In contrast, from February 1996, South African passport holders are now able to obtain entry visas at the port of entry instead of having to apply to the Zimbabwean High Commission in Pretoria before departure.

A NOTE ON METHOD

The survey results presented in this chapter are based on interviews conducted in February-March 1997 with 947 Zimbabweans. Thirty-two survey areas were randomly selected from a list of national population census enumeration areas, 17 of them in rural areas and 15 in urban areas. There were somewhat more male (56%) than female respondents (44%) in the sample. All the respondents were Africans by race. This is not surprising for two reasons. Firstly, the size of the non-African population in Zimbabwe is very small, a mere 1.2% of the total population according to the results of the 1992 national population census. Secondly, the sample areas that were randomly selected did not include the urban high-income suburbs or rural large-scale commercial farms, the two areas where non-Africans generally live in Zimbabwe.

The sampling strategy and field methodology employed are described in greater detail in Appendix A. The questionnaire and aggregate summary of the results of the survey are provided in Appendix B. A profile of the sample population is provided in Table 4.1.

It must be noted, however, that the sample did not include those people who have already moved to South Africa permanently or temporarily, and would therefore not be available for an interview. This caveat is important because it limits the conclusions that can be drawn about why Zimbabweans go to South Africa and what they do while they are there. In other words, one cannot assume that the resident population of Zimbabwe has had the same experiences as those Zimbabweans currently out of the country. Nevertheless, the sample is drawn from a large, representative survey of resident Zimbabweans and provides invaluable information about previous cross-border activities from one of South Africa's largest neighbours.

SURVEY RESULTS

Who goes to South Africa from Zimbabwe?

Analysis of the data shows that only 22% of the respondents had ever been to South Africa. Of those who had been to South Africa, men were only slightly more likely to have visited than women. Thus, 128 men (23% of the total males in the sample) said they had been to South Africa at least once in their lives, compared with 82 women (19% of the females in the sample). This result contradicts a public perception widely held in Zimbabwe that it is now predominantly females who are participating in periodic cross-border movements for purposes of informal trading. However, there was a significant difference between males and females in terms of usual place of residence. Urban women were almost twice as likely to have been to South Africa than either their rural counterparts or the male respondents. Two-thirds of the females who said they had visited South Africa were from urban areas, compared with only 40% of the males.

For males and females, the largest proportion of those who had been to South Africa were in the 26–35 age categories (Table 4.2). However, while 87% of the

TABLE 4.1: A PROFILE OF THE SAMPLE POPULATION IN ZIMBABWE

Number of interviews	947
Gender (%)	
Male	56
Female	44
Race (%)	
African	99
White	–
Coloured	–
Age (%)	
15–24	26
25–44	50
45–64	17
65+	6
Urban or rural (%)	
Urban	55
Rural	45
Marital status (%)	
Married	66
Separated/divorced/abandoned	5
Widowed	3
Unmarried	25
Household status (%)	
Household head	34
Spouse	26
Child	20
Other family	7
Other	13

Note: Figures in tables may not add to 100% due to rounding. A single dash (–) signifies a value of greater than zero but less than 0.5%.

females were under 45 years, males tended to be more widely spread across all age groups. Almost three-quarters of the females were in the 26–45 category compared with only 49% of the males. Among the older men who had been to South Africa are included those who had been there a long time ago as migrant mine workers, and had since returned home either because of old age or upon expiry of their contracts. In the current situation of high unemployment and rampant inflation, it is the younger age categories – both males and females, but more so females – with young families to support – who are likely to be most hard hit and therefore to seek amelioration in many varied ways, including cross-border migration.

TABLE 4.2: AGES OF RESPONDENTS WHO HAVE VISITED SOUTH AFRICA (%)

Age group	Males	Females
Up to 25	23	17
26–35	32	44
36–45	17	26
46–55	10	6
56–65	7	2
Over 65	10	1
Age unknown	1	4

Note: N = 264.

Three-quarters of both male and female respondents who had been to South Africa were married (Table 4.3). Another 3% of the males and 9% of the females were separated, divorced or widowed. Similar results were obtained by Moyo (1996), in a study of a rural community in south-western Zimbabwe with a high level of cross-border labour migration to South Africa, where 72% of the migrants were married. Cross-border travel is thus being done by people with family responsibilities at home. This is an important consideration for immigration policy formulation by the South African authorities. Family responsibilities at home are likely to weigh heavily against long-term or permanent migration to South Africa. As will be shown later, of crucial importance are the length of stay in South Africa and the reasons for going there, nullifying the fear that these people may decide to stay there permanently. On the other hand, 26% of the males and 15% of the female respondents who had been to South Africa were single. Permanent or semi-permanent migration, whether through legal or non-legal means, is likely to occur among this unmarried group with fewer social and family responsibilities at home.

The questionnaire also sought information about the education qualifications of the respondents. Migration of educated people constitutes a loss of human resources on the part of the sending country; conversely, it represents a significant economic gain to the receiving country. On the other hand, if migration is only short-term or circulatory, there is no detrimental transfer of human resources between the countries, although it may have

TABLE 4.3: MARITAL STATUS OF RESPONDENTS WHO HAVE VISITED SOUTH AFRICA (%)

Marital status	Males	Females
Married	71	75
Separated/divorced	2	5
Widowed	1	5
Never married	26	15

Note: N = 264.

other socio-economic impacts on both sending and receiving countries such as the trade balance or foreign exchange transfers. The results from this survey show that the largest proportion of both male and female respondents who had been to South Africa had received at least some secondary school education (Table 4.4). Half the males and 61% of the females reported that they had been educated up to secondary school level; a further 8% and 2%, respectively, had been educated to tertiary level. Not unexpectedly, a larger proportion of males than females had been educated to tertiary level. Clearly, cross-border movement involves a relatively well-educated segment of the Zimbabwean adult population who are not only able to access the bureaucratic process of getting the necessary travel documents before departure, but will be able to negotiate their way in a foreign country.

TABLE 4.4: HIGHEST EDUCATIONAL LEVEL OF RESPONDENTS WHO HAVE VISITED SOUTH AFRICA (%)		
Education level reached	Males	Females
No schooling	9	9
Some primary schooling	15	12
Completed primary school	19	16
Some high schooling	38	49
Completed high school	12	12
University/other tertiary	8	2
Note: N = 209.		

There were notable differences between males and females in terms of their employment status in Zimbabwe at the time of the survey. One-third of the males said they were employed in the formal sector, compared with only 10% of the females (Table 4.5). A little more than half of the males were unemployed, with nearly one-quarter saying they were not actively looking for work. On the other hand, almost 80% of the females were unemployed and a little more than half said they were not looking for work (including homemakers). However, not more than 10% in both groups reported themselves as employed in the informal sector. Those people engaged in cross-border export/import presumably do not see themselves as falling in the same category as vendors and hawkers who spend the day selling their goods from fixed or mobile stalls, respectively.

TABLE 4.5: EMPLOYMENT STATUS OF RESPONDENTS WHO HAVE VISITED SOUTH AFRICA		
Employment status	Males (%)	Females (%)
Employed – formal sector	35	10
Employed – informal sector	7	10
Unemployed – looking for work	31	27*
Unemployed – not looking for work	23	52*
Others eg pensioners/students	4	1
Note: * = includes homemakers. N = 200.		

How often and how do they travel?

The mean number of lifetime visits to South Africa was six, with a maximum of 50 visits. Those who had been to South Africa were further asked how frequently they had visited that country during the past five years. A little more than one-third (35%) of all the respondents said that they visited South Africa once every few months or more frequently. This high frequency of visiting is not necessarily an indication of intent to migrate – legally or otherwise – but, as will be shown later, is related to the purpose of the visits.

Females have made more frequent visits than males over the past five years (Table 4.6). Some 45% of the women reported that they visited South Africa once a month or more and 59% visited every few months or more. In contrast, only 10% of the males travelled every month and 20% at least once every few months. Thus, for those women who are involved in cross-border movement to South Africa, it has become a regular way of life. On the other hand, nearly half of the men had visited South Africa only once a year or less during the past five years.

TABLE 4.6: FREQUENCY OF VISITS TO SOUTH AFRICA DURING THE PAST FIVE YEARS		
Frequency	Males (%)	Females (%)
More than once a month	2	12
Once a month	8	33
Once every few months	10	14
Once or twice a year	31	20
Less than once a year	22	9
Only once	27	12
Note: N = 166.		

Further evidence that much of the cross-border movement from Zimbabwe to South Africa is circulatory, with no intention of staying there indefinitely, is that the average length of stay per visit was found to be fewer than two weeks for 45% of all the visitors during the past five years. Up to 70% stayed for less than one month. Only 6% stayed for more than one year, the longest reported stay being 5.5 years. In general, women stay for much shorter periods in South Africa than men (Table 4.7). Almost two-thirds of the females stayed for less than two weeks, compared with only one-third of the males. Almost 90% of the females return to Zimbabwe within one month. In contrast, a little over two-fifths of the males stayed for more than one month. At the other end of the scale, almost 9% of the males who had been to South Africa said that they had stayed an average of one year or more during the past five years.

Those respondents who said that they had been to South Africa were asked how they had got there on their most recent visit. Public transport was the most frequently used mode of transport by both males and females, notably buses, trains and "combis" (ie 10–15-seater minibuses) (Table 4.8). However, there

TABLE 4.7: AVERAGE LENGTH OF STAY IN SOUTH AFRICA DURING VISITS IN THE PAST FIVE YEARS

Length of stay	Males (%)	Females (%)
Up to two weeks	33	62
3 to 4 weeks	24	25
1 to 3 months	14	6
3 to 6 months	3	1
6 months to 1 year	17	3
More than once a year	9	3

Note: N = 174.

TABLE 4.8: MODE OF TRANSPORT USED DURING THE MOST RECENT VISIT TO SOUTH AFRICA

Mode	Males (%)	Females (%)
Bus	37	32
Train	12	35
"Combi"	12	23
On foot	21	5
Private car	10	4
Plane	7	1
Bus/train and on foot	2	0

Note: N = 200.

seems to be a difference between males and females in terms of the most preferred modes of public transport. Choice of transport mode for females appeared more restricted than for males, with two-thirds of the women using either buses or trains. Males, on the other hand, had a wider choice of public transport, with at least 10% of the respondents saying they had used either buses, trains, "combis" or driven in private cars. The most popular mode for males was the bus, used by 37% of the respondents. Another 7% of the males (compared with 1% of the females) had flown on their last visit to South Africa.

Overall, public transport by bus, train and "combi" was used by 72% of the travellers. Those are the preferred modes of transport by low-income groups because of their lower fares. The expanding cross-border transport services are regulated by the state in both countries to some extent through the granting of permits and the requirement for some form of passenger insurance cover, they operate from known points within urban areas, and they pass through official border crossing points. Most of the respondents would have passed through Beitbridge (Zimbabwe) and Messina (South Africa), the only official direct crossing point for overland travellers between the two countries.

From the viewpoint of the immigration and border control authorities, it is those who walked part of or the entire journey from their areas of origin into

South Africa who would be cause for concern (the "on foot" category in Table 4.8). Most of the respondents in this category were males. Twenty-one percent of them said they went on foot, while another 2% used either bus or train for part of their journey and then walked across the border. Five percent of the female respondents said that they had also walked across the border. It is not known whether these people used legal crossing points or not when they crossed the border on foot. During 1996, immigration authorities of the two countries agreed to open two informal crossing points in addition to Beitbridge, one west and the other east of the town. The two crossing points are intended to facilitate the movement of rural people living in districts along the border. Under the system, temporary permits valid for up to 21 days are issued even to non-passport holders allowing the permit holder to travel up to 50 kilometres on the other side of the border. Most of the people who use the informal crossing points will be visiting relatives on the other side, or going to work as labourers on commercial farms in South Africa's Northern Province. Twenty (61%) of the 33 respondents who had walked across the border came from the two districts of Beitbridge and Chiredzi which are adjacent to the Limpopo River. The other 11 also came mostly from districts in the south of the country, notably Chipinge, Gwanda and Zaka, suggesting that at least some of this pedestrian traffic was legal.

There are indeed Zimbabweans who cross into South Africa "on foot" without legal documents. Monitoring of press and police reports on this activity over the past few years supports the finding in this survey that it is mostly males who cross the border in this way and that it reaches its peak around December-January. This is the time when those Zimbabweans staying "illegally" in South Africa want to come home for Christmas and go back after New Year (Moyo, 1996). Tragically, this is also the time when the Limpopo River may be running high, resulting in some of these "border-jumpers" being drowned or attacked by crocodiles, with such incidents being widely reported in the press.

Why do they go to South Africa?

Asked about the purpose of their most recent visit, the most frequently cited reason by the majority of the female respondents (65%) who had been to South Africa was shopping or to sell and buy goods for subsequent importation into Zimbabwe (Table 4.9). Visiting family or friends was the only other noteworthy reason for travelling to South Africa, given by 16% of the female respondents. These two factors alone accounted for 81% of the responses from females. It has already been noted that the majority of women stayed in South Africa for only up to two weeks at a time. This gender difference is in keeping with the primary reason for travel, namely informal trading. A fortnight provides sufficient time for them to dispose of whatever wares they have brought with them, and then purchase those goods they want to take back to Zimbabwe. The results also confirm a public perception in both countries that it is mostly women who engage in informal cross-border trading.

In contrast, although informal trading was also the principal reason given by

TABLE 4.9: PURPOSE OF MOST RECENT VISIT TO SOUTH AFRICA DURING THE PAST FIVE YEARS		
Purpose of visit	Males (%)	Females (%)
Shopping/buying and selling goods	32	65
Work	20	3
Look for work	21	1
Visit family/friends	11	16
Business	8	8
Holiday	3	4
Medical treatment	2	1
School/college/university	3	1
Note: N = 191.		

the male respondents (32%), those who had gone to South Africa either to look for work or to work were well represented as well (Table 4.9). Reasons pertaining to work in South Africa were given by a little more than 40% of the male respondents, compared with only 4% of the females. A potentially permanent or semi-permanent migration stream, legal or otherwise, would only come from these two work-related categories. All the other reasons given in Table 4.9 for the most recent visit represent short-term circulatory trans-border movements, primarily for small-scale informal trading, or for family and other personal reasons.

CONCLUSION

It is clear from the results presented in this study that the typical Zimbabwean man/woman who has been going to South Africa during the past few years does not fit into the public stereotype that has been portrayed in that country. She/he is typically a middle-aged family person who uses cross-border migration as one strategy for the survival of her/his family, particularly where this is an urban household. The majority of these people are engaged in a purpose-specific circulatory migration process, but one in which they are only spending very short periods of time in South Africa.

These findings raise the question of what policy alternatives South Africa should adopt in future, alternatives that range from draconian policy, which seeks greater closure of national boundaries (rigidly enforcing controls and expulsion, and running contrary to the SADC proposal for greater freedom of movement for people within the region), to a humane option that takes cognisance of the issues raised in this chapter and seeks to facilitate better living conditions in the home countries of the migrants. This latter option will not take away South Africa's right to deal effectively with undocumented immigrants who cross national boundaries "illegally" or overstay and break the conditions of their original entry permits regarding employment. The point has been made elsewhere that "it is important to distinguish between short-term, purpose-orient(at)ed cross-border migration of the sort described by most respondents in this research, and long-term permanent immigration" (McDonald *et al*, 1998: 34). This, then, would make it possible to regularise those short-term cross-border migrants who might otherwise be forced to use illegal means of getting into and/or staying in South Africa. It is also important to recognise that any new (im)migration policy should be framed in a manner consistent with South Africa's current and future role within the region, and include related issues such as the quest for balanced regional trade and development among SADC member countries, and regional economic integration.

Finally, this chapter has also attempted to contribute towards a better understanding of the population geography of Zimbabwe by profiling the persons that have been involved in cross-border movements between this country and South Africa, but more research is clearly needed in this area. For instance, it has been suggested that the majority of those who travel to South Africa are going to sell and buy goods for subsequent resale back home. But we do not as yet know the significance of this trade to the economies of the two countries. We do not know, for example, the benefits, if any, of this trade to South Africa in terms of export earnings over and above those reported in the standard national accounts statistics, or the extent of the benefits to Zimbabwe in terms of the social support that the affected households get from such trade which would otherwise be borne by the state. Another issue that requires further investigation is the extent to which cross-border trade is contributing towards the economic empowerment of women and reducing their dependence on the wage incomes of their spouses.

ACKNOWLEDGEMENTS

The author thanks Lazarus Zanamwe of the Department of Geography and Environmental Science, University of Zimbabwe, for his assistance with the fieldwork on which this chapter is based.

REFERENCES

Buthelezi, M, 1997, "After amnesty: The future of foreign migrants in South Africa", keynote address at a Southern African Migration Project (SAMP) conference on amnesty in Pretoria, June.

Cheater, A, and Gaidzanwa, R, B, 1996, "Citizenship in neo-patrilineal states: Gender and mobility in Southern Africa", *Journal of Southern African Studies*, 22, No.2.

Crush, J, 1997, "Covert operations: Clandestine migration, temporary work and immigration policy in South Africa", *SAMP Migration Policy Series*, No.1. Cape Town and Kingston: Southern African Migration Project.

De Villiers, R, and Reitzes, M, (eds), 1995, *Southern African migration: Domestic and regional policy implications*, Workshop Proceedings, No.14. Johannesburg: Centre for Policy Studies.

Fultz, E, and Pieris, B, 1998, "The social protection of migrant workers in South Africa", *ILO/SAMAT Policy Paper* No.3. Geneva: International Labour Organisation.

Gibbon, P, 1995, *Structural adjustment and the working poor in Zimbabwe*. Uppsala: Nordiska Afrikainstitutet.

Government of Zimbabwe, 1991, *Zimbabwe: A framework for economic reform, 1991–1995*. Harare.

Government of Zimbabwe, 1998, *Framework for the second phase of the Public Service Reform Programme*. Harare.

Institute for Futures Research, 1996, "Migration processes, systems and policies, with special emphasis on South African international migration", *IFR Occasional Paper*, No.25. Stellenbosch: IFR, University of Stellenbosch.

MacGarry, B, 1994, *Double damage: Rural people and economic structural adjustment in a time of drought*. Gweru: Mambo Press.

Maduna, P, 1995, "Illegal immigrants as a domestic issue", in R, de Villiers and M, Reitzes (eds), *Southern African migration: Domestic and regional policy implications*. Johannesburg: Centre for Policy Studies.

McDonald, D, Gay, J, Zinyama, L, Mattes, R and De Vletter, F, 1998, "Challenging xenophobia: Myths & realities about cross-border migration in Southern Africa", *SAMP Migration Policy Series*, No.7. Cape Town and Kingston: Southern African Migration Project.

Moyo, G, 1996, "Cross-border migration in a border region: A study of Ndolwane Ward, Bulilimamangwe District", unpublished dissertation. Department of Geography, University of Zimbabwe.

Mudimu, G, D, 1996, "Urban agricultural activities and women's strategies in sustaining family livelihoods in Harare, Zimbabwe", *Singapore Journal of Tropical Geography*, 17, No.2. Kent Ridge: Department of Geography, National University of Singapore.

Smith, D, W, and Tevera, D, S, 1997, "Socio-economic context for the householder of urban agriculture in Harare, Zimbabwe", *Geographical Journal of Zimbabwe*, No.28.

South African Institute of Race Relations, 1997, *South Africa Survey 1996/7*, Johannesburg.

Southern African Development Community, 1996, *The Draft Protocol on the Free Movement of Persons in the Southern African Development Community*. Gaborone.

Tevera, D, 1995, "The medicine that might kill the patient: Structural adjustment and urban poverty in Zimbabwe", in D, Simon, W, van Spengen, C, Dixon and A, Narman (eds), *Structurally adjusted Africa: Poverty, debt and basic needs*. London: Pluto Press.

Zinyama, L, M, 1990, "International migrations to and from Zimbabwe and the influence of political changes on population movements, 1965-1987", *International Migration Review*, 24, No.4.

ENDNOTES

1 An earlier version of this chapter was published in the *Geographical Journal of Zimbabwe*, No. 29, 1998.
2 A White Paper on International Migration was released on 30 March 1999.

Chapter Five

Namibians on South Africa: Attitudes towards cross-border migration and immigration policy

by Bruce Frayne and Wade Pendleton

After a successful round of public opinion surveys on cross-border migration in Lesotho, Mozambique and Zimbabwe (McDonald et al, 1998), the survey was extended to Namibia. The questionnaire used in Namibia is identical to that used in the other three countries and therefore offers important comparative information as well as data specific to Namibia.

The intent of the survey was to record respondents' attitudes towards migration and immigration policy with specific reference to South Africa. It also attempts to document people's experiences with migration and immigration to South Africa as well as their future plans and ideas in this regard. Further enriching the analysis are questions regarding cross-border migration between Namibia and its neighbours other than South Africa (that is, Angola, Zambia, Zimbabwe and Botswana). Although not the central theme of this study, these additional findings are briefly described in the chapter.

The chapter begins with a brief historical background of Namibia in order to place the country's relationship with South Africa in a regional context. In particular, it is important to note that the lengthy history of migrant labour to South Africa, a typical feature of the other countries, is not as strongly evident in Namibia, which altered to some degree the characteristics of cross-border movements between the two countries.

This analysis is followed by a very brief explanation of the methodology that was used for Namibia and describes the sample size and demographics of the respondents.

The key findings of the survey are then explored and comparisons are made with similar data from Lesotho, Mozambique and Zimbabwe. Looking to the future, migration trends from Namibia to South Africa are then considered, and important regional policy questions investigated. Finally, a summary of the key findings, which emerged from a more rigorous analysis undertaken for the Namibian data, is presented.

In summary, only a minority of Namibians has any desire to move permanently or temporarily to South Africa. Of those who do want to go, the propensity to migrate from Namibia to South Africa is determined in large part by socio-economic status, with the wealthier and better-educated sectors of society being more mobile and having a greater desire and likelihood to visit and live in South Africa. One important conclusion to draw from this finding is that South Africa does not appear to be facing a "flood" of migration from the poorest sectors of Namibia's population. Indeed, the contrary appears to be true, with relatively few (and relatively skilled and better-educated) Namibians making their way to South Africa.

HISTORICAL BACKGROUND TO MIGRATION IN NAMIBIA

Namibia has an unusual relationship with South Africa (for a detailed discussion, see Bley, 1971; Goldblatt, 1971; Pool, 1991; and Grotpeter, 1994). Unlike other countries in the region, Namibians did not have to go to South Africa in order to experience apartheid. Rather, from 1915 to 1990, South Africa occupied Namibia, bringing with that occupation people, policies, ideologies, religion, culture, language, trade, commerce, manufacturing and industry. Some of the major Namibian population groups whose ancestors migrated from South Africa include: the various Nama groups, the only remaining descendants of the once great Khoi-Khoi who inhabited South Africa prior to European occupation; the Basters as well as the descendants of various Orlam groups who came from the northern Cape; coloured people from the Cape (people of mixed African and white ancestry); and Afrikaners. Some Germans remained in Namibia after the defeat of Germany during World War I, and other Germans migrated to Namibia from Germany and South Africa. Thus, many Namibians have strong historical links with South Africa.

The major African Namibian populations migrated to Namibia from central Africa some time after the fifteenth century, and they include the Herero (including Himba and Mbanderu) and the Owambo (a collective term for eight different related ethnic groups). The Namibian Tswana population derives from cross-border migration from Botswana in the recent past. The Damara and various hunter/gatherer populations generally referred to as Bushmen or San are probably Namibian in origin.

Germany colonised and occupied South West Africa (as Namibia was called until independence) from 1890 until 1914. The initial South African occupation of South West Africa occurred after the defeat of Germany in the First World War under a mandate from the League of Nations. After the United Nations was established in 1948, it tried unsuccessfully for several decades to revoke South Africa's administration of the country. Only in 1989 did the United Nations establish its presence in the country and supervise elections. In 1990 Namibia became independent.

During South Africa's administration of the country, it was ruled as though it was a fifth province of South Africa. South Africa introduced policies and laws that were virtually identical to those in force in South Africa. In some ways, the administration of apartheid in Namibia was stricter than in South Africa because of the small size of the population and the remoteness of the country.

During the period of South African administration of the country the links between Namibia and South Africa became very strong. All major paved roads, railway lines and airline routes led to South Africa. Many white South Africans moved to Namibia and a commercial farming sector was established which took over about 40% of the land in the country. As towns were established and the capital, Windhoek, began to grow, the South African administration designated these towns primarily for white occupation. Africans were only allowed to reside in towns if they were employed.

Rural African Namibians were required to live in communal areas located in the north, east, south and west of the country. These communal areas received virtually no development assistance, and movement from the communal areas to the towns and commercial farming area was limited and controlled. The area north of the commercial farming area was closed to white occupation, and a "veterinary" cordon fence was established along this boundary preventing cattle and people from crossing. The South African police patrolled the country and enforced the myriad of laws and regulations that restricted people's freedom of movement and other human rights.

Lasting for more than 20 years, the South African Defence Force, together with the South West African Territorial Force, fought a war with the military wing of the South West African People's Organisation (SWAPO), known as the People's Liberation Army of Namibia (PLAN), for the liberation of Namibia. The conflict was fought primarily along the Namibian border with Angola and Zambia. Many people were required to move by the military forces and the effects on the rural population were often devastating. The attitudes of many rural people in the Namibian north about South Africa have been influenced by their experiences of the South African Defence Force and the Namibian War of Liberation.

After 1980, most of the apartheid laws in Namibia were abolished, but many of the social and economic practices of apartheid remained. Even after independence the legacy of apartheid can still be seen in urban townships ("locations"), occupied largely by poor Africans, and the dual system of land tenure (no freehold land ownership in communal areas and no freehold land ownership of commercial farmland and urban land). The Namibian population also continues to be exposed to extensive media information about South Africa. They purchase and make use of products manufactured in South Africa, watch television programmes about South Africa, meet many South Africans, and some have also visited, worked, and have relatives or friends in South Africa. The attitudes and opinions revealed in the survey in Namibia are therefore the result of a complex history of relations between the two countries.

A NOTE ON METHOD

Namibia is a large, sparsely populated and heterogeneous country. These factors alone provide significant barriers to successfully conducting nationally representative survey research. In the case of this project, both budget and time factors constrained achievement of the ideal of national representation, and certain geographic areas and sectors of the population had to be omitted from the sample.[1]

The survey also wanted to capture the opinions, attitudes and possible plans of those without obvious ties and close proximity to South Africa. In addition, cross-border migration is an important issue with other countries, besides South Africa, and some sense of this dynamic needed to be captured, as it has relevant policy and development implications. Analyses of migration patterns from the 1991 Population Census (Tvedten and Mupotola, 1995; Melber, 1996; and Miranda, 1998), together with relevant studies and cumulative knowledge about migration in Namibia, provided a rational basis on which to make decisions regarding areas of selection.

The sample was derived by selecting sites from the most significant areas of migration as well as sites where migration was less likely. The selected areas include major typologies of land use and population in Namibia. The sample includes representative areas where experience of South Africa would be likely as well as areas where such experience would be lower. The resultant sample was drawn from the following categories: northern rural communal areas; northern communal towns; and central, southern and coastal towns (see Table 5.1).

The number of household interviews (600) was determined largely by a trade-off between budget limitations and the minimum number required as a valid sample from the three typologies identified in the literature and data review.

The sampling strategy and field methodology employed are described in greater detail in Appendix A. The questionnaire and aggregate summary of the results of the survey are provided in Appendix B. A profile of the sample population is provided in Table 5.2.

TABLE 5.1: SAMPLE AREAS AND NUMBER OF RESPONDENTS FOR EACH AREA					
Total number of interviews: 600					
Northern rural communal	Number of interviews	Northern communal towns	Number of interviews	Central, southern and coastal towns	Number of interviews
Caprivi	50	Katima Mulilo	50	Windhoek	50
Owambo	50	Rundu	50	Katutura	50
		Oshakati	50	Rehoboth	50
				Luderitz	50
				Keetmanshoop	50
				Walvis Bay	50
				Karasburg/Warmbad	50
	Total: 100		Total: 150		Total: 350

TABLE 5.2: A PROFILE OF THE SAMPLE POPULATION IN NAMIBIA	
Number of interviews	600
Gender (%)	
Male	49
Female	51
Race (%)	
African	73
White	7
Coloured	20
Age (%)	
15–24	27
25–44	51
45–64	17
65+	5
Urban or rural (%)	
Urban	84
Rural	17
Marital status (%)	
Married	52
Separated/divorced/abandoned	4
Widowed	5
Unmarried	40
Household status (%)	
Household head	36
Spouse	24
Child	21
Other family	17
Other	3

Note: Figures in tables may not add to 100% due to rounding. A single dash (–) signifies a value of greater than zero but less than 0.5%.

NAMIBIAN MIGRATION TO SOUTH AFRICA

Migration to South Africa

Namibia's unique relationship with South Africa has shaped patterns of cross-border migration between the two countries. The first important observation is that 38% of the Namibian sample have been to South Africa, which is significantly higher than the other countries, with the obvious exception of Lesotho (see Table 5.3).

When location and race are considered, a predictable picture begins to emerge. Ninety-seven percent of visitors to South Africa are urban residents, which exceeds the sample proportion of urban areas by 13%, suggesting that it is urban rather than rural people who are largely the visitors. While 42% of the visitors are Africans, they are also primarily urban.

Of those Africans surveyed in the northern communal areas only 8% had been to South Africa. In addition, the coloured and white populations (who have the strongest historical, economic and cultural ties with South Africa) comprise 58% of those who had visited South Africa at least once in their lives (even though they make up only 27% of the sample population). Again, these people are predominantly urban residents.

Namibian men only slightly outnumber women as visitors while for Zimbabwe, and especially Mozambique, men are more likely to have been to South Africa. This may be explained by the very limited labour migration from Namibia to serve South African economic needs.

TABLE 5.3: PROFILE OF VISITORS TO SOUTH AFRICA				
	Namibia	Lesotho	Mozambique	Zimbabwe
Been to South Africa? (%)				
Yes	38	81	29	22
No	62	19	71	88
Gender (%)				
Male	56	54	88	61
Female	44	46	12	39
Urban or rural (%)				
Urban	97	62	44	92
Rural	4	39	56	8
Age (%)				
15–24	16	20	14	17
25–44	51	50	46	58
45–64	26	29	34	17
65+	7	2	6	9
Marital status (%)				
Married	68	68	74	73
Separated/divorced/abandoned	3	5	3	3
Widowed	4	9	4	2
Unmarried	26	18	19	22
Household status (%)				
Household head	46	52	66	40
Spouse	28	27	9	25
Child	16	17	18	22
Other family	8	1	5	5
Other	2	3	3	8
Home ownership (%)				
Live with others/illegally occupy	2	–	4	4
Accommodation as part of job	3	–	1	1
Rent	18	15	8	16
Own	77	84	87	78

TABLE 5.3 (cont.): PROFILE OF VISITORS TO SOUTH AFRICA				
	Namibia	Lesotho	Mozambique	Zimbabwe
Income/household member/per year (%)				
R160 or less	7	19	17	11
R161–450	5	14	18	19
R451–1200	9	22	11	12
R1200+	79	45	55	58
Level of employment activity (%)				
Inactive	27	15	22	30
Looking for work	15	32	29	28
Part-time	11	19	17	9
Full-time	48	34	32	33
Level of education (%)				
No schooling	4	8	18	9
Some primary school	14	38	30	14
Primary school completed	4	17	14	18
Some high school	34	25	24	41
High school completed	23	9	10	12
Post-grad and further	21	2	4	6
Race (%)				
African	42	99	95	99
White	18	–	1	–
Coloured	40	–	4	–

Note: N = 2 900.

The age, marital status, home ownership and employment profile of Namibian visitors is similar to that of the other countries. About 50% are between 25 and 44 years of age, about half are married and heads of households, about three-quarters own their home and almost 60% are employed full- or part-time. However, Namibian visitors are generally better educated and have higher personal household income levels than those from the other countries.

Most Namibians who visit South Africa do so only once or twice a year (see Table 5.4). Almost 90% of all visits are for less than a month, with 14 being the average number of lifetime visits, which is greater than Mozambique and Zimbabwe but significantly less than Lesotho.

TABLE 5.4: LENGTH AND FREQUENCY OF VISITS TO SOUTH AFRICA				
Number of visits (%)	Namibia	Lesotho	Mozambique	Zimbabwe
Average number of visits in lifetime	14	68	5	6
Average number of visits in the last five years	4	20	2	6
Frequency of visits (during past five years) (%)				
More than once a month	1	19	10	6
Once a month	–	13	1	18
Once every few months	9	21	12	12
Once or twice a year	25	18	25	26
Less than once or twice a year	38	17	19	18
I have been just once	27	12	33	21
Average length of stay (%)				
Less than a month	87	66	32	71
Between 1 and 3 months	6	8	9	9
Between 3 and 6 months	3	6	9	2
Between 6 months and a year	1	9	20	11
More than 1 year	3	10	31	6

Note: N = 1 199.

Migration to other SADC countries

South Africa is not, of course, the only destination for Namibians. Namibia is also bordered by Angola, Zambia, Zimbabwe and Botswana. Generally speaking, the largest concentrations of Namibia's population live along these borders, not along those with South Africa. In addition, there is much similarity among the people living on either side of these borders. This is particularly true along the northern borders where socio-economic systems are truncated in many instances by these borders.

It is therefore no surprise to learn that 14% of the sample have visited Angola, and that 89% of these visitors are Africans. Sixty-nine percent of these visitors live in the northern areas and are in close proximity to the border. Twelve percent of the sample have visited Zambia, and again the majority are from the northern communal areas and towns.

The profile for visiting Botswana and Zimbabwe is a little different, with more white and coloured Namibians visiting these two countries. Also, in contrast to the visitors to the northern countries of Angola and Zambia, 37% and 46% of visitors from Namibia are from the central and southern towns (including Luderitz and Walvis Bay).

Reasons for migration to South Africa

By far the most important reasons cited for going to South Africa were to visit friends and family and to go on holiday. In fact 63% of visitors to South Africa go for these reasons alone. In contrast, only 11% of the sample visited South Africa for work purposes (see Table 5.5).

The findings are significantly different from those of the other three countries. Twenty-five percent of respondents in Lesotho go to work or to look for work, with 29% and 68% in Zimbabwe and Mozambique respectively. Namibia's remoteness from the big urban centres of South Africa also ensures that very few

TABLE 5.5: REASONS FOR VISITING AND LEAVING SOUTH AFRICA				
	Namibia	Lesotho	Mozambique	Zimbabwe
Purpose of most recent visit (%)				
Look for work	2	8	22	14
Work	11	17	46	15
Buy and sell goods	2	3	2	21
School	1	1	1	1
Study at university/technikon	3	–	–	1
Shopping	1	19	4	21
Business	7	2	2	8
Visit family or friends	44	34	12	13
Holiday/tourism	19	2	5	3
Medical treatment	4	6	4	2
Other	6	9	2	4
Reason for return (%)				
Returned after holiday	24	35	16	26
Wanted to come back	44	15	22	25
Family reasons	18	8	9	7
Sick/injured	–	5	3	1
Contract ended	4	2	18	9
Retired from job	–	2	3	3
Lost job or retrenched	2	11	10	2
Found job at home	1	1	1	1
Travel documents expired	1	4	2	5
Expelled/deported from SA	–	1	11	4
Studies ended	2	–	–	1
Goods sold out	1	–	2	8
Other	4	18	5	8

Note: N = 1 199.

people go there to shop, which differs again from the other countries, particularly Lesotho and Zimbabwe. Namibia also has the advantage of a well supplied retail sector, thus reducing the need for Namibians to travel to South Africa specifically to shop.

Of those respondents who travelled to South Africa for work purposes, only four respondents went there to look for work. Of the 11% who went to work in South Africa, more than half (51%) had arranged employment before they left Namibia. Virtually all of the people who went to work are urban males, married, own homes, and represent a relatively stable sector of the population.

Approximately 85% of the Namibian sample reported that they returned from South Africa because their holidays ended, for family reasons, or that they simply wanted to come back. It is noteworthy that losing work, a completed contract and deportations are significant reasons for people leaving South Africa to return to Lesotho, Zimbabwe and Mozambique. These factors are of limited significance for Namibia, with zero deportations being reported.

Perhaps the most significant findings are that those who go to South Africa are neither the destitute of the country, nor are they looking for work. Certainly the claim by the South African government that South Africa is being swamped by the neighbouring poor does not apply to Namibia (McDonald *et al*, 1998).

Almost all of the respondents who visited South Africa went by road or air. Only two people claimed to have crossed the border by foot (see Table 5.6). Given the remote and hostile environment near to the Namibia/South Africa border, the opportunities for people to cross undocumented from Namibia into South Africa are few. In any event, there is little need to do this as temporary entry permits for travel to South Africa are readily issued at the border to people in possession of a valid Namibian passport. In the past, when Namibia was administered by South Africa, there was no border-crossing control and no documents were necessary.

These findings are supported by the information available from Statistics South Africa on Namibians in South Africa and cross-border movements between the two countries. In 1996, 200 523 Namibians entered South Africa legally. Of these, only 5 569 (3% of the total) over-stayed their visas (Government of South Africa, 1998), providing further evidence that traffic between the two countries is

TABLE 5.6: METHODS OF TRAVEL TO SOUTH AFRICA ON MOST RECENT VISIT				
Method (%)	Namibia	Lesotho	Mozambique	Zimbabwe
On foot	1	4	14	14
Bus	19	17	20	35
Plane	9	–	3	5
Car	59	10	19	8
Horse or donkey	–	–	1	1
Train	9	5	38	19
Combi or taxi	3	63	4	16
Other	–	1	1	2
Note: N = 1 199.				

indeed highly legalised. In 1996, there were only 84 deportations of Namibians from South Africa. Further evidence of the present limited number of Namibians living illegally in South Africa is the fact that only 91 Namibians applied for the amnesty (77 successful) offered recently by the South African government to SADC citizens who had lived in South Africa since at least 1991 (Crush and Williams, 1999).

Given the findings of the survey, and the corroborating statistics from South Africa, it seems that there are indeed very few undocumented border crossings into South Africa by Namibians. Current estimates by the South African government are that there are less than 20 000 undocumented Namibians in South Africa. The findings presented here would certainly not lead us to challenge these figures.

Factors in migration decision-making

When asked what the most important reason might be that would cause them to go to South Africa in future, substantially fewer Namibians (24%) cited jobs, compared to Lesotho (53%), Zimbabwe (35%) and Mozambique (40%). Namibia has the highest percentage of people who would go to South Africa for educational purposes and the lowest percentage who would go for shopping purposes. Health care appeared to be about as important to Namibians as it is for people in Lesotho and Mozambique (about 10%). Trade, as a reason, is highest for Zimbabwe and Namibia, at about 8–9% (see Table 5.7).

In sharp contrast to the reasons people would consider going to South Africa, 23% of the respondents cited "peace" as the most compelling reason for remaining in Namibia. The second most important reason given for remaining in Namibia was safety for oneself and family (19%). The third most important response was that the respondents grew up in the country (12%). Personal

TABLE 5.7: FACTORS IN THE MIGRATION DECISION-MAKING PROCESS				
	Namibia	Lesotho	Mozambique	Zimbabwe
Most important reason for going to SA [ie conditions seen to be better in SA] (%)				
Land	–	–	1	2
Water/food	–	1	2	1
Houses	2	–	–	1
Jobs	24	53	40	35
Treatment by employers	1	–	1	1
Trade	9	1	4	8
Overall living conditions	9	2	14	5
Safety of self and family	1	1	1	–
Crime	1	–	1	–

TABLE 5.7 (cont.): FACTORS IN THE MIGRATION DECISION-MAKING PROCESS				
	Namibia	Lesotho	Mozambique	Zimbabwe
Most important reason for going to SA [ie conditions seen to be better in SA] (%)				
Peace	1	–	–	1
Education/schools	21	9	7	2
Health care	9	10	14	3
Place to raise your family	1	–	–	–
Diseases/HIV/AIDS	–	–	1	–
Freedom	1	–	–	1
Democracy	–	–	–	–
Travel documents	–	–	1	1
Shopping	7	18	9	26
Nothing	8	1	–	8
Other	7	4	5	8
Most important reason for remaining in own country [ie conditions seen to be better in home country] (%)				
Land	6	42	17	14
Water/food	1	3	4	3
Houses	2	6	6	2
Jobs	2	2	3	1
Treatment by employers	–	–	1	–
Trade	–	1	–	–
Overall living conditions	5	7	5	5
Safety of self and family	19	1	13	12
Crime	7	5	4	6
Peace	23	10	18	23
Education/schools	2	1	1	2
Health care	1	–	–	1
Place to raise your family	4	1	5	5
Diseases/HIV/AIDS	–	2	–	1
Freedom	8	10	3	6
Democracy	2	1	1	1
Travel documents	–	–	6	1
Shopping	–	–	–	–
Grew up here	12	2	–	11
Other	6	6	12	8
Note: N = 2 900.				

safety and a peaceful environment are strong motivating factors for Namibians to remain at home. Also interesting is that for Namibians, land is the least important reason to remain in the country, in sharp contrast to Lesotho, Mozambique and Zimbabwe. However, the urban dominance of the sample may explain this difference.

Thus, while jobs are certainly considered an important reason for going to South Africa, they are by no means the key factor. There are a variety of factors which both induce people to move and hold people back, and which demonstrate that the migration decision-making process is undoubtedly diverse and complex.

FUTURE MIGRATION TRENDS FROM NAMIBIA

Perceived impact of migration on Namibia

In stark contrast to the other countries, Namibians clearly feel little personal impact from the migration of people to South Africa. Likewise, Namibians feel that migration to South Africa has little or no impact on their families. More people are of the opinion, however, that migration to South Africa has some negative impact on community and country (Table 5.8).

In Lesotho, Mozambique and Zimbabwe, the impact on people personally, and on family, community and country, was generally felt to be significant. In the case of Mozambique and Zimbabwe, the majority felt the impact positively with somewhat more ambiguity in Lesotho. Namibians do not necessarily feel that migration to South Africa is of direct benefit to either themselves, their families or their communities, and that it may have some negative consequences for the country as a whole. Indeed, Namibians appear to be ambivalent about migration to South Africa. These results would indicate a propensity not to choose to migrate, or to encourage others not to do so, as the benefits are not apparent to the respondents. However, people may be just as likely not to discourage anyone who may indicate a wish to go to South Africa.

Likelihood of moving to South Africa

In keeping with the findings for Lesotho, Mozambique and Zimbabwe, nearly two-thirds of Namibian respondents indicated that they would be able to go to South Africa if they wanted to. However, only 17% of the Namibians said that they had a strong or moderate desire to move to South Africa "permanently" (significantly lower than the other countries) (see Table 5.9). When asked about the likelihood of their actually doing so, the figure dropped to 12% (comparable with Mozambicans and Zimbabweans who show little desire to go and live in South Africa permanently). The largest response category was that it is "very unlikely".

When asked about living in South Africa for a "short period of time (up to two years)", the responses were slightly more favourable. Some 43% of Namibians

TABLE 5.8: PERCEIVED IMPACT OF MIGRATION ON PERSON/FAMILY/COMMUNITY/COUNTRY				
	Namibia	Lesotho	Mozambique	Zimbabwe
Personal impact (%)				
Very positive	4	11	22	13
Positive	13	41	47	35
No impact	63	12	21	46
Negative	15	27	8	4
Very negative	2	8	–	1
Don't know	3	2	3	2
Impact on family (%)				
Very positive	2	10	19	11
Positive	13	37	51	34
No impact	63	13	17	46
Negative	15	27	9	5
Very negative	3	6	–	1
Don't know	5	7	4	3
Impact on community (%)				
Very positive	1	9	9	10
Positive	10	41	51	40
No impact	48	4	15	25
Negative	19	25	12	6
Very negative	4	9	1	1
Don't know	18	12	12	19
Impact on country (%)				
Very positive	3	10	12	10
Positive	12	37	47	36
No impact	30	3	7	14
Negative	24	28	17	12
Very negative	10	12	2	3
Don't know	22	10	15	25

Note: N = 2 900.

TABLE 5.9: DESIRE AND LIKELIHOOD OF MOVING TO SOUTH AFRICA				
	Namibia	Lesotho	Mozambique	Zimbabwe
Ability to go to SA if desired (%)				
Yes	62	64	76	68
No	37	35	17	31
Don't know	1	–	8	1
Desire to go and live permanently in SA (%)				
A great extent	6	17	14	9
Some extent	11	8	18	11
Not much	15	9	15	12
Not at all	67	66	46	67
Don't know	1	–	7	2
Desire to go and live temporarily in SA (for up to two years) (%)				
A great extent	12	15	15	22
Some extent	31	35	42	28
Not much	15	10	19	15
Not at all	41	39	19	34
Don't know	2	1	6	2
Likelihood of going and living permanently in SA (%)				
Very likely	4	11	3	4
Likely	8	14	11	8
Neither likely nor unlikely	6	3	13	7
Unlikely	19	5	36	19
Very unlikely	61	64	33	59
Don't know	3	4	5	3
Likelihood of going and living temporarily in SA (%)				
Very likely	7	16	6	13
Likely	28	42	34	26
Neither likely nor unlikely	6	2	20	7
Unlikely	18	5	20	16
Very unlikely	40	32	15	32
Don't know	2	4	6	5

Note: N = 2 900.

have a strong or moderate desire to go to South Africa for a short period. When asked about the "likelihood" of living in South Africa for a short period, the responses were polarised, with a large proportion of people saying it was "very unlikely" (see Table 5.9), but with 35% saying that it was "likely" or "very likely" that they might live in South Africa for a limited period. These results are consistent with those for other countries in the region. Some 43% of Namibians have a strong or moderate desire to go to South Africa for a short period (with a likelihood of 35%). These figures are consistent with those for other countries in the region.

Confirming the ephemeral interest of Namibians in South Africa, some 81% of Namibians have no desire to become permanent residents of South Africa, with 86% having no wish to become a citizen of the country either. Even fewer people indicated a desire to retire in South Africa or to be buried there (see Table 5.10). These patterns of response are broadly consistent with those for Mozambique and Zimbabwe (with people from Lesotho showing greater, though far from overwhelming, interest).

In sum, South Africa remains a place of interest for a significant minority of Namibians, but not as a place to go to permanently. The findings of the survey confirm that for Namibians, like other SADC country citizens, home is best, and South Africa is not a preferred place to live. In keeping with the stereotypes discussed in McDonald *et al* (1998) for Zimbabwe, Lesotho and Mozambique, fears of settlement in South Africa by significant numbers of migrants from Namibia appear to be ill-founded.

TABLE 5.10: DESIRE TO STAY IN SOUTH AFRICA PERMANENTLY				
	Namibia	Lesotho	Mozambique	Zimbabwe
Interest in permanent residence in SA (%)				
Yes	17	33	14	12
No	81	62	83	87
Don't know	2	6	3	1
Interest in SA citizenship (%)				
Yes	12	34	7	14
No	86	60	90	85
Don't know	2	6	3	1
Interest in retiring in SA (%)				
Yes	11	28	4	6
No	87	67	95	91
Don't know	2	6	2	2
Interest in being buried in SA (%)				
Yes	7	17	1	3
No	91	77	96	95
Don't know	3	6	3	2
Note: N = 2 900.				

Future migration patterns

The demography of future migration is, of course, notoriously difficult to assess, reflecting the complex and diverse dynamics of the migration process. Tables 5.11 and 5.12 on the following pages compare Namibia with Lesotho, Mozambique, and Zimbabwe in this regard. For all four countries, the highest response categories for short-term migration to South Africa are "likely" and "very unlikely", with younger cohorts being more likely than older people to migrate.

Men are marginally more likely to go than women (48% versus 41%). Those with experience of South Africa are more likely to go than those who have none (54% versus 38%). Better-educated Namibians are also more likely than people with less education to go for a short-term visit. The same is true for those who already have family in South Africa, as well as those who have a favourable impression of the country. These figures once again support the notion that South Africa is of interest as a short-term migration destination for Namibians. However, there are clear differences along lines of gender, experience, age and education. Even then, more than half of the population has little or no interest in going to South Africa.

ATTITUDES TOWARDS MIGRATION AND IMMIGRATION POLICY

Citizenship and belonging

Namibians have a strong attachment to their own country. Table 5.13 indicates that most Namibians "agree" or "strongly agree" that they are proud to be called a citizen of their country (97%). Namibian citizenship is an essential component of identity and self-definition. The strong feelings of national identity are very similar to the levels observed in Zimbabwe, Mozambique and Lesotho.

The rating of government performance is not as positive as feelings of pride and national identity. However, 67% of Namibians interviewed still approve or strongly approve of the performance of government over the last year, 51% have confidence that the government can be trusted to do the right thing, and 61% are satisfied or very satisfied with democracy in Namibia. All of this suggests that the Namibian government enjoys significant legitimacy and that political discontent is not particularly widespread at present.

The confidence levels in government are most similar to those in Zimbabwe, although the Zimbabwean levels of satisfaction would likely be lower today given the political turmoil in that country since the survey was conducted. Levels of distrust are higher in Lesotho and Mozambique, though in the latter case there is a high level of satisfaction with the functioning democracy. The survey results suggest that people are relatively satisfied with living in Namibia at the present time. Deeper loyalty to Namibia, strong national identity and an absence of widespread political dissatisfaction are all factors that would discourage Namibians from looking over the fence for greener pastures.

TABLE 5.11: LIKELIHOOD OF SHORT-TERM MIGRATION TO SOUTH AFRICA FROM NAMIBIA					
	Very likely	Likely	Neutral	Unlikely	Very unlikely
Total sample (%)	7	28	6	18	40
Gender (%)					
Male	13	35	9	16	27
Female	9	32	8	15	36
Age (%)					
15–24	15	40	9	13	22
25–44	10	35	10	17	28
45–64	10	24	6	15	46
65+	6	18	4	13	59
Employment (%)					
Inactive	11	32	9	16	33
Looking for work	15	40	7	14	24
Part-time	10	38	13	12	27
Full-time	10	29	9	17	35
Education (%)					
No schooling	5	27	9	17	42
Some primary school	11	32	9	14	34
Primary school completed	13	32	7	13	37
Some high school	13	36	9	15	26
High school completed	11	37	8	17	26
Post-grad and further	13	36	11	19	21
Been to SA? (%)					
Yes	16	38	5	12	29
No	8	30	11	18	32
Family in SA? (%)					
None	10	30	7	17	37
Few	12	29	11	13	25
Most	16	34	11	17	22
Almost all	27	24	5	22	22
Overall impression of SA (%)					
Very favourable	21	38	6	13	22
Favourable	9	39	10	18	25
Neutral	7	26	14	14	39
Unfavourable	7	31	5	15	42
Very unfavourable	8	12	11	13	57

Note: N = 600.

TABLE 5.12: LIKELIHOOD OF PERMANENT MIGRATION TO SOUTH AFRICA FROM NAMIBIA					
	Very likely	Likely	Neutral	Unlikely	Very unlikely
Total sample (%)	4	8	6	19	63
Gender (%)					
Male	6	11	8	21	53
Female	5	9	6	19	61
Age (%)					
15–24	9	14	9	23	45
25–44	4	11	8	20	57
45–64	5	6	5	17	68
65+	4	1	3	16	77
Employment (%)					
Inactive	6	10	7	21	57
Looking for work	7	14	7	20	52
Part-time	5	12	10	20	54
Full-time	5	8	7	20	60
Education (%)					
No schooling	3	8	9	18	62
Some primary school	6	8	6	17	63
Primary school completed	4	10	7	19	60
Some high school	6	11	8	23	52
High school completed	7	15	6	23	50
Post-grad and further	6	12	8	25	50
Been to SA? (%)					
Yes	8	12	6	16	58
No	4	10	8	23	55
Family in SA?					
None	4	9	6	19	62
Few	7	12	8	21	52
Most	7	14	9	28	42
Almost all	13	26	3	18	40
Overall impression of SA					
Very favourable	12	12	8	19	49
Favourable	4	12	8	23	53
Neutral	3	8	11	21	58
Unfavourable	2	9	3	18	69
Very unfavourable	3	1	8	12	76

Note: N = 600.

TABLE 5.13: PRIDE OF CITIZENSHIP AND GOVERNMENT APPROVAL RATINGS BY RESPONDENTS				
	Namibia	Lesotho	Mozambique	Zimbabwe
It makes me feel proud to be called a citizen of my country (%)				
Strongly agree	62	81	58	61
Agree	35	14	40	34
Neither agree nor disagree	1	1	1	2
Disagree	2	3	2	3
Strongly disagree	–	1	–	–
Don't know	–	–	–	–
Being a citizen of my country is an important part of how I see myself (%)				
Strongly agree	54	79	47	52
Agree	43	13	45	40
Neither agree nor disagree	1	1	6	3
Disagree	1	5	3	3
Strongly disagree	–	2	–	1
Don't know	1	–	–	1
Rating of government performance over the past year (%)				
Strongly disapprove	9	27	8	9
Disapprove	22	17	50	19
Approve	51	33	22	50
Strongly approve	16	12	4	12
Don't know	3	10	17	10
How often can you trust government to do what is right? (%)				
Just about always	15	21	17	11
Most of the time	36	12	18	37
Only some of the time	37	40	49	34
Never	6	23	8	9
Don't know	5	4	9	9
Are you satisfied with democracy in your country? (%)				
Very dissatisfied	8	32	8	10
Dissatisfied	18	24	20	17
Satisfied	49	27	45	45
Very satisfied	19	13	7	10
[Respondent's country] is not a democracy	3	1	4	4
Don't know	2	4	16	15

Note: N = 2 900.

Borders

Despite the similarities with other countries on questions of pride, national identity and democracy, Namibians feel differently about national borders (see Table 5.14). Whereas many people in Lesotho, Zimbabwe and Mozambique "agree" or "strongly agree" with the assertion that freedom of movement is a fundamental human right that transcends national boundaries, 57% of the Namibian sample "disagree" or "strongly disagree".

Namibians are equally divided on the issue of the artificiality of borders. The pattern duplicates that in Zimbabwe and Mozambique. Only in Lesotho, as expected, is there an overwhelming sentiment about the artificiality of boundaries. A clear majority of Namibians, as in the other three countries, believe that people on opposite sides of an international boundary are different from one another. Eighty percent of Namibians (the highest of the four countries) believe it is very important for a country to have borders that differentiate it from other states.

The general Namibian belief in the integrity and importance of state boundaries shows important differences across racial lines. Coloureds feel more strongly that crossing borders freely is a basic human right than do white or African Namibians, and that borders are artificial. In contrast, white Namibians tend to feel that borders do not separate people of different backgrounds and character (possibly reflecting their historical affinity with white South Africa). Nonetheless, the majority of Namibian respondents, from all racial groups, are not supportive of free cross-border movements, and they consider national pride and national borders as an integral and important part of their identity as Namibians. On the question of "free movement" of people in the region, responses were more polarised. Thirty-eight percent of the respondents agreed or strongly agreed with the notion of free movement in the Southern African region, whereas 52% disagreed or strongly disagreed with the proposition.

Immigration to Namibia

The survey indicates that while Namibians favour both foreign investment in Namibia and cross-border trade, they do not support the free movement of people into the country. The respondents' opinions in this regard tend to reflect their own economic and socio-political experiences. For example, with some 70% of Namibia's population involved in (semi-) subsistence crop and livestock farming, and given the marginal productive value of much of the country's farmland and the history of land dispossession, it is not surprising that there is a perceived shortage of land.

Thus, when asked whether or not Namibia should allow other Southern Africans to farm in the country, it is not surprising that 80% either disagreed or strongly disagreed with the idea. Likewise, 59% felt that there should be strict limits on foreigners entering the country. On the other hand, more than half of the respondents agreed or strongly agreed that Namibia should allow Southern Africans to trade and invest in the country.

TABLE 5.14: ATTITUDES TOWARDS BORDERS				
	Namibia	Lesotho	Mozambique	Zimbabwe
It is a basic human right for people to be able to cross from one country into another without obstacles (%)				
Strongly agree	13	61	16	23
Agree	28	20	34	39
Neither agree nor disagree	2	–	6	4
Disagree	42	16	28	25
Strongly disagree	15	1	10	5
Don't know	2	2	6	4
It is ridiculous that people from this country cannot freely go to another country, all because of some artificial border (%)				
Strongly agree	12	56	10	12
Agree	27	20	28	27
Neither agree nor disagree	7	–	14	12
Disagree	29	20	34	34
Strongly disagree	13	2	9	7
Don't know	3	2	6	8
People who live on different sides of borders between two countries are very different from one another (%)				
Strongly agree	12	33	11	11
Agree	40	35	33	31
Neither agree nor disagree	8	1	16	10
Disagree	26	25	29	37
Strongly disagree	11	3	4	7
Don't know	4	4	8	5
It is very important for my country to have a border that clearly differentiates it from other countries (%)				
Strongly agree	35	24	25	30
Agree	45	20	41	41
Neither agree nor disagree	4	1	8	7
Disagree	9	46	14	11
Strongly disagree	7	8	2	5
Don't know	1	2	10	6
Note: N = 2 900.				

South African immigration policy

The strong respect for borders and territorial integrity among Namibians is mirrored in their assessment of the rights of the South African government to set its own immigration policy. Some 58% of the Namibian sample even felt that the South African government should place strict limits on the number of foreigners they allow into South Africa (see Table 5.15), which is only slightly lower than what South Africans themselves think about the issue (see Chapter 7).

Moreover, 36% of Namibians think that "illegal" residents in South Africa should be sent back to their home countries – a higher proportion than in Lesotho, Zimbabwe or Mozambique. And finally, Namibians are more inclined than Basotho, Mozambicans and Zimbabweans to say that amnesty should not be offered to "illegal immigrants" in South Africa.

Surprisingly, given the existence of SADC and arguments within South Africa for immigration preferences for SADC citizens, Namibians do not see any particular reason why South Africa should show preferences for people from the region (only 39% in favour) or even from Namibia itself (40% in favour). These figures are not dissimilar to those in the other countries, suggesting that a regional consciousness, if indeed it even exists, has a long way to go before it permeates people's views about migration and immigration.

Non-citizens' rights in South Africa

Most Namibians take a fairly liberal approach to the question of rights for non-South Africans living in South Africa. On the whole, they think that non-South Africans should have the same rights as South African citizens to employment, medical services, housing and education.[2] Most also agree that non-South African citizens should enjoy the same basic human rights as citizens (see Table 5.16), with the exception of the right to vote (60% opposed).

Namibians, like their South African counterparts, are generally supportive of basic civil liberties and human rights for migrants in South Africa – despite their strong support for retaining borders and controlling cross-border movements – but do not expect temporary migrants to receive the full political privileges of South African citizenship.

Incorporation and free movement

Despite their relatively conservative attitude towards immigration policy, more than half (56%) of the Namibian sample hold that the preferred policy should be freedom of movement of people and goods between Namibia and South Africa. Only 29% of respondents think that Namibia and South Africa should remain totally independent from each other. Although this figure is substantially higher than reported for Lesotho, Mozambique and Zimbabwe, it is, nevertheless, a minority of the sample.

TABLE 5.15: ATTITUDES TOWARDS SOUTH AFRICAN IMMIGRATION LAWS				
	Namibia	Lesotho	Mozambique	Zimbabwe
Which one of the following do you think the SA government should do? (%)				
Let anyone into SA who wants to enter	19	68	13	22
Let people into SA as long as there are jobs	21	25	67	35
Place strict limits on the number of foreigners	54	6	16	36
Prohibit all people entering into SA from other countries	4	–	1	4
Don't know	2	1	4	4
What should the SA government do about people from other Southern African countries in the country? (%)				
Send them all back to their own country	5	2	2	11
Send back those who don't contribute to economic well-being	11	12	28	23
Send back those who have committed serious crimes	41	68	59	30
Send back those who are in SA without the government's permission	36	10	8	27
The government should not send back any people	5	6	2	8
Don't know	3	1	2	1
Amnesty for foreigners living illegally inside the country (%)				
Strongly disagree	14	11	11	21
Disagree	31	18	20	21
Neither agree nor disagree	11	1	17	7
Agree	22	32	39	27
Strongly agree	15	37	5	15
Haven't heard enough about it	2	1	3	2
Don't know	6	1	6	7

TABLE 5.15 (cont.): ATTITUDES TOWARDS SOUTH AFRICAN IMMIGRATION LAWS				
	Namibia	Lesotho	Mozambique	Zimbabwe
Special treatment for other SADC country citizens (%)				
Strongly disagree	12	21	5	16
Disagree	36	45	20	33
Neither agree nor disagree	9	3	17	10
Agree	27	20	37	25
Strongly agree	12	9	5	7
Hanen't heard enough about it	1	1	6	1
Don't know	2	2	10	7
Special treatment for Namibians (%)				
Strongly disagree	11	20	5	16
Disagree	34	43	24	35
Neither agree nor disagree	11	3	16	12
Agree	20	19	31	21
Strongly agree	20	15	16	10
Haven't heard enough about it	1	1	1	1
Don't know	3	–	8	6

Note: N = 2 900.

TABLE 5.16: ATTITUDES TOWARDS RIGHTS FOR NON-CITIZENS				
The SA government should offer people from other African countries in SA:	Namibia	Lesotho	Mozambique	Zimbabwe
The same chance at a job as South Africans (%)				
Strongly disagree/disagree	21	6	14	20
Neither agree nor disagree	5	–	5	6
Strongly agree/agree	72	94	79	69
Haven't heard enough about it/don't know	2	–	3	5
The same access to medical services as South Africans (%)				
Strongly disagree/disagree	5	2	10	11
Neither agree nor disagree	3	–	3	4
Strongly agree/agree	89	98	84	80
Haven't heard enough about it/don't know	2	–	3	5

TABLE 5.16 (cont.): ATTITUDES TOWARDS RIGHTS FOR NON-CITIZENS				
The SA government should offer people from other African countries in SA:	Namibia	Lesotho	Mozambique	Zimbabwe
The same access to a house as South Africans (%)				
Strongly disagree/disagree	16	10	14	17
Neither agree nor disagree	4	–	11	6
Strongly agree/agree	77	90	73	71
Haven't heard enough about it/don't know	3	0	2	6
The same access to education as South Africans (%)				
Strongly disagree/disagree	6	3	12	13
Neither agree nor disagree	2	–	5	6
Strongly agree/agree	89	97	79	76
Haven't heard enough about it/don't know	3	–	4	6
The right to vote in SA elections (%)				
Strongly disagree/disagree	60	33	65	55
Neither agree nor disagree	8	1	10	6
Strongly agree/agree	27	65	15	27
Haven't heard enough about it/don't know	6	2	9	12
The right to become a permanent resident of SA (%)				
Strongly disagree/disagree	26	17	49	40
Neither agree nor disagree	10	2	18	12
Strongly agree/agree	58	80	29	38
Haven't heard enough about it/don't know	6	1	5	10
The right to become a citizen of SA (%)				
Strongly disagree/disagree	28	15	54	39
Neither agree nor disagree	10	2	18	12
Strongly agree/agree	57	81	23	38
Haven't heard enough about it/don't know	5	–	5	11

Note: N = 2 900.

Of the small number who thought that the countries should join together (13% of the sample), opinions are relatively equally divided between Namibia becoming a province of South Africa and the Northern Cape province of South Africa becoming a part of Namibia.

TABLE 5.17: ATTITUDES TOWARDS POLITICAL INCORPORATION				
	Namibia	Lesotho	Mozambique	Zimbabwe
Policy preferences (%)				
The two countries join together under one government	13	41	7	9
Both countries keep their own government, but complete freedom of movement of people and goods across the border	56	39	67	72
Total independence between the two countries	29	19	22	16
Don't know	2	1	5	3
Preferences of those favouring incorporation (%)				
Your country becoming a new province within SA	31	45	43	28
Your country becoming part of [nearest SA province]	13	12	7	16
[Nearest SA province] becoming part of your country	30	39	14	25
Don't know	27	4	36	31
Note: N = 2 900, 493.				

DETERMINANTS OF VARIATION IN NAMIBIAN ATTITUDES

In order to understand the results of the Namibian survey better, a rigorous statistical analysis was undertaken of 38 key questions and considered against 14 profile variables. While these do not represent the complete data set, they are a comprehensive analysis of key issues. Table 5.18 provides a summary of the trends identified and the degree to which these variables influence people's opinions and attitudes on the 38 questions, based on an inspection of the percentage difference in responses.[3] The trends uncovered in the analysis show quite clearly the dominant factors that influenced the Namibian sample's opinions of, and attitudes towards, migration and immigration. The discussion that follows refers exclusively to the Namibian data set.

TABLE 5.18: SUMMARY OF THE TRENDS IN THE NAMIBIAN DATA BY DEMOGRAPHIC VARIABLE

Profile variable	% of questions influenced
Race	71
Age	45
Income	37
Education	34
Urban versus rural	34
Location	32
Likelihood of short-term migration to SA	32
Likelihood of long-term migration to SA	29
Home ownership	18
Economic activity	16
Household status	16
Impression of SA	13
Marital status	13
Gender	8

The significance of race

Race is by far the most influential variable affecting attitudes. In 71% of the questions, race influenced the response given. The chi-square test found that race was significant in at least 15 of the 38 questions identified. The strongest correlation with race was for opinions on whether or not people wanted to become permanent residents of South Africa, to become citizens of South Africa or to retire or be buried in the country.

Africans showed the least interest in settling in South Africa permanently, but it is noteworthy that the overwhelming majority of Namibians from all racial categories have no interest in these possibilities. While the reasons for these differences are not entirely clear from this survey, the historical and cultural links between South Africa and coloured and white Namibians are stronger than those between the various groups of northern African Namibians.

The significance of age

Although not as important as race, age is a key variable influencing people's attitudes and opinions about migration to South Africa. The trend suggests that the older people get, the less interested they are in migration, and yet the less they are satisfied with their own government's performance and system of rule.

Although a lack of satisfaction with various aspects of national governance might be expected to influence people positively to migrate in search of more favourable conditions, age appears to directly counter this likelihood. The most statistically significant correlations were observed between age and the questions of who visits South Africa, and whether or not respondents want to become permanent residents or citizens of South Africa.

The significance of income

As might be expected, income is an important variable in determining behaviour and opinion. The trend from the Namibian data is for higher-income groups in the population to be more mobile, have more choice, and be more likely to visit or live in South Africa for a short period of time. The relationships with the most significant correlations were found to be between income, the questions of who visits South Africa, and issues concerning borders. From a developmental point of view, these people may be more attractive to South Africa and represent a bigger loss for Namibia since they tend to be educated, employed and urban.

The significance of education

Like income, education influences many of the questions identified. With better education comes greater mobility and a greater desire to visit or live in South Africa. Also, better-educated people feel that they are more likely than their less educated counterparts to actually live in South Africa in the foreseeable future. Notwithstanding this trend in the data, the correlation coefficients were generally weak.

The significance of location

There can be no doubt that the location (urban/rural) of the respondents also influenced their responses. Urban dwellers are more likely to visit and to stay permanently in South Africa. The correlation coefficient is strongest between the urban/rural variable and the question of who visits South Africa, the importance of borders to differentiate people, South Africa's returnee policy, the question of amnesty for illegals, rights relating to access to medical care and education, the right to vote and to become a permanent resident and citizen. This finding is supported by the opinions and behaviour of urban versus rural residents in the survey. The urban residents are the more mobile of the two groups, and it is they who are more liberal towards most of the issues described.

Location in the country (eg north versus south) is also an important factor. The trend is for those people living in the central, coastal and southern towns of Namibia to be more inclined to move between Namibia and South Africa, with residents of the northern communal towns being less likely, and the rural communal dwellers being the least likely to move. The most significant statistical correlation is between location and the questions of who visits South Africa. Location is strongly correlated with additional questions, the most interesting being respondents' attitudes towards government and border, policy and amnesty issues. Rural dwellers tend to be more conservative, and are more satisfied with and trusting of their government. This again supports the hypothesis that rural people, despite their relatively unfavourable circumstances, are not ready migrants to South Africa.

The significance of attitude

The likelihood of short-term migration to South Africa from Namibia increased with the level of dissatisfaction with Namibia's democracy. Of course, a positive desire to go to South Africa influenced people's likelihood too, as did the number of friends and family they had in South Africa. What is most compelling in this analysis is that Namibians have little desire at all to become permanent residents or citizens of South Africa. The correlation coefficient for these variables is strong. The same is true for retirement, and most Namibians answered "no" when asked these questions. From a policy perspective, these responses support the argument that people from Namibia, and indeed the region, have no strong desire to move to South Africa on a permanent basis (McDonald *et al*, 1998).

Namibian people's impressions of South Africa indicate that those who have been to South Africa are more favourable in their impression of the country. What is more interesting is that those with the least favourable impressions tended, more than those with favourable impressions, to feel that Namibian borders were important. Similarly, people favoured Namibia's independence more if they had a less favourable impression of South Africa, as is evident by the trend analysis and the test for significance. People who were positive about South Africa were more in favour of supporting migrants' rights to permanent residence and citizenship in South Africa. The strongest correlation measured was between people's impression of South Africa and their desire to live in the country, whether or not they wanted to become permanent residents, citizens, or to be buried there.

The significance of home ownership

Home ownership is an interesting variable, as it influences, in particular, the degree to which Namibians visit South Africa and their desire to live there, both in the short term and permanently. Owners certainly visit South Africa more than non-owners and are more critical of government. However, it also seems from the trend that investment in the home and security of tenure militate against migration, while a lack of investment, or ability to invest, and insecure tenure (illegal occupation) appear to increase the likelihood of migration. However, this must be considered against the other factors that are positively correlated with migration, including income and education. These latter two factors are important variables and appear more relevant than a lack of tenure security.

The insignificant variables

Economic activity appears surprisingly weak in its general influence on the range of questions posed in this survey. As a predictor of migration, the employed – with higher income, education and mobility – are certainly more able to go to South Africa, and actually visit more often, than the unemployed, although it is the unemployed who are more desirous of going to South Africa for a short term. The test for significance was disappointing using chi-square, with few cases and weak correlation coefficients. This is largely the result of too many categories for the economic activity variable, and it is likely that a substantial recoding of the data would draw out stronger relationships than those observed, supporting the trend identified.

Household status is generally not significant as an independent variable, although it is noteworthy that heads of households and spouses are the least interested in considering moving to South Africa, or becoming a permanent resident or citizen of the country. The strongest correlation reported was between household status and visits to South Africa.

The test for marital status provided no results. However, the trend indicates that married people are less likely to want to go to South Africa, or to become permanent residents, than single and separated/divorced people. This is not surprising, as married people tend to be less mobile than single and separated/divorced people and are more settled in a place.

Surprisingly, gender was the least influential demographic variable on the 38 questions selected from the survey for this analysis. (Marital status failed the test for significance in all cases, but it had higher percentage responses than the gender variable.) Although not unusual, more men reported going to South Africa to work than women (17% and 2%, respectively). The most statistically significant relationship, although still weak, was between gender and questions on South African returnee policy.

CONCLUSIONS AND POLICY IMPLICATIONS

Perhaps the most significant outcome of the Namibian survey is the low propensity of the Namibian population to migrate to South Africa. It is clear from the findings that it is the more stable and wealthier sectors of Namibian society who are the cross-border visitors to South Africa, not the poor and destitute. Also, it is urban residents who go to South Africa, not rural dwellers.

The pattern of internal migration in Namibia is for rural migrants to move to urban places within Namibia, often in a step-wise fashion, and not to travel directly to South Africa or any other neighbouring country. The exception is the movement of rural people over the northern borders of the country, but this is a reflection of familial and economic links with people living in these neighbouring countries, rather than a tendency for the rural population to want to migrate out of Namibia. Given that nearly 70% of Namibia's population is rural, and that it is the more affluent and mobile urban sectors that move, this suggests that there is not likely to be an exodus of people from Namibia to South Africa now or in the foreseeable future.

An important adjunct to this picture is the fact that most cross-border migration with South Africa is short-term and for non-economic purposes. In addition, the overwhelming majority of Namibians have no desire to become permanent residents or citizens of South Africa and have no intention of retiring there either. These factors again reinforce the emerging trend that South Africa is not threatened with a flood of migration from other countries in the Southern African region and should address immigration policy reform accordingly.

Namibians indicated in the survey that, in general, they do not favour the removal of borders. Rather, they appear to favour a policy of non-integration, border controls and the strict maintenance of a Namibian national identity. Yet there is also support for the free movement of goods and services within the SADC region as well as support for improving the ease with which people can move between countries. Thus, while ease of movement is considered important, Namibians also want to see a strict limit placed on foreigners entering Namibia and even South Africa.

Namibians did not support undocumented migration, and were of the opinion that "illegal migrants" in South Africa should be sent home. Certainly, this opinion is reflected in Namibia's own domestic actions in this regard. Criminality is a concern for South Africa, and this is also the case in Namibia, where ease of cross-border movement is erroneously associated with a lack of control and a consequent rise in serious crime. While amnesty was not supported as an option for undocumented migrants, Namibians were supportive of civil liberties and basic human rights for migrants in South Africa, particularly with regard to issues of equality and access to services.

It would seem that Namibia is no less concerned than many other countries around the world about controlling the negative aspects of undocumented and unmanaged migration. However, there is clear support for greater regional integration and improved access to countries within the southern African region on a legal basis. This is an encouraging situation, and bodes positively for continued efforts at improving the well-being of both Namibia and the Southern African region as a whole.

ACKNOWLEDGEMENTS

The authors wish to give special thanks to Christa Schier who undertook all aspects of data entry, processing and management under considerable pressure. This chapter is testimony to her expertise and diligence. Data entry was done by R. Katzao, K. Matengu, S. Nangulah, J. Shapaka, N. Ndalikokule, E. Isaacks, F. Shilongo, S. Shipanga, and B. Kauahuma.

The following people worked as enumerators in the field, and the project benefited from their consistency and hard work in collecting the data: R. Katzao, D. Gowaseb, G. Stephanus, E. Isaacks, K. Matengu, P. Sisinyize, C. Mahoshi, J. Mamili, F. Shilongo, A. Vatileni, S. Nangulah, J. Shapaka, B. Kauahuma, F. Shikesho, F. Xamises, D. Siteketa, J. Chapwa, C. Shilima, R. Ihemba.

Thanks are also due to the staff of the Social Sciences Division (SSD) of the University of Namibia's Multidisciplinary Research Centre who provided a high standard of supervision in the field, including K. Stephanus, S. Mafwila, M. Naanda, M. Shapi and G. van Rooy. As always with a project of this nature, the greatest debt is to those people who gave freely of their time and knowledge, agreeing to be interviewed at length. The authors' heartfelt thanks go to all participants in all areas of Namibia, both rural and urban.

BIBLIOGRAPHY

Bley, H, 1971, *South West Africa under German rule, 1884–1914*. London: Heinemann.
Crush, J, and Williams, V, 1999, *The new South Africans? The immigration amnesties and their aftermath*. Cape Town: Idasa.
Goldblatt, I, 1971, *History of South West Africa*. Cape Town: Juta.
Government of South Africa, 1998, http://www.statssa.gov.za/releases/demograp/jan99/p0351.htm. Pretoria: Statistics South Africa.
Grotpeter, J, 1994, *Historical dictionary of Namibia*. Metuchen, NJ and London: The Scarecrow Press.
McDonald, D, Gay, J, Zinyama, L, Mattes, R, De Vletter, V, 1998, "Challenging xenophobia: Myths and realities about cross-border migration in Southern Africa", *SAMP Migration Policy Series*, No. 7. Cape Town: Kingston: Southern African Migration Project.
Melber, H, 1996, "Urbanisation and internal migration: Regional dimensions in post-colonial Namibia", NEPRU Working Paper, No. 48. Windhoek: Namibian Economic Policy Research Unit (NEPRU).
Miranda, A, 1998, "A note on migration in Namibia, based on the 1991 Census". Unpublished paper.
Pool, G, 1991, *Samuel Maherero*. Windhoek: Gamsberg Macmillan.
Tvedten, I, and Mupotola, M, 1995, "Urbanisation and urban policies in Namibia", SSD Discussion Paper, No. 10. Windhoek: Social Sciences Division, Multi-Disciplinary Research Centre, University of Namibia.

ENDNOTES

1   The omitted areas included: the commercial farms, which are disproportionately expensive to survey and yield little information as a percentage of the total Namibian population; remote and sparsely settled communal areas; and some major communal areas. A trade-off had to be reached between a nationally representative sample and a selection of important areas, without consciously biasing the sample only in favour of likely cross-border migrants.
2   It is worth noting that the question does not differentiate legal from undocumented immigrants.
3   The chi-square test was used to determine the statistical significance between each of the demographic variables and the questions. The strength of correlation was evaluated with a contingency coefficient (cc) for valid chi-square tests. The failure of the chi-square test to show significance is not necessarily an indication of no statistical significance. In many cases, there are too many categories with too few cases in each for the test to be valid. Nonetheless, based on the findings of the survey reported thus far, it appears that the chi-square test has approximated the general trends and patterns observed.

Chapter Six

Women on the move: Gender and cross-border migration to South Africa from Lesotho, Mozambique and Zimbabwe

by Belinda Dodson

Immigration policy is one of the last bastions of sovereign state power in an increasingly globalised world. Capital and information flow more or less freely across state borders. It is only when actual human bodies become involved that national drawbridges are raised. Relations of power and access to resources determine who moves where, when, how and why (Hyndman, 1996: 151–2). Men and women have differential access to power and resources across a range of scales, from the local to the global, and thus face different opportunities and constraints in determining their patterns of mobility. Nowhere, perhaps, is this truer than in migration to South Africa from other Southern African countries. Yet the links between gender and *international* migration in the region remain poorly understood (see for example Bozzoli, 1993; Murray, 1981).[1]

In an attempt to redress the imbalance, this chapter examines the contemporary experiences of women in relation to such cross-border migration from three countries in the region (Lesotho, Mozambique and Zimbabwe) and compares these experiences to those of men. Among the questions it seeks to answer are:
- **Who migrates?** How do the characteristics of female migrants differ from those of male migrants? Are they from similar backgrounds in terms of age, position in the household and educational status?
- **Why do women migrate to South Africa?** Do men and women cite the same factors influencing their decision to migrate? What is the relative importance of economic and social motives?
- **What are the spatial and temporal patterns of female compared to male migration?** Do men and women go to the same places in South Africa? Do

women cross borders more or less often? Is their migration more likely to be short-term rather than long-term or permanent?
- **How do women move?** Do they take their migration decisions independently or are they subject to decisions taken by (male) others? Do they move as individuals, or do they tend to migrate with male partners or in family or other groups? Do women use the same mode of transport as men to cross the border? Are women more or less likely to migrate illegally?
- **How does the economic behaviour of female migrants differ from that of men?** How do they support themselves in South Africa? Are women more or less likely than men to remit earnings to family members in their home country?
- **What are the social experiences of women migrants?** Are they more or less likely to describe their experiences in South Africa in positive terms?
- **How do men and women perceive the impacts of migration (male and female) at the individual, household, community and national scale?**

Although the questions seem straightforward, their answers reveal a complex set of gender relations and gender-specific behaviour. While there are many interesting similarities, the differences between male and female respondents are at least as significant.

The gender-neutral language used by officials, researchers and the media to describe migration and migrants – although intended to be non-sexist – effectively acts to discriminate against women. Real migrants, and the people they leave behind, are not sexless "persons", "migrants" or even, in official parlance, "aliens", but men and women, husbands and wives, fathers and mothers, sisters and brothers, sons and daughters, homosexuals and heterosexuals, friends and lovers. Their very decisions to migrate are often motivated precisely by their gender identities, roles and relations. So too are the decisions of the South African state whether to admit people as legal (im)migrants. Gender must therefore be thoroughly and explicitly addressed in formulating new migration policy.

GENDER AND MIGRATION IN INTERNATIONAL CONTEXT

Migrancy in Southern Africa needs to be placed in an international context if it is to be meaningfully interpreted. One of the legacies of apartheid-era isolation has been a tendency to stress the uniqueness of the South African experience. But international comparisons and the application of theories developed elsewhere in the world can help to shed light on the patterns and processes operating in this region. Particularly helpful is the large and growing literature on gender, migration and development (Chant, 1992, 1998; Moodie and Ndatshe, 1995; Campani, 1996; Hyndman, 1996).

Sylvia Chant (1992: 192–8) has identified eight characteristics of the gendering of migration that are found in most developing country contexts:
- Men are more mobile than women, and it is women who are more often "left behind";

- Women left behind are often disadvantaged by male out-migration;
- Men's migration is undertaken more independently than that by women;
- Men migrate "in ways that are linked much more directly with access to employment";
- Men move further and to a wider range of destinations;
- Migrant women "have fewer employment opportunities than migrant men in destination labour markets";
- Men migrate across a wide range of ages, whereas female migrants tend to be young;
- In terms of both social and economic links, women "maintain more enduring ties between areas of origin and destination".

In the Southern African region, the traditional pattern of cross-border migration has been impermanent (if long-term) labour migration of black males to South Africa from other Southern African countries (Crush, Jeeves and Yudelman, 1992; Jeeves and Crush, 1997). These men generally return to their countries of origin on completion of their contracts on South African mines or farms, and this system remains essentially intact. Yet it is likely that parallel female migration to South Africa has been underestimated, being of tenuous legality and therefore deliberately covert (see for example Miles, 1991; Cockerton, 1995).

Robin Cohen (1997) has recently noted six global trends in migration patterns that relate to post-apartheid South Africa:
- Refugee migration;
- Immigration shopping;[2]
- Undocumented workers;
- Independent female migration;
- Skilled transients;
- Unskilled contract workers.

Each, of course, has gender implications specific to particular historical and geographical contexts. Noting that the last category – almost entirely male – is at present the most common form of migrancy in Southern Africa, Cohen predicts an increase in the other five categories. With regard to women he writes:

> Many studies of migration have dealt with women as a residual category, as those "left behind". Where they crossed a border, women have generally been treated as dependent or family members. They were effectively the baggage of male workers. However, even historically, we are beginning to turn up evidence that women were more independent actors than had previously been thought.

Although he does not hazard a guess at the South African numbers, nor how these might have changed over time, he comments that "independent female migration from inside the country and from outside is now highly visible", including 'traders, maids, prostitutes and waitresses entering from neighbouring countries". Far from being exceptional, this type of female migration is common between a number of countries around the world (Chant and Radcliffe, 1992). Indeed the "feminisation" of international migration seems to be a worldwide trend, and there is little reason to believe that Southern Africa should be an exception (Campani, 1996).

Female migration into South Africa from outside the country appears to have undergone a significant increase since 1994. The lack of data makes it impossible to put a number on this increase, and much of it may represent an increase in visibility rather than volume, but it certainly warrants attention by both researchers and policy-makers.

Despite its importance, female migration has been "hidden from history" and from policy. There is a fundamental reason for recentring gender in the analysis of migration. As Chant and Radcliffe (1992: 2–3) point out, "gender-differentiated population movement may be significant in a whole range of ways to societies undergoing developmental change". Understanding the gender dimensions of Southern African migration provides insights into the wider transformation of the region's society and economy in the post-apartheid era. This, in turn, suggests a range of possibilities for positive development interventions that could improve the lives of women and men alike.

This chapter therefore seeks to retrieve women from a dual marginalisation:
- Their insecure legal status as migrants to South Africa, where many of them are technically "illegal" or "undocumented" (Reitzes, 1997);
- Their marginalisation in research and policy-making, where they are either relegated to footnotes or erased altogether through the use of gender-neutral language to describe what are in reality markedly gendered patterns and processes.

The chapter uses survey data collected by the Southern African Migration Project (SAMP) in Lesotho, Mozambique, and Zimbabwe in mid-1997 (see Chapters 1–4 for an analysis of this data on a country-by-country basis and Appendices A and B for a description of research methodology and a summary of aggregate results). A total of 2 300 interviews were completed in the three countries, 1 014 of which were with women (339 in Lesotho, 258 in Mozambique, 417 in Zimbabwe; the data from Namibia was not available at the time of writing).

The next section of the chapter analyses this empirical data on a gender basis and provides detailed demographic and attitudinal profiles of the women interviewed. Although limited by the closed-ended response options of the methodology, the survey provides a very large and comprehensive set of data on women and cross-border migration in the region and allows for country comparisons.[3] The chapter then moves on to suggest a number of measures that might be adopted in the construction of more gender-aware and non-sexist migration policy in South Africa in particular.

It must be noted, however, that these survey results represent the attitudes and experiences of women who were resident in their home country at the time of the interviews. The data, therefore, cannot claim to be representative of the thousands of women who were outside of the various countries, perhaps in South Africa, at the time of interviews.

GENDER AND MIGRATION IN POST-APARTHEID SOUTH AFRICA

The role of gender in migration patterns and processes

There are three dominant prevailing stereotypes of Southern African migration to South Africa. The first is an image of a highly formalised system of male migrant labour to the mines. The second stereotype is one of an uncontrolled post-apartheid invasion of "illegal immigrants" seeking a better life in the new South Africa. A third stereotype, largely arising from the first two, is that all migrants are male.

The first stereotype is an accurate representation of reality, although there exist a number of myths and misconceptions about how the system operates *and* about the migrants themselves (see Moodie and Ndatshe, 1995, 68–81; Sechaba Consultants, 1997; De Vletter, 1998).[4] A previous SAMP publication debunks the second stereotype, concluding that most Southern Africans are content to remain in their own countries and that those who do migrate are "hardly the stuff of desperate, uneducated criminals threatening South African society" (McDonald *et al*, 1998: 10). With regard to the third stereotype, the survey in Lesotho, Mozambique and Zimbabwe shows that the cross-border migrant is frequently, and perhaps increasingly, likely to be a woman.

Before analysing the survey results, there are two important caveats. Firstly, although the surveys were conducted according to rigorous methodological standards, the questionnaire was not designed primarily to elicit information about gender.[5] This makes it difficult to determine fully the gendered nature of migration in the region. Further survey work that focuses explicitly on gender and migration is therefore highly recommended.

Secondly, certain in-built spatial (eg urban/rural) and temporal (eg agricultural season) factors served to render the survey sample biased towards men. The sampling method was designed to select a nationally representative sample of the adult population in each country.[6] If women made up at least 50% of the population, and if men were more likely to have migrated to South Africa, and thus be physically absent from the locations in which the survey was conducted, the sample should have been more than 50% female. But the highest proportion of women was only 49% (in Lesotho).[7] In Mozambique and Zimbabwe the figures were 39% and 44%, respectively. One possible explanation is that women's responsibility for much of the household's agricultural and domestic labour may have made them less likely to be available when the interviewer called. The sampling bias may thus itself reflect the implication of gender in household relations and the division of labour, which gives rise to gendered personal geographies and temporalities.

Nevertheless, despite these caveats, the survey constitutes a valid enough national sample to provide a reliable source of information on women's experience of migration, although it cannot be taken as numerically accurate, nor used to predict or extrapolate the incidence of female migration in any quantitative sense.

Who goes to South Africa?

The gender bias in migration is immediately apparent in the basic demographic breakdown of the survey sample populations. Males are under-represented relative to females in the age categories 15–24 and 25–44, the economically active age groups from which migrants are typically drawn. The male bias in migration also shows up in respondents' answers to the question of whether they had ever been to South Africa (see Table 6.1). The smallest gender difference was found in Lesotho, where 86% of the male respondents and 76% of the female respondents had visited South Africa at least once in their lives.

Lesotho also had the highest overall incidence of visits to South Africa (81%). Mozambique had the largest gender difference, with 41% of the men and only 9% of the women reporting previous visits to South Africa. In Zimbabwe, with the lowest overall incidence of cross-border visits (23%), 25% of the men and 20% of the women reported experience of such travel. These gender differences throw into relief the broader differences among the three countries in the nature, pattern and motives of migration to South Africa. They also suggest that men and women go to South Africa for different reasons, and this is borne out by analysis of several other variables.

Other socio-economic indicators show interesting differences between men and women, reflecting women's generally disadvantaged position in the Southern African context. Compared to the men, women had lower levels of literacy and education, were less likely to be in formal, remunerated employment, and were less likely to own property (except indirectly through marriage). Although a similar percentage of men and women (63% and 61%, respectively) gave their marital

TABLE 6.1: MIGRATION EXPERIENCE BY GENDER						
	Male (%)			Female (%)		
Age breakdown of sample						
15–24	26			30		
25–44	46			51		
45–64	22			15		
65+	5			4		
Ever been to SA						
No	53			64		
Yes	48			36		
Ever been to SA (by country)	Les.	Moz.	Zim.	Les.	Moz.	Zim.
No	14	59	75	24	92	80
Yes	86	41	25	76	9	20

Notes: Tables may not add to 100% due to rounding. A single dash (–) signifies a value greater than zero and less than 0.5%. N = 2 300. Les. = Lesotho, Moz. = Mozambique, Zim. = Zimbabwe.

status as "married or living together" (see Table 6.2), women were more likely to report being separated, divorced, abandoned or widowed. Although the question was not raised directly, it is likely that many such incidences of marital breakdown are related to male out-migration.

When socio-demographic variables are broken down by whether or not respondents have ever been to South Africa (for whatever reason or duration of visit), a number of possible causal relationships emerge that might explain women's migration behaviour (see Tables 6.2, 6.3 and 6.4). In terms of marital status (see Table 6.2), married women and widows were more likely than unmarried or divorced/abandoned women to have visited South Africa. This is similar to the situation for men, although currently absent migrants could, by definition, not be included in the survey, so the male figures especially are biased towards returnees or non-migrants.

In the unmarried category, the gender difference is most marked. Of the men who had been to South Africa, 23% were unmarried, whereas only 13% of the women who had been to the country were unmarried. Migration is thus related to marital status, with older, married women being more likely to have made cross-border visits – including, of course, visits to husbands living and working in South Africa. Widows, although they make up only a small proportion of the sample (10% of women surveyed), comprise 13% of the women reporting personal experience of migration to South Africa. This too is likely to be related to husbands having lived and perhaps died there.

In terms of their status in the household (Table 6.3), women who classified themselves as "child" or "other family" were far more likely not to have visited South Africa than those describing their status as "spouse" or "head of household". The latter category had the highest level of migration experience. This lends weight to the argument that female migration cannot be viewed simply as an adjunct to male migration, but is often undertaken independently of a male spouse and may even represent a means of female empowerment (although, of course, some women may have reported their status as *de facto*

TABLE 6.2: MIGRATION EXPERIENCE BY MARITAL STATUS				
Marital status of sample	Male (%)		Female (%)	
Unmarried	32		23	
Widowed	2		10	
Separated/divorced/abandoned	4		6	
Married	63		61	
Ever been to SA?	No	Yes	No	Yes
Unmarried	40	23	29	13
Widowed	1	3	8	13
Separated/divorced/abandoned	4	3	7	6
Married	55	71	57	69
Note: N = 2 300.				

TABLE 6.3: MIGRATION EXPERIENCE BY HOUSEHOLD STATUS				
Household positions of sample	Male (%)		Female (%)	
Household head	57		18	
Spouse	4		48	
Child	26		20	
Other family	7		6	
Other	6		8	
Ever been to SA	No	Yes	No	Yes
Household head	46	69	14	25
Spouse	4	3	43	56
Child	32	21	24	14
Other family	9	4	9	2
Other	9	4	10	4
Note: N = 2 300.				

"head of household" precisely because of absent migrant husbands). In either case, this finding supports the idea of the female migrant as "responsible citizen", engaging in short-term migration to South Africa for reasons related to household reproduction.

The breakdown of "level of education" by gender also reveals the types of men and women who migrate. For the men in the sample, experience of migration to South Africa decreased as level of education increased (see Table 6.4). Men who were functionally illiterate or educated only to primary school level were over-represented in the category of males who reported having made at least one visit to South Africa, while men with secondary or tertiary education were under-represented (although, again, this category would have been missing men who were currently absent).

While the same picture emerged for women with tertiary education, there were significant gender differences in the other categories. Whereas 15% of men who had visited South Africa at least once in their lives had no schooling, the same was true of only 3% of women. Women who had visited South Africa tended to be those with at least primary or some secondary education, with education seeming to encourage cross-border travel.

In Zimbabwe and Mozambique, there was also a gender difference in the geographical origin of migrants. Women who reported visiting South Africa came mostly from urban areas, while males with migration experience tended to come from rural areas. In Lesotho, by contrast, there was a rural bias in both male and female respondents.

The above analysis suggests that in general female migrants are more sophisticated than their male counterparts. These differences reflect different motives for male and female migration, together with the different opportunities and constraints facing men and women, both in South Africa and in the countries

TABLE 6.4: MIGRATION EXPERIENCE BY EDUCATIONAL STATUS				
Educational status of sample	Male (%)		Female (%)	
No schooling	11		9	
Some primary school	26		27	
Primary school completed	16		19	
Some high school	32		36	
High school completed	9		8	
Post-grad and further	6		2	
Ever been to SA	No	Yes	No	Yes
No schooling	9	15	13	3
Some primary school	19	32	26	29
Primary school completed	17	15	18	20
Some high school	39	24	35	36
High school completed	9	9	6	10
Post-grad and further	7	5	2	1
Note: N = 2 300.				

surveyed. McDonald *et al* (1998: 8–13, 21–4) draw attention to various positive attributes of potential migrants to South Africa. A gendered analysis suggests that these attributes relate especially to women with migration experience, whose marital status, household position and level of education are far removed from the common negative stereotypes.

What factors encourage or discourage women's migration to South Africa?

A key element of the surveys was the part that investigated the potential to migrate through a series of questions on "push" and "pull" factors in the respondents' home countries and in South Africa. Here again, although there are broad similarities between men and women, there are also a number of revealing differences (see Table 6.5).

Men and women cited the same reasons for staying in their home country rather than migrating to South Africa: access to land; water and housing; better levels of safety; peace; freedom and democracy; and the ties of family and friends. Even when pressed to identify the single most important attraction of home, there was remarkable concurrence between male and female respondents.

A slight gender difference emerged when respondents were asked to rate, on a four-point scale, their level of concern with a range of factors that might discourage them from migrating to South Africa. Although they agreed on the broad categories of concern, men tended to express lower levels of concern than women in response to almost every suggested deterrent, including leaving behind assets and family members, not having family or friends in South Africa

TABLE 6.5: FACTORS ENCOURAGING AND DISCOURAGING MIGRATION TO SA		
Most important reason given for staying in home country	**Male (%)**	**Female (%)**
Land	22	25
Water	2	1
Food	1	2
Houses	4	4
Jobs	2	2
Living conditions	5	6
Safety of self and family	10	8
Crime	5	5
Peace	17	18
Education/schools	2	1
Health care	-	1
Place to raise a family	4	3
Freedom	7	6
Democracy	1	1
Other	18	17
Most important reason given for wanting to go to SA		
Jobs	53	28
Trade	3	7
Living conditions	7	7
Education/schools	5	6
Health care	6	12
Shopping	13	25
Other	19	15
Concerns about "someone close" going to SA		
Have an affair in SA	3	3
Get injured	28	30
Be victim of a crime	21	18
Be involved in crime	6	5
Get a disease	8	10
Have second family	3	6
Never come back	18	17
Other	13	11
Perceptions of South Africans views of foreign migrants		
Very negative	15	18
Negative	27	25
Neither positive or negative	13	12
Positive	35	35
Very positive	11	11
Note: N = 2 300.		

and not being assured of accommodation or employment. It would therefore seem that the migration *potential* of women is currently lower than that of men.

In contrast to the situation for what might be termed migration retardants, the "pull" factors encouraging migration displayed considerable gender variation. Jobs, trading opportunities, shopping, education and health care were consistently seen by both men and women as being better in South Africa than in their home country. When asked what would actually motivate them to go to South Africa the overwhelming majority of men cited employment, while women were almost as likely to cite shopping (25%) as jobs (28%). A range of goods available in South Africa, including many foodstuffs, are either unavailable or more expensive in the countries surveyed, so there is sound economic justification for crossing the border to make purchases.

Other migration motives cited more frequently by women than by men included trade, health care and education. It would thus seem that while there are strong motives for both men and women to travel to South Africa, gender-specific social and economic roles are reflected in existing and potential migration behaviour. In economic terms, and supported by restrictions on the employment of foreign women, most men would go to South Africa to work, most women to buy and/or sell goods. Women were also more likely to express multiple motives for migration. This, of course, relates to their responsibility for a wide range of household productive and reproductive functions, rendered even more complex by the "stretching" of households across international borders by male migrant absenteeism.

Somewhat surprisingly, given their differences in migration behaviour, there was remarkable agreement between men and women when it came to specific concerns about "someone close to you" going to South Africa. The main concerns expressed by people of both sexes were that the migrant might get injured, be a victim of crime, never come back, catch a disease, have an affair or start a second family. This indicates a broadly realistic view of the migration experience, with both men and women alert to the potential risks and costs as well as the benefits.

There was also remarkable concurrence between men and women in their rating of South Africans' perceptions of people who go there from other Southern African countries, with an interesting bimodal distribution of positive and negative responses. Again, this suggests a realism about migration that would seem to negate the stereotype of millions of would-be migrants threatening to swamp South Africa's society and economy.

What are the spatial and temporal patterns of women's migration?

The term "migration" covers a wide range of spatial and temporal patterns of movement, from short-distance shopping trips lasting a few days to long-distance, long-term contract labour over several years. As the survey demonstrates, the dominant forms of migration to South Africa differ markedly between men and women. Already evident from the discussion above, these differences are borne out by respondents' answers to questions concerning their actual and anticipated migration behaviour (see Table 6.6).

Respondents were asked whether they had any desire to live in South Africa, with separate questions for permanent (immigration) or short-term (migration) residence. The majority of men and women replied strongly in the negative for permanent residence, with women being more negative than men. There was also a gender difference for short-term residence, with some 60% of men, and only 46% of women saying they would like to go and live in South Africa for a

TABLE 6.6: DESIRE AND LIKELIHOOD OF MIGRATING TO SOUTH AFRICA		
Desire to live in SA permanently	Male (%)	Female (%)
Not at all	59	67
Not much	13	11
To some extent	15	10
To a great extent	14	12
Desire to go to SA for a short period (up to two years)		
Not at all	26	39
Not much	15	14
To some extent	38	31
To a great extent	21	15
Likelihood of living in SA permanently		
Very unlikely	52	59
Unlikely	21	20
Neither likely nor unlikely	8	7
Likely	12	10
Very likely	7	5
Likelihood of leaving home country for a short period (up to two years)		
Very unlikely	24	31
Unlikely	14	14
Neither likely nor unlikely	9	9
Likely	35	31
Very likely	14	10
Don't know	5	5
Desire to retire or be buried in SA		
Do you want to retire in SA? (% who said yes)	11	14
Do you want to be buried in SA? (% who said yes)	7	8
Note: N = 2 300.		

period of up to two years. A similar pattern emerged in response to a question about their likelihood of ever living in South Africa, again asked separately about permanent and short-term residence. Here, too, men and women responded largely in the negative for permanent residence, but slightly more men than women regarded it as likely that they might end up spending some time living in South Africa. Migration potential is thus once more demonstrated to be lower amongst women than men.

Neither men nor women expressed a great desire to attain South African citizenship or permanent residence status, with a roughly 80/20 split of "no" to "yes" answers for both genders in both categories. Even more tellingly, neither male nor female respondents had much wish to retire to South Africa, still less to be buried there. Clearly ties to "home" are strong. This was further evident in respondents' expressed desire for return visits should they ever reside in South Africa, with most men and women saying that they would return "frequently". Even, perhaps especially, those with strong migration experience or potential thus seek to retain a transnational lifestyle and identity rather than become fully, or permanently, South African.

The different pattern and purpose of male and female migration shows up clearly in the duration of both anticipated and actual visits to South Africa (see Table 6.7). For hypothetical future migration, the question on duration of visit was phrased as follows: "Imagine that you decided to go and stay in South Africa. How long would you want to stay?" In categories ranging from "a few days" up to "a few months", the anticipated length of stay for women exceeded that for men. There was an almost equal response rate between men and women in the categories "six months" and "six months to a year", but a heavy male bias towards the longer time periods. In other words, women are more likely to make short trips while men are more likely to make extended trips.

This gender difference was also evident in frequency and duration of actual visits to South Africa in the previous five years. Women had made more frequent visits of shorter duration, most lasting one month or less. Most men had stayed a month or more. Those men who had stayed longer than a month commonly reported periods of residence in South Africa lasting 48 to 52 weeks – the typical year-long migrant labour contract. Thus, gender difference in migration timing arises from the different motives for male and female migration: men for employment purposes, requiring stays of months or years; women for buying and selling goods, visiting family members and accessing services such as health care, requiring only short visits of a few days or weeks.

There is a corresponding geography to these temporal differences. When asked hypothetically where they would like to migrate to, men and women gave strikingly similar responses: Gauteng came up most frequently, followed by Cape Town, Durban, Welkom and Bloemfontein, and then by a number of smaller towns in the Free State, Mpumalanga, KwaZulu-Natal, Northern and North-West provinces (the five South African provinces most proximate to the three countries surveyed).

However, when asked where they actually went on their last visit to South Africa, gender differences in migration geography *did* show up, displaying

TABLE 6.7: FREQUENCY OF VISITS AND LENGTH OF STAY IN SOUTH AFRICA		
Length of stay for hypothetical future visits to SA	Male (%)	Female (%)
A few days	3	6
A few months	4	9
One month	1	4
A few months	8	11
Six months	7	7
Six months to a year	17	17
A few years	40	29
Indefinitely	21	17
Frequency of actual visits in the past 5 years		
More than once a month	13	17
Once a month	10	15
Once every few months	18	17
Once or twice a year	21	21
Less than once or twice a year	20	15
I have been just once	19	16
Duration of actual visits in the past 5 year		
1 week or less	23	35
2–4 weeks	26	42
1–6 months	15	15
6 months to 1 year	17	4
Longer than a year	19	4

Note: N = 2 300.

marked difference from the desired destinations. Respondents reported visits to a wide range of places, some as specific as a particular mine and others as general as a city or province. Nevertheless certain patterns emerge.

Rather than the major cities, which is where people say they would like to go, most migration seems to be to mining and other small towns. Men tended to migrate to places of employment, notably the mines of the Witwatersrand and the Free State. Women, by contrast, travelled to places offering opportunities to buy and sell: either the major cities (mostly in Gauteng) or towns near the border with Lesotho, Zimbabwe or Mozambique. This gendered geography was explicit in respondents' stated reasons for selecting a destination. Men overwhelmingly cited job availability. Women, in addition to employment, gave the presence of friends and family and the availability of cheap goods and better shopping as their reasons for choosing to go to a particular place.

All of this suggests that the status quo, with heavily male-biased labour migration, is deeply entrenched. People in neighbouring countries are realistic rather than optimistic about life "on the other side of the fence", and most, especially women, would prefer to remain in their home countries.

Male migration, even when it is long-term, is not permanent, nor do most male migrants wish it to become so. Female migration is a response to difficult circumstances in the home countries, but is perceived and practised as a temporary and expedient tactic to alleviate some of those difficulties rather than as long-term relocation. Greater job opportunities in their home countries, along with general social and economic upliftment and better availability of goods and services, would remove much of the motivation for male and female migration, serving to reunite divided households and allow people from Lesotho, Zimbabwe and Mozambique to remain at home where they wish to be.

Logistics of female migration

Not only do men and women display different patterns of migration, but the logistics of male and female migration differ too. Some of the key differences are summarised in Tables 6.8 and 6.9.

For a start, the decision to migrate is much less likely to be taken independently by women. Some 65% of women said that if they were to migrate the decision would be taken for them by someone other than themselves. The equivalent figure for men was only 38%. Perhaps reflecting their relative lack of independence, or alternatively an indication of stronger family commitment, women were slightly more likely than men to say they would migrate with other family members, or send for family members once they got to South Africa.

A higher number of men (78%) than women (63%) were of the opinion that they would be able to go to South Africa if they wanted to, further indication of the greater social constraints on women's mobility. Family members were said to be likely to discourage women from migrating while encouraging men to do so, meaning that even those women with the inclination to go to South Africa face added obstacles relative to their male peers.

A further constraint on women's migration is their relative lack of knowledge and information about South Africa and how to get there. Women were less likely to know how to obtain travel documents, how to get to South Africa safely and cheaply, how to get a job or how to find a place to go on arrival. For the most part, women's information was at best secondhand, gleaned from people who had been to South Africa. Twenty-eight percent of the men surveyed could report personal experience as their main source of information about the country, compared with only 18% of women. Combined with family discouragement, fear of the unknown must serve as a powerful deterrent to female migration.

Even more revealing than answers to the questions about hypothetical migration were the gender differences in reported migration behaviour for the person's most recent cross-border visit (see Table 6.9). Interestingly, and significantly for

TABLE 6.8: DECISION-MAKING AND MIGRATION		
Who would make the final decision if you were to go to SA permanently?	Male (%)	Female (%)
Myself	62	35
Another person	38	65
Would you be able to go to SA if you wanted to?		
No	22	37
Yes	78	63
Would your family encourage or discourage you from going?		
Strongly discourage	19	26
Discourage	19	23
Neither discourage nor encourage	12	10
Encourage	27	24
Strongly encourage	24	18
Sources of information about SA		
I don't know anything about SA	4	7
My own experiences in SA	28	18
Meeting South Africans in [respondent's home country]	2	2
Others who have been to SA	35	39
Others about SA	5	7
Television	3	5
Newspapers	5	2
Magazines	2	1
Radio	15	19

Note: N = 2 300.

TABLE 6.9: LOGISTICS OF MIGRATION		
Ability to obtain passport before departure from home country	Male (%)	Female(%)
Yes	86	95
No	14	5
Mode of transport on most recent visit to SA		
On foot	11	5
Bus	23	19
Plane	2	1
Car	11	4
Train	16	11
Combi or taxi	33	55

Note: N = 2 300.

policy purposes, women appear to have a higher incidence of legal migration than male migrants. Ninety-five percent of women who had been to South Africa, compared with 86% of men, had a valid passport before leaving their home country on their last visit.

Both of these figures are quite high, and certainly challenge the stereotype that most Africans from the region enter South Africa "illegally", but the figures also demonstrate once more the degree to which women's migration in particular contradicts the stereotype. The real incidence of undocumented migration may have been under-reported in the survey due to respondents' concerns with confidentiality, but there is little reason to believe that the relative gender picture would be any different. If anything, the truth might have revealed an even higher incidence of undocumented migration among men.

Also interesting, although without straightforward explanation, are the different modes of transport used by men and women. More than half the women on their most recent trip to South Africa had travelled by minibus taxi, whereas men's mode of transport was more evenly divided between minibus taxi, bus and train. What this difference could indicate is the greater spontaneity and shorter duration of women's visits, with the more formalised, longer-term labour migration of men being more compatible with less flexible modes of transportation. Men were also more likely than women to have travelled by car, by plane or on foot, although in all cases the percentages were relatively small. Again, the perception of migrants fording rivers and sneaking through fences to gain "illegal" access to the country seems to be contradicted by the survey findings.

What this section shows is that women come to South Africa not as undocumented, would-be immigrants but as legal migrants. While this is also true of men, it would appear to be even truer of women, who make short visits to South Africa by legal means and for legitimate purposes. Given that women wishing to migrate face added deterrents and obstacles at home, there would appear to be little justification for any further discrimination against them in South African migration policy.

Economic and social aspects of women's migration

A number of factors have already indicated gender-specific motives for migration, with men migrating for more narrowly economic reasons while women tend to combine economic and social motivations for visiting South Africa. But what do men and women actually do when they get to South Africa? Here the gender differences are striking and unambiguous (see Table 6.10).

Sixty-three percent of men interviewed have worked in South Africa at some point, compared with only 16% of women. The most common reason cited by men for going to South Africa on their most recent visit was to work or look for work (50%), with mining being the most common occupation stated. For women, the order was, firstly, visiting family or friends, secondly, shopping, thirdly, buying and selling goods, fourthly, for medical care and only then to work or look for work (10%). Reasons given for returning home from South

TABLE 6.10: REASONS FOR VISITING SOUTH AFRICA AND RETURNING HOME		
	Male (%)	Female (%)
Have you worked in SA in the past? (Yes)	63	16
Purpose of most recent visit to SA		
Look for work	17	3
Work	33	7
Buy and sell goods	4	10
Shopping	13	23
Business	3	3
Visit family or friends	17	38
Holiday or tourism	3	3
Medical care	2	8
Other	8	5
Reason for returning home		
Returned after holiday or visit ended	21	43
Wanted to come back home	17	20
Family reasons	8	8
Sick/injured	5	1
Contract ended	10	1
Retired from job	3	1
Lost job or retrenched	14	–
Travel documents expired	3	6
Expelled or deported from SA	5	–
Goods sold out	2	3
Other	12	17
Note: N = 971.		

Africa are related to these gendered migration motives. Men were more likely than women to state that they had lost their job, their contract had ended or they had become ill or injured, while women were more likely to say simply that their holiday or visit had ended.

A less clear picture emerged when respondents were asked about hypothetical future migration as opposed to actual recent migration (see Table 6.11). When asked what job they might want to do in South Africa, men's first choice of occupation was mining, followed by industry and trading. This closely matches their actual patterns of employment in existing migration. Women, when asked the same question, mostly expressed a preference for vending and hawking, followed by industry, trading, starting their own business and being a domestic worker.

Although the question was a leading one, women can evidently at least imagine the possibility of working in South Africa, even those who have not done so in the past. This suggests that there may be considerable latent migration potential among women, but in the absence of legislative reform and the expansion of legal employment opportunities in South Africa for female SADC citizens, this latent potential will remain just that. Furthermore, while some of the occupations stated might "take jobs away from South Africans", women's commonly expressed wish to trade or start their own business suggests a strong

TABLE 6.11: JOB PREFERENCES AND REMITTANCES		
Job preferences		
Type of job preferred (first mention)	Male (%)	Female (%)
Vendor/hawker	5	18
Trader	8	10
Miner	23	1
Mechanic	7	1
Industrial worker	9	12
Farm worker	2	3
Start own business	4	6
Teacher	3	4
Doctor	1	1
Nurse	1	3
Domestic worker	–	5
Remittances		
If you were working in SA would you send money home?		
Yes	91	89
No	9	11
To whom would you send money?		
Parents	43	49
Grandparents	2	2
Spouse	36	12
Children	11	27
Sister/brother	4	5
Other – family members	2	2
Other – non-family	2	3
Note: N = 2 300.		

entrepreneurial urge that might well create jobs and generate income for South African citizens (on the employment potential of foreign-owned small enterprises, see Rogerson, 1997).

When asked about remittances, and contrary to what might have been expected, women seem no more or less likely than men to send money back to their home country.[8] Rather tellingly, 90% of respondents stated hypothetically that they would send money home should they migrate to South Africa in future, whereas only a third of respondents who had actually worked in South Africa claim to have remitted any of their earnings.

Some gender distinction is apparent in the different people to whom money would be sent, with men most frequently listing their parents and spouse while women gave parents and children as the likely recipients. Clearly men are expected to be the primary breadwinners, and it would be unusual for a woman to remit money to a male partner. Here again, migration behaviour is shown to be grounded in socially constructed gender roles and relations.

Men's and women's social experiences with regard to migration differ widely, but this was not explored in the survey beyond trying to ascertain people's general impressions of South Africa. Here there was broad consensus between men and women, although women were slightly more likely than men to describe their impressions of South Africa as being unfavourable or very unfavourable. There was closer gender concurrence in the perceptions held by those men and women who had direct personal experience of South Africa, with 79% of men and 80% of women who had visited the country rating their experience as either positive or very positive. Women who had not been to South Africa had more negative impressions, again indicating a fear of the unknown that is surely a deterrent to female migration.

One revealing gender difference was in the reported incidence of friends resident in South Africa, with 59% of all the women surveyed, but only 36% of the men replying that they had no friends living there. Given that the existence of social networks in the destination country lends powerful encouragement to migration, this is an additional deterrent facing potential female migrants. It is also indicative of the longer-established tradition of male migration, with men living more transnational lives.

TABLE 6.12: EXPERIENCES WITH MIGRATION AND IMPRESSIONS OF SOUTH AFRICA		
Rating of personal experience in SA (%)	Male	Female
Very negative	8	6
Negative	10	9
Neither positive or negative	4	5
Positive	47	50
Very positive	32	30
General impressions of SA (%)		
Very unfavourable	4	8
Unfavourable	11	12
Neither favourable nor unfavourable	12	12
Favourable	45	45
Very favourable	29	23
Note: N = 971.		

It is important, in identifying such gender similarities and differences, not to lose sight of the fact that men's and women's migration streams are linked. The men who migrate to work in South Africa are the husbands, brothers, fathers and sons of the women surveyed. Their remitted earnings make an important contribution to household economies in their home countries. Much of the women's cross-border movement is for the purpose of "visiting family and friends", including male partners and other relatives living in South Africa. The information on which women make their migration decisions and choices comes largely from friends and family members who have themselves been to South Africa, most of whom are likely to be men.

Migration should thus be seen in terms of household production and reproduction strategies, as a collective endeavour rather than as a set of isolated individual choices and practices. If men's migration is largely economically based while that of women relates to a wider range of social and economic factors, this is because the societies in the countries surveyed attach particular social and economic roles and responsibilities on the basis of gender. That said, migration could be a means of challenging and undermining social norms; this may be particularly true for women, who can employ migration as a means of social and economic empowerment. Democratic migration policy should therefore be based on relations between men and women, on families, households and communities, and not simply on genderless, atomistic "persons".

The impact of migration

The impact of migration is difficult to assess in any absolute or objective sense, especially by those actually involved. Not only does it touch on virtually every aspect of life, but it represents a combination of costs and benefits that are not easy to disentangle, still less to weigh up. How, for example, does one calculate the benefit of economic gains obtained at the social cost of disrupted family lives? Respondents were asked to try and evaluate the impact of people from their country going to South Africa in four categories – ie impact on the respondent personally, on their family, their community and their country. In each category, respondents were asked to rate the impact on a five-point scale from "very negative" to "very positive".

Given that migration behaviour itself is so strongly gendered, one would expect a difference between men's and women's perceptions of the impact of migration. Yet overall, the ratings of the impact of migration, at every scale from the personal to the national, were strikingly similar across gender – and surprisingly positive (see Table 6.13). More than 50% of both men and women rated the impact of migration as "positive" or "very positive". Women were slightly more likely to rate the impact as negative, and men slightly more likely to rate it as very positive, but the differences were small.

In terms of personal and family impact, some 30% of both genders felt it had "no impact", and fewer than 20% rated it "negative" or "very negative". Going up the geographical scale to community and national levels, negative ratings increased for both men and women, but this was matched by a decrease in the "no impact" rather than the "positive" categories. Indeed it was at the community level that the incidence of "positive" and "very positive" ratings was highest, at just more than 60% of both men and women. The highest incidence of "negative" and "very negative" responses occurred at the national scale, so clearly people are conscious of the effect of countries "losing" labour and skills to South Africa.

Breaking down the answers according to whether respondents had themselves been to South Africa reveals a much more complicated picture. The most highly positive ratings of migration seem to come from men who have been to South Africa and women who have not. This seeming paradox is simply resolved: many

TABLE 6.13: PERCEIVED IMPACT OF MIGRATION		
Impact of migration on you personally	Male (%)	Female (%)
Very negative	2	4
Negative	11	14
No impact	29	28
Positive	41	41
Very positive	16	14
Impact of migration on your family		
Very negative	2	3
Negative	12	16
No impact	30	27
Positive	42	42
Very positive	14	13
Impact of migration on your community		
Very negative	4	4
Negative	16	16
No impact	19	19
Positive	51	50
Very positive	11	11
Impact of migration on your country		
Very negative	6	8
Negative	22	24
No impact	11	10
Positive	48	48
Very positive	14	11
Note: N = 2 300.		

of the women without migration experience are married to men with migration experience, so it is likely that their opinions are coming via their husbands.

The impact of female migration is much more ambiguous, and the personal experience is clearly difficult for many women. At every scale, from the personal to the national, the highest incidence of "negative" and "very negative" responses came from women who had been to South Africa. Yet even for this group of women, there were more positive than negative responses, especially at family and community level. This suggests that overall the impact of migration is still considered to be beneficial, and that women are prepared to endure personal difficulties in order to secure benefits for their families and wider communities.

Certainly people seem to be generally aware of the tensions between the costs and benefits of migration: how costs to individuals can bring benefits to families; and how benefits to families and communities might translate into costs to broader national development. Of course households are unlikely to forfeit personal gain for national development, and this is precisely the "Catch 22" situation that South African migration policy should be trying to address. The objective of policy should be to facilitate migration that can be beneficial to both source ánd recipient countries, harnessing human mobility as an agent for the exchange of goods, services, ideas and skills that drives the development process.

POLICY IMPLICATIONS AND RECOMMENDATIONS

Understanding women's migration experience

The analysis in this chapter suggests a number of ways in which Southern African women's experience of migration differs from that of men. These are summarised here – firstly, by answering the questions set out in the introduction, and secondly, by comparing the survey findings with the international observations made by Chant (1992).
- Migration to South Africa is still heavily male-biased, with a far lower incidence of migration experience among female respondents. Those women who do have migration experience tend to be married, older women rather than younger, single women, whereas male migrants come from a wider range of age groups and marital status categories. Female migrants tend to be better educated than their male counterparts, with lack of education seeming to discourage female mobility while encouraging male mobility.
- Men and women migrate to South Africa for different reasons. Men go primarily in search of employment, whereas women's migration is driven by a wide range of social and reproductive factors in addition to economic incentives. Even the economic motives for migration are gender-specific, with women going to South Africa largely to trade and men to work, most in formal employment. Thus migration is closely tied to socio-economic roles and responsibilities allocated on the basis of gender.
- Related to the differences in the purpose of migration, men and women tend to go to different destinations in South Africa. Male migration is closely tied

to places of employment, notably the mines, whereas female migration is to towns and cities offering opportunities for informal sector trade and the procurement of a range of goods and services.
- The decision process and logistics of female and male migration differ. Women are less likely to migrate independently and are more likely to be subject to the will of a (male) parent or partner in determining whether they migrate. In addition, although women's migration cannot be seen merely as an adjunct to male migration, women's migration is still commonly tied to that of men, with many women travelling to South Africa for the express purpose of visiting male family members. Women from the three countries surveyed visit South Africa for shorter time periods, and are more likely than men from these countries to migrate legally.
- The social and economic behaviour of people migrating to South Africa is gender-specific, reflecting the different motivations and patterns of male and female migration. Men are more likely to have established social networks in South Africa, reflecting their longer periods of stay in single locations and their ties to workplace-based social structures.
- Men participate more formally in the South African economy, while women's migration experience is shaped by the temporary and contingent social and economic interactions that are involved in trading and retail activity.
- Both genders, migrants and non-migrants alike, hold generally favourable impressions of life in South Africa, although they would still generally prefer to remain in their home country.

The impacts of migration, both positive and negative, are well understood by the men and women affected. Rather than the women "left behind", however, it was women with personal migration experience who were more likely to rate the impact of migration as negative. The economic benefits of migration are achieved at considerable social cost, with disruptions to family and community life. Both male and female respondents were also well aware of the national cost of migration through the loss of skills to the local economy, but nevertheless continue to support and participate in migration as a rational household reproduction strategy in a situation of limited alternative options.

The survey findings show that the Southern African experience closely parallels that of other developing countries. As elsewhere, men in Southern Africa are more mobile than women, and it is women who are more often left behind. The women left behind are disadvantaged in various ways by male out-migration, which may bring in earnings but adds to women's productive and reproductive responsibilities at home.

Certainly men's migration in the region is undertaken more independently than women's, although both are better understood as part of a "household strategy" approach.[9] As in the international experience more generally, male migration to South Africa is more closely tied to employment, and women have fewer legal employment opportunities than men in the South African labour market.

Related to these gender-specific motivations for migration, men move further and to a wider range of destinations, with women's migration often being no more than a quick cross-border shopping trip. The different age profiles of male and female migrants are rather difficult to determine from the survey data, although it is certainly clear that men migrate across a wider range of ages than women. Also difficult to determine from this particular survey is whether the Southern African experience conforms with the international norm of women "maintain(ing) more enduring ties between areas of origin and destination" (Chant, 1992: 198). Both genders clearly retain strong ties to home, including ties between husbands and wives separated by the "stretching" of households across international borders. If the legal and social restrictions on women's mobility are relaxed, and women come to engage more directly and fully in cross-border migration, the "feminisation" of migration may well lead to changes in the social linkages between places of origin and destination, although whether this is a weakening or a strengthening remains to be seen.

Two fundamental points emerge clearly from the survey data:
- The migration experience in Southern Africa is deeply and profoundly gendered. To a long-established tradition of male labour migration is being added a growing stream of female migrants, coming to South Africa for a number of different reasons, both social and economic. Gender inequalities and discrimination have until now constrained women's migration, which can be an important mechanism of female empowerment.
- The different motives and patterns of male and female migration arise from structural determinants in the social and economic fabric of source and recipient countries. Any sound migration policy therefore has to go hand-in-hand with regional development initiatives. Just as development can alter migration patterns, so migration can itself be an agent of development. It is in this broader context that democratic, non-sexist migration policy must be formulated.

Policy implications

The policy implications of the survey findings for gender and migration are numerous, and are outlined here only in the most general terms. In this section, a number of broad guidelines for policy on gender and migration are presented. This is followed by a section in which the South African government's Draft Green Paper on International Migration is subjected to a gender-aware, critical reading, with further suggestions being put forward on how the policy proposals in the Green Paper might be made more gender-sensitive.[10]
- The most important lesson is that if there are indeed "good" and "bad" migrants in terms of their impact on South African society and economy, then female migrants from the three important source countries discussed here are generally "good". Those who have previously travelled to South Africa are law-abiding, responsible, entrepreneurial and resourceful women, who employ cross-border movement as a mechanism for their own and their families' betterment.
- Current migration policy, together with a host of entrenched social norms and practices, discriminates against women in all sorts of ways, limiting their

life choices and restricting their physical and socio-economic mobility. Migration policy should instead aim to facilitate female migration, thus aiding women's empowerment and allowing them to become agents of development both in their home countries and in South Africa. This is not to suggest that female migration should be unrestricted, but that controlled female migration, particularly that of a short-term nature, can be harnessed as a powerful force for regional development. It can also be harnessed for the reduction of socio-economic inequalities between the South African core and its neighbouring periphery. Migration policy should aim to increase rather than decrease the range of options available to women in the range of productive and reproductive responsibilities that they bear.

- Policy must be formulated not in terms of atomistic, genderless "persons" or "migrants" but in terms of men and women with specific biological, legal and social relationships. Cross-border migration, even when undertaken by individuals, takes place within a social framework, with implications for families, households and communities. Policy must not merely accommodate but actively encourage the links between migrants and their families and communities "back home" – for example, by making it easy for migrants to make return visits and for family and friends to visit foreign migrants in South Africa. There should certainly be a special class of multiple-entry visa for women (or men) to visit spouses working in South Africa.
- Another category of female migrant that could be actively encouraged is those women who come to South Africa for the purposes of trading and shopping. The latter activity certainly injects cash into the South African economy, and while there are complaints that foreign informal-sector traders undercut their South African counterparts, this competition must surely be seen as part of the movement towards freer trade in the SADC region (Peberdy and Crush, 1998). Although hard evidence is limited, it is likely that women from neighbouring countries who bring goods into South Africa to sell then spend a large proportion of their earnings in the South African retail sector, thus making a positive economic contribution overall.
- Repatriated profits and remittances can make a positive impact on the economies of the women's country of origin, thereby facilitating local development and ultimately reducing the incentives for more permanent out-migration. Again, while the flow of imports into the country cannot be allowed to proceed completely uncontrolled, restrictions on the cross-border movement of people and goods should certainly be eased, particularly for small- and medium-scale traders.
- Rather more vexing is the question of foreign women being allowed to work in South Africa. Survey results show potentially increased flows of women into the South African labour market should restrictions on their employment be lifted, with many female respondents expressing a desire to be employed as domestic workers, for example. With unemployment in South Africa at high levels, especially for black women, to allow more foreign labour into the country could have deleterious social and economic consequences for South African citizens.

- That said, the perpetuation of male foreign migrant labour on mines and farms, to the virtual exclusion of female migrant labour, is clearly discriminatory.[11] Equitable opportunity for legal participation in the South African labour market by citizens of other Southern African countries, while difficult to achieve, should nevertheless be one of the objectives of migration policy, with particular attention to the expansion of opportunities for women in occupations where they could make a positive contribution to the South African economy.
- As part of wider regional development assistance, the South African government could also be fostering the education and training of women in neighbouring countries, from basic literacy to vocational and professional training. Not only would this facilitate local development in those countries, but it would also mean that women are less discriminated against by the strict application of education and skills criteria for entry into South Africa – although, of course, care would have to be taken to avoid exacerbating the regional "brain drain".
- In formulating and drafting policy and legislation, the adoption of gender-neutral language to describe and control what are in reality gender-specific processes and types of behaviour can effectively serve to discriminate against women. Nowhere, for example, should the term "spouse" be used, where "husband" or "wife" (or even "same-sex partner") is intended to be either included or excluded. Further, the drafting of non-sexist migration policy must be carried into the actual day-to-day implementation of that policy by the officials who ultimately decide who is or is not permitted access into the country, for it is at this level that the most insidious forms of gender discrimination often operate.

Each of the above recommendations has specific development implications, both for South Africa and for neighbouring countries. While it is a common view that migration undermines development, with a loss of skills from source countries and an over-supply of labour in the recipient country, the pattern of "to-and-fro" migration practised by Southern African women can serve to facilitate positive socio-economic change, providing an effective mechanism for the exchange of money, goods and ideas across borders. Carefully formulated, gender-sensitive migration policy can thus make a direct contribution not just to women's upliftment, but towards wider regional integration and development.

The Green Paper: Gender-neutral or gender-blind?

The 1997 *Draft Green Paper on International Migration* provides a blueprint for a democratic, non-discriminatory immigration policy for post-apartheid South Africa (RSA, 1997). Yet a gender-aware reading of the Green Paper reveals a number of implicit anti-female biases. The broad philosophy of the proposed migration policy is that economic criteria of labour demand and democratic criteria of human rights should determine who can and cannot enter South

Africa. But as the following discussion will show, neither labour demand nor human rights can be regarded as gender-neutral, particularly in the Southern African context where discrimination against women is deeply culturally ingrained and where women are systematically denied rights and opportunities granted to men.

The Green Paper begins by identifying three streams of cross-border migration: immigrants, migrants and refugees. The very title of the document is significant, deliberately referring to "international migration" rather than immigration *per se* so as to move away from the implication of permanence in the latter phrase. The reasons for this distinction lie partly in the history of male contract labour migration to South Africa, discussed above. It was also designed as a corrective to the pervasive stereotype that every foreign African in South Africa is an immigrant who wishes to stay.

However, aside from an acknowledgment of the persistence of the historical male bias into the present, the Green Paper is curiously gender-blind in its recommendations for the "migrant" category, essentially arguing for the perpetuation of labour migration in a new and more humane guise.[12] While the temporary work schemes proposed could, in theory, be more gender-inclusive than the current system, there is no explicit recognition of this fact.

Furthermore, the Green Paper argues that for both temporary migration and permanent immigration there should be "rules of entry driven by labour-market need", admitting "individuals who have desirable skills, expertise, resources and entrepreneurial will" (RSA, 1997: 19). As Southern African women are routinely denied the opportunity to acquire such skills and resources, they are automatically disadvantaged by the application of such criteria for (im)migration eligibility. Nor is it made clear anywhere whether Southern African labour migrants would be allowed to bring their partners and families with them to South Africa, beyond an endorsement of "border passes to eligible persons to ease the flow of legally-sanctioned temporary visitation of *bona fide* family members across our borders" (RSA, 1997: 26).[13]

The proposed policy of "flexible labour quotas" for the employment of foreign migrants, extending beyond mining and agriculture to include other spheres of economic activity, might in theory open up opportunities for women (RSA, 1997: 23). But such opportunities are likely to be limited in scale and scope. Many women have skills or work in sectors where work is individualised and not amenable to large-scale recruitment. One area in which female migration might be positively favoured is in the recommendation that cross-border trading, including small-scale and informal sector trading, be facilitated by more relaxed SADC trade policies. As the SAMP survey shows, such trading is one of the key motives for visits to South Africa by women from neighbouring countries.

The final category of SADC-origin temporary migrant considered is that of students, where again there is likely to be a heavy bias in favour of males. As in the other categories, immigration eligibility criteria do not have to be explicitly sexist to discriminate against women.

The category of general immigration to South Africa is dealt with in similarly gender-blind terms. Here too there is likely to be discrimination in favour of men in both the specification and the application of the proposed skill- and wealth-based admission criteria. Everywhere in the world, but particularly in Africa, women's access to the resources and opportunities required to achieve their full economic potential is restricted through a variety of mechanisms. On average, relative to men, women own less property, have less access to capital, and are less educated, not through any fault of their own but through socially institutionalised gender discrimination. Immigration criteria based on wealth, property ownership and skills thus automatically have an anti-female bias. The very word "entrepreneur", which recurs throughout the document, to most people still conjures up an image of male prosperity.

This economic discourse is in contrast to the human rights-based language contained in the section on refugees, the "third stream" of international migrants and the only category in which gender is given explicit, if still partial, treatment. In the section summarising the current situation, one reads:

> The majority of people who are asylum-seekers are young men in their 20s who have fled African countries such as Angola, Somalia, Zaire, Liberia, Rwanda and Ethiopia. Significant numbers of asylum-seekers have also arrived in recent months from Pakistan, India and Bangladesh (RSA, 1997: 32).

In many countries, both in Africa and elsewhere, women are a category particularly at risk and especially vulnerable to the effects of the famines, wars and natural disasters that commonly initiate major flows of refugees. Why, then, are most of the refugees who find their way to South Africa male rather than female? Do these men leave behind female partners, parents and children who remain victims of "serious human rights violations" in their country of origin? Of course, there is a danger in emphasising women's vulnerability that they might become "ghettoised" into the "refugee" category, regarded as temporary sojourners in South Africa awaiting ultimate repatriation, while men can more readily be admitted as mainstream immigrants.

If refugee policy is couched in language of risk and vulnerability, with women being identified as a group especially in need of protection, an unintended consequence may be the further marginalisation of women rather than protection of their human rights. The male bias of current refugee flows nevertheless demands that the gender implications of refugee policy be given careful consideration.

These gender-based reservations notwithstanding, the Green Paper represents a considerable advance on the present situation regarding migration policy. Nevertheless, great care will have to be taken in the drafting of legislation and formulation and execution of policy if gender discrimination is to be avoided, not just in language but in practice. In fact, the use of gender-neutral language can serve to conceal or even perpetuate existing discrimination, thus being quite counter-productive if the aim is to achieve gender equity. Gender differences are entrenched in past and present patterns of migration to South Africa, and any policy that is blind to this reality is fundamentally flawed.

CONCLUSION

This chapter has attempted to elucidate the perceptions and experiences of Southern African women with regard to cross-border migration to South Africa. Contrary to the common stereotypes, women coming to South Africa from neighbouring countries do so for the most part legally and for legitimate purposes. They visit their husbands, friends and relations; buy and sell goods; and access services that are either less readily available or of lower standard in their countries of origin. Far from being a threat, many of their activities are of benefit to the South African economy.

Women's migration also provides benefits to their families and communities at home, as well as mitigating the social costs of male labour migration. Present migration policy discriminates against women, and even the Draft Green Paper contains a number of recommendations that implicitly favour men. There can be no justification for further discrimination against women; indeed policy should instead be seeking to facilitate female migration as an agent of positive social and economic change in the region.

Allowing women freer access to South Africa would encourage the exchange of goods, services and ideas, which constitutes the very engine of development, and there is little to suggest that a more open migration policy would result in an unmanageable influx of women, or men, into the country. Properly managed, female migration to South Africa could be a mechanism for reducing both spatial and gender-based inequalities in the region, empowering women to be agents of development both in their home countries and in South Africa itself.

REFERENCES

Bozzoli, B, 1993, *Women of Phokeng: Consciousness, life strategy and migrancy in South Africa, 1900–1983*. Portsmouth: Heinemann.

Campani, G, 1996, "Women migrants: From marginal subjects to social actors", in Cohen, R, (ed), *The Cambridge survey of world migration*, Cambridge: Cambridge University Press.

Chant, S (ed), 1992, *Gender and migration in developing countries*. Chichester: Wiley.

Chant, S and Radcliffe, S, 1992, "Migration and development: the importance of gender", in Chant, S, (ed), *Gender and migration in developing countries*. Chichester: Wiley.

Chant, S, 1998, "Households, gender and rural-urban migration: Reflections on linkages and considerations for policy", *Environment and urbanisation*, 10 (1). London: International Institute for Environment and Development.

Cockerton, C, 1995, "Running away from the land of the desert: Women's migration from colonial Botswana to South Africa, c.1895–1966", PhD thesis. Kingston, Ontario: Queen's University.

Cohen, R, 1997, "International migration: Southern Africa in global perspective", in J. Crush and F, Veriava (eds), *Transforming South African immigration policy*. Cape Town and Kingston: Southern African Migration Project.

Crush, J, Jeeves, A and Yudelman, D, 1992, *South Africa's labour empire: A history of black migrancy to the gold mines*. Cape Town/Boulder: David Philip Publishers/Westview Press.

Crush, J, 1998, "It strikes a good balance", *Crossings*, 2(1). Cape Town: SAMP/Idasa.

De Vletter, F, 1998, "Sons of Mozambique: Mozambican miners and post-apartheid South Africa", *SAMP Migration Policy Series*, No.8. Cape Town and Kingston: Southern African Migration Project.

Hyndman, J, 1996, "Border crossings", in *Antipode*, 29(2). Oxford: Blackwell Publishers.

Jeeves, A and Crush, J (eds), 1997, *White farms, black labor: The state and agrarian change in Southern Africa, 1910–1950*. London, New York and Pietermaritzburg: James Currey, Heinemann and University of Natal Press.

McDonald, D, Gay, J, Zinyama, L, Mattes, R and De Vletter, F, 1998, "Challenging xenophobia: Myths and realities about cross-border migration in Southern Africa", *SAMP Migration Policy Series*, No.7. Cape Town and Kingston: Southern African Migration Project.

Miles, M, 1991, "Missing women: A study of female Swazi migration to the Witwatersrand, 1920-1970", MA thesis. Kingston, Ontario: Queen's University.

Moodie, D, with Ndatshe, V, 1995, "Town women and country wives: Housing preferences at Vaal Reefs Mine", in J, Crush and W, James (eds) *Crossing boundaries: Mine migrancy in a democratic South Africa*. Cape Town/Ottawa: Idasa/International Development Research Centre (IDRC).

Murray, C, 1981, *Families divided: The impact of migrant labour in Lesotho*. New York: Cambridge University Press.

Peberdy, S and Crush, J, 1998, "Trading places: Cross-border traders and the South African informal sector", *SAMP Migration Policy Series*, No.6. Cape Town and Kingston: Southern African Migration Project.

Reitzes, M, 1997, "Undocumented migration to South Africa: Dimensions and dilemmas", in J, Crush and F, Veriava (eds), *Transforming South African immigration policy*. Cape Town and Kingston: Southern African Migration Project.

Rogerson, C, M, 1997, "International migration, immigrant entrepreneurs and South Africa's small enterprise economy, *SAMP Migration Policy Series*, No.3. Cape Town and Kingston: Southern African Migration Project.

RSA (Republic of South Africa), 1997, *Draft Green Paper on International Migration*. Pretoria: Government Printer.

Sechaba Consultants, 1997, "Riding the tiger: Lesotho miners and permanent residence in South Africa", *SAMP Migration Policy Series*, No.2. Cape Town and Kingston: Southern African Migration Project.

ENDNOTES

1 Women's migration *within* countries has been better documented, as has the impact of male labour migration on women left behind.

2 By "immigration shopping" Cohen means the active targeting of potential immigrants with specified skills, as practised by the Australian and Canadian governments.

3 It should also be noted that most SAMP research directly addresses issues of women and migration, and a number of important findings have been highlighted from various case study reports (eg Peberdy and Crush, 1998; Gay, 1998; De Vletter, 1998).

4 Accompanying the formal movement of male contract workers is a growing informal movement of female migrants to the mining areas (see Moodie, 1995: 68–81).

5 For example, certain questions were left unasked, or were asked in ways that obscure or downplay the gender question. Questions were asked about parents, grandparents and "immediate family members" migrating, but not specifically about husbands (or wives).
6 For logistical reasons, in Mozambique only the southern half of the country was surveyed.
7 The Lesotho team made an individual decision to select a sample in which men and women were equally represented. In Zimbabwe and Mozambique, the samples were selected randomly from the entire population. The author's observations about in-built sampling bias therefore apply only to the latter two countries.
8 International experience suggests women are more frequent remitters, although amounts are lower because of lower earning potential.
9 Understanding both men's and women's migration in terms of "household strategies" approach must be the starting point for democratic, non-sexist migration policy (see Chant, 1998).
10 The White Paper on International Immigration, released at the end of March 1999 (after this chapter was written), reflects no effort to acknowledge or address the deeply gendered nature of cross-border migration.
11 For example, the bilateral labour agreements between South Africa and neighbours Mozambique, Lesotho, Swaziland and Botswana represent the main means of legal access to the South African labour market. The primary beneficiary of the bilaterals (and for whom they are designed) is the South African mining industry, which hires only male contract workers. A small number of female agricultural workers (in Lesotho and Zimbabwe) are recruited under the bilaterals. However, the South African government is now privately threatening to terminate such arrangements. No such threats have been made to male mine migrancy.
12 The Green Paper, as did the Labour Market Commission before it, recommends that the bilaterals should be scrapped. The reason given is interesting: that they discriminate against some South African employers (which is true), and not that they discriminate against female migrants (which is equally true).
13 According to one commentator, "temporary residence and work permits issued to SADC citizens should not prevent them from bringing dependents", although this is nowhere explicitly stated as such in the Green Paper, a fact that has produced some confusion (see Crush, 1998: 5).

Chapter Seven

What about the future? Long-term migration potential to South Africa from Lesotho, Mozambique and Zimbabwe

by Donald M. Taylor and Kelly Barlow

Previous chapters have focused on the migration experiences and attitudes of people in Lesotho, Mozambique, Namibia and Zimbabwe, based on their responses to questions at a given point. But what happens if circumstances change? What happens, for example, if a respondent was gainfully employed and living in a safe community on the day the survey was conducted, but in the future loses his or her job, or political instability spreads throughout his/her country, or there is a boom in the South African economy? The military intervention by South African troops in Lesotho and the political crisis in Zimbabwe are good examples of changes that have already occurred in two of the countries surveyed. Any of these circumstances might be sufficient to change the respondent's perspective on migration completely.

In this chapter an attempt is made to use survey results to project into the future, and in so doing hope to provide policy-makers with answers to the question of how changing conditions in the future might impact on migration. Our challenge, therefore, is to translate responses to a survey taken at a given point into information that might offer insights that extend through time.

Because our optic is future-orientated, we approach the survey data from a different perspective. Rather than focusing on those respondents who said they had been to South Africa, we will concentrate instead on those who say they "intend" to go to South Africa in the future. This analysis is not as reliable as discussions in previous chapters, since there is no guarantee that the respondent will act on his or her stated "intention". However, it does help to build a profile of those respondents who are most likely to go to South Africa, and determine what this may mean for immigration policy in future. And because policy-makers are particularly interested in who might be coming to South Africa permanently, we have decided to focus on those respondents who said they intend migrating to South Africa on a long-term basis.

The discussion will focus on survey results in Lesotho, Mozambique and Zimbabwe (the Namibian data was not available at the time of writing).

LONG-TERM MIGRATION

In the questionnaire, respondents were asked whether they "want" to go to South Africa for an extended period and how "likely" it was that they would go. Responses to these questions were placed on a five-point scale, ranging from "no interest" in going (1) to "very high interest" in going to South Africa (5). Using this scale it was possible to divide respondents from each of the three nations into two groups: those who are interested in long-term migration (a rating of 4 or 5) and those who are not (a rating of 1 or 2). Any respondent who was unsure of his or her intention (3) was left out of the analysis.

What emerges clearly for all three countries is that the majority of the respondents have no intention of immigrating to South Africa. Only 31% of respondents from Lesotho, 40% from southern Mozambique, and 23% from Zimbabwe are inclined towards long-term migration. The country that stands out is Mozambique, with the largest percentage of respondents serious about long-term migration. However, this percentage is likely inflated due to sampling in Mozambique being limited to the provinces that are closest to South Africa, while the sampling in the other two countries was nation-wide.

Of those who do intend migrating, it might be expected that the best predictor of future migration potential is whether or not the person has already been to South Africa. However, the results presented in Table 7.1 present a different picture. In all three countries, there are large numbers of respondents who have already been to South Africa and have no intention of returning. There are equally large numbers who have never been to South Africa, but who are seriously contemplating long-term migration.

But since the focus of this chapter is on intentions, and not past behaviour, it is most important to assess the seriousness and consistency with which interviewees responded to questions about future places. Specifically, respondents were asked whether or not they would like to become a permanent resident or citizen of South Africa in future. It would be expected that those who intend migrating for a lengthy period might wish to become permanent residents or citizens as well.

TABLE 7.1: A COMPARISON OF THOSE WHO HAVE BEEN TO SOUTH AFRICA AND THOSE WHO INTEND LONG-TERM MIGRATION TO SOUTH AFRICA						
	Lesotho		Mozambique		Zimbabwe	
	Been to SA	Not been to SA	Been to SA	Not been to SA	Been to SA	Not been to SA
Intend to migrate (%)	25	6	12	28	7	16
Do not intend to migrate (%)	56	13	18	42	17	60
Note: N = 2 300.						

The results of these questions are summarised in Table 7.2 by comparing those who intend migrating with those who do not. Two points will be highlighted here. Firstly, consistently and dramatically, those from any of the three countries who intend long-term migration are far more interested in becoming a permanent resident or citizen of South Africa than those who have no interest in long-term migration.

Secondly, there are important country differences. In Lesotho the results reflect the observations made in Chapter 2 that "much of South Africa is, to the Basotho, simply an extension of their own country of Lesotho" and, indeed, more than 40% of Lesotho's population would seriously endorse joining South Africa (at the time of the interviews). This reality is captured by the results in Table 7.2. Among those Basotho who intend migrating, 78% wish to become permanent residents and 71% desire South African citizenship. For those who do not wish to migrate, interest in permanent residence and citizenship is minimal. For Zimbabwe and Mozambique, on the other hand, interest in permanent residence and citizenship is considerably lower, even among those who intend long-term migration in the future. The lack of interest among Mozambicans in formalising their status in South Africa is particularly noteworthy. Migrants from Mozambique appear to be in search of satisfying well-defined needs such as work, with little focus on social integration in South Africa.

TABLE 7.2: RESPONDENTS WHO WISH TO BECOME PERMANENT RESIDENTS OR CITIZENS OF SOUTH AFRICA						
	Wish to become permanent residents of SA			Wish to become citizens of SA		
	Les.	Moz.	Zim.	Les.	Moz.	Zim.
Intend to migrate (%)	78	22	34	71	13	37
Do not intend to migrate (%)	16	10	5	17	4	8
Notes: N = 2 300. Les. = Lesotho, Moz. = Mozambique, Zim. = Zimbabwe.						

THE DEMOGRAPHIC PROFILE OF A MIGRANT

Common sense, and the experiences of many immigrant-receiving nations, would suggest that there are a number of basic demographic characteristics that define the prototypical long-term immigrant: it is usually a *young, single man* with *above-average education*. This stereotypical profile highlights the reality that the mobility associated with migration requires that a person be unconstrained by such factors as long-term attachments to family, community and meaningful long-term employment. Less agreement surrounds the inclusion of education as part of the prototype. Many immigrant-receiving countries select on the basis of education and training; thus, it is no surprise that the prototypical immigrant has higher than average education. For South Africa, the role of education is less clear, since to date there has not been a formal immigration policy that screens for education.

How does the profile of a young, single man who is educated fit the long-term migration intentions of those from Lesotho, Mozambique, and Zimbabwe? We can examine the impact that each element in the stereotype has on people's intentions in order to validate the stereotype.

Age

In Table 7.3, the average age of those who intend migrating on a long-term basis is contrasted with that of those who do not. Two features of the results are noteworthy. Firstly, for all three nations the stereotype of the prototypical migrant is supported. The tendency is for those who intend migrating to be younger. There are, however, important differences among the countries. The age differential is least pronounced for Lesotho, perhaps suggesting that moving between Lesotho and South Africa is a normal, common experience. In Lesotho, migration may not be limited to those who are younger, but is open to almost everyone. The age factor is most pronounced for Zimbabwe. Since the focus here is on long-term migration, it may be that to uproot oneself from a relatively diverse and regularised economy is reserved for the most mobile. These differences among the three countries notwithstanding, it is clear that long-term migration is preferred by the young.

TABLE 7.3: AVERAGE AGE OF THOSE WHO INTEND MIGRATING ON A LONG-TERM BASIS			
	Lesotho	Mozambique	Zimbabwe
Intend to migrate	33	31	29
Do not intend to migrate	36	35	36
Note: N = 2 300.			

Gender

Table 7.4 presents the proportion of male and female respondents who say they plan to migrate to South Africa on a long-term basis, and it is clear that for all three countries men are more likely than women to claim they intend migrating to South Africa. In this sense the stereotype is reinforced. But there are some important qualifications to the stereotype pattern that need to be underscored. In Lesotho, men only modestly outnumber women in terms of long-term plans for migration. Again this underscores the extent to which mobility across the border between Lesotho and South Africa is normal. For both Mozambique and Zimbabwe it would appear that the percentages for men are relatively high (64%). However, in the case of Mozambique this percentage is almost identical to the proportion of men who claim they have no intention of migrating to South Africa. Only for Zimbabwe do we see a definite bias in favour of men. It is here that we may see the classic pattern of long-term immigration being

TABLE 7.4: MEN AND WOMEN WHO INTEND MIGRATING COMPARED WITH THOSE WHO DO NOT INTEND MIGRATING

	Lesotho		Mozambique		Zimbabwe	
	Male	Female	Male	Female	Male	Female
Intend to migrate (%)	55	45	64	36	64	36
Do not intend to migrate (%)	50	50	62	38	54	46

Note: N = 2 300.

largely the domain of men. This is not to say that women are not migrating to South Africa, but perhaps for shorter periods of time (for a more detailed discussion of these gender dynamics see Chapter 6).

Marital status

Is it mainly those who are single who intend migrating? The answer again is "yes", but only a *very qualified* "yes". The results depicted in Table 7.5 indicate that for all three countries it is single people, rather than those who are married, who tend to migrate. However, for Lesotho and Zimbabwe the percentage of single potential migrants is at or below 50%. Thus, for these countries at least half who wish to migrate are married. For Mozambique, the stereotypical image of the single migrant (77%) is confirmed, but this too is qualified by the fact that many who do not wish to migrate (67%) are also single. In other words, the stereotypical image for Mozambique exists simply because there are so many single people, not because of an overwhelming tendency for only single people to migrate.

TABLE 7.5: SINGLE RESPONDENTS WHO INTEND MIGRATING ON A LONG-TERM BASIS

	Lesotho	Mozambique	Zimbabwe
Single respondents who intend to migrate (%)	45	77	51
Single respondents who do not intend to migrate (%)	33	67	32

Note: N = 2 300.

Education

The final factor associated with our stereotype of the prototypical long-term migrant is that of education. The results, depicted in Table 7.6, are consistent with the experiences of most immigrant-receiving countries, with one major exception: Mozambique. For Lesotho and Zimbabwe, it is the more highly-educated respondents that tend to want to migrate. This profile is consistent with the experiences of other nations, however much it conflicts with the often expressed views held by South Africans – that most immigrants are desperately poor and uneducated. It is interesting to note in Chapter 1 that for Lesotho, it was less educated men who had worked in South Africa in the past. The present analysis indicates that when it comes to future, long-term migration, it is the more educated respondents who are contemplating such a move. It may well be that opportunities for less educated migrants are limited and that only the more educated can hope to be successful in South Africa.

The case of Mozambique is noteworthy in that it represents the only deviation from the pattern. Although the difference is small, it is less educated Mozambicans who indicate a desire to migrate to South Africa on a long-term basis. These results are easily interpretable given the long period of instability in Mozambique and the country's relatively weak economy. Thus, Mozambique shows a deviation from the worldwide pattern, and indeed the pattern for the other two countries that contribute the bulk of the newcomers to South Africa.

TABLE 7.6: EDUCATION AND MIGRATION						
	Average number of years of education			% of respondents who have at least finished high school		
	Les.	Moz.	Zim.	Les.	Moz.	Zim.
Intend to migrate	7	6	10	11	11	23
Do not intend to migrate	7	6	9	9	14	12
Note: N = 2 300.						

THE YOUNG, SINGLE, EDUCATED, MALE MIGRANT: STEREOTYPE OR REALITY?

The results thus far confirm that it is young, single men who intend migrating on a long-term basis from the three countries surveyed. But the stereotype of the potential immigrant cannot be fully appreciated by analysing elements one at a time. Thus, we conclude our analysis by combining all the elements contained in the stereotype, as represented in Figure 7.1.

For each of the countries, three results are presented in the form of bar graphs. Beginning our analysis with Lesotho, the first bar on the graph represents the extent to which the entire sample intends migrating to South Africa permanently. Their intentions are reflected on a scale ranging from 1 to 5, where 1 indicates no intention to migrate, 3 indicates uncertainty, and 5 indicates complete certainty to migrate. The bar for the entire sample indicates that even for Lesotho, where movement across the border into South Africa is highly regular and normal, respondents are not inclined to consider permanent migration to South Africa.

When we examine the intentions of young, single, educated men (bar 2), we notice that the possibility for migration has been raised considerably to a point just above (2.5). This result is higher than the sample as a whole but still below the neutral mark. As a point of contrast we present the profile for older, married, less educated women and find that they are far less disposed to migrate.

It is clear that for Lesotho the stereotype is confirmed; it is young, single, educated men who are prone to consider long-term migration. However, the results also indicate that the stereotypical elements are not sufficient to explain the tendency to migrate. Even when all elements are combined, the tendency to migrate is still below the neutral position on the scale.

The results for Mozambique point to its unique position in terms of migration to South Africa. Firstly, we note from Figure 7.1 that the entire sample is more inclined towards migration than is the case for Lesotho. Clearly, people from the southern provinces of Mozambique are more motivated to migrate to South Africa. Not surprisingly, when we combine the stereotypical elements for respondents from Mozambique which, unlike the other two countries, includes those who are less educated, the intention to migrate rises to a point above neutral on the scale. While these combined stereotypical elements are still not sufficient to produce extremely high ratings, it is clear that among the three countries, it is young, single, less educated men from Mozambique who are most likely to contemplate long-term migration to South Africa.

The results for Zimbabwe stand out in terms of the conservatism with which permanent migration is considered. The entire sample is not particularly predisposed to migrate, and even the stereotypical respondents do not reach the neutral (3) position on the scale. Some of this conservatism no doubt arises because the entire nation of Zimbabwe was covered by the sampling, including the more northern provinces, which are much further from the South African border.

Overall, then, the stereotype of the prototypical immigrant has been confirmed. Despite wide geopolitical differences among the three countries, it is young, single men who are prone to long-term migration. The one clear exception is Mozambique where it is less educated respondents (not more educated) who are prone to migrate, and stereotypical respondents from Mozambique stand out as especially prone to consider migration. Indeed, it is only demographically stereotypical respondents from Mozambique who indicate strong intentions to migrate.

The intention to migrate, however, involves much more than the stereotypical demographic profile. When we examine each of the elements separately, despite the stereotype being largely confirmed, there was always a substantial percentage of respondents who belied the stereotype. That is, there was a significant minority of older people, married people, and women who indicated their intention to migrate to South Africa. Moreover, even when all the demographic elements are combined, and even considering the more motivated respondents from Mozambique, the expressed intention to migrate remains relatively modest. The challenge is to explore factors beyond the stereotyped demographic characteristics that would prompt respondents to migrate with complete certainty.

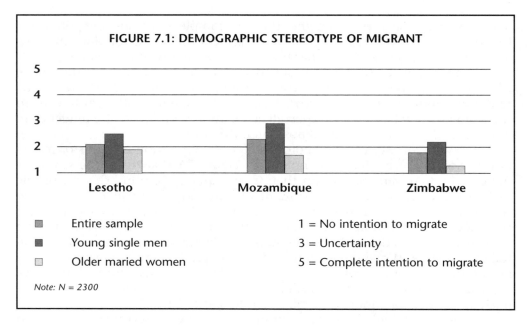

IS IT ALL ABOUT JOBS?

It is obvious that immigrant-receiving countries offer newcomers what they perceive to be a better quality of life, and often it is the opportunity for more and better jobs that instigates the migration process. South Africa is no exception, and it is clear that favourable economic conditions in South Africa are a critical factor.

Beyond economic conditions, social and political conditions in the host country compared to the contributing country may play a pivotal role. But are these the critical conditions that will prompt someone to migrate permanently to South Africa? The question needs to be addressed for two reasons. Firstly, the relative importance of each condition needs to be determined so that policy-makers can anticipate the immigration implications of changing conditions in either country. Secondly, even when comparative conditions are attractive to newcomers, why do so few actually take the step to emigrate? A knowledge of the key decision-making factors would allow policy-makers to predict the flow of migration more accurately. (See Figure 7.2.)

In order to address this issue respondents were asked to compare their own country with South Africa on 20 different dimensions that ranged from the availability of jobs, to the prevalence of HIV/AIDS, from health care and education, to political stability. In order to organise the vast number of comparisons into overriding themes, a factor analysis was performed that yielded six distinct themes. These themes are: *basic necessities* (land, water, food, housing), *social programmes* (education, health care), *economic opportunities* (jobs, trade, employers), *safety* (family, crime), *disease* (diseases, AIDS), and *political stability* (peace, freedom, democracy).

For each of the items that comprise the six themes, respondents were asked about the extent to which conditions were better in their own country, better in South Africa, or approximately the same. Respondents expressed their comparative judgement on a five-point scale and the results are depicted in Figure 7.2. The results confirm that the one set of conditions that all respondents agree is better in South Africa is economic opportunities, including availability of jobs, good wages as well as good treatment by employers. Respondents from Lesotho and Mozambique also believe that social programmes are superior in South Africa, whereas those from Zimbabwe feel their own country has better programmes.

Equally striking is the consensus among respondents that for all other themes, conditions are better in their own country. Although people are drawn to South Africa because of economic opportunity and, to some extent, superior social programmes, on the other four dimensions respondents firmly believe that conditions are better in their own country.

But the fact that most respondents agree that South Africa is a land of economic opportunity does not explain why some choose to seek such opportunities and others do not. We might expect that those who intend migrating see economic conditions in South Africa as particularly favourable compared to their own country, whereas those who do not intend migrating see only modest differences in favour of South Africa. When we make such a comparison surprising results emerge. In Lesotho there is a modest tendency for those who intend migrating to judge conditions in South Africa to be vastly superior to those in their own country. However, this is a modest tendency, and for Mozambique and Zimbabwe there is little or no difference in comparative judgements between those who intend migrating and those who do not.

Clearly, then, the availability of jobs is not the key issue. Everyone appears to recognise that South Africa offers economic opportunity and no doubt such favourable conditions are a necessary condition for attracting newcomers. But those who choose to migrate are not the ones who have an inflated view of conditions in South Africa.

Policy-makers often fear that improving economic conditions in their own country will invite a flood of newcomers. Apparently this is not the case. Of course, newcomers are more likely to gravitate to nations that offer economic opportunity, but as has been underscored in previous chapters, it is only a small minority of people from nations such as Lesotho, Mozambique and Zimbabwe that actually choose to leave their country with the intention of migrating for any length of time. The critical factor for making such a decision does not appear to be any exaggerated view about the favourability of economic conditions in South Africa.

Whether or not respondents intend migrating to South Africa, they are aware that South Africa offers economic opportunity. Can we therefore gain any insights into what type of people choose long-term migration by exploring more concrete questions such as "would they know where they might get a job" and "what type of job would they look for if, and when, they migrated to South Africa"?

The answer to the first question is summarised in Table 7.7 where we contrast those who intend migrating with those who do not, in terms of their knowledge about where to obtain employment. The results are indeed consistent with peoples' intentions, so those who intend migrating feel they know where in South

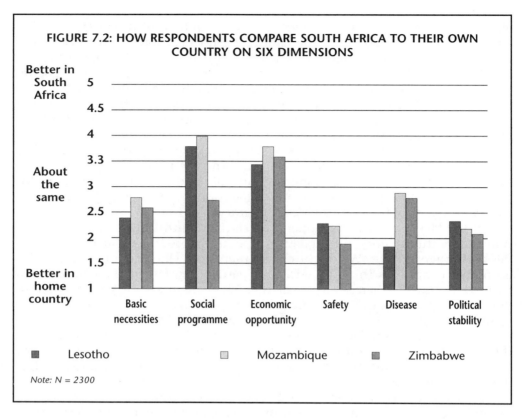

Africa they might gain employment. However, even for those who intend migrating the percentage with such knowledge is not strikingly high. Not surprisingly, the highest percentage is for Lesotho, but even here only 42% of those who intend migrating claim they know where they might get a job. In contrast, for Mozambique those who plan to migrate are not particularly knowledgeable about where to get a job. This finding is important because respondents from Mozambique who are particularly interested in long-term migration tend not to be well educated, and from Table 7.7 we learn that they are not especially knowledgeable about where to obtain employment in South Africa.

The next question is explored in Table 7.8 where the preferred job for those who intend migrating is contrasted with those who do not wish to do so.

One set of notable contrasts arises in all three countries in the informal sector.

TABLE 7.7: RESPONDENTS WHO CLAIM THEY KNOW HOW TO GET A JOB IN SA			
	Lesotho	Mozambique	Zimbabwe
Intend to migrate (%)	42	21	23
Do not intend to migrate (%)	36	20	16
Note: N = 2 300.			

Those who intend migrating, be they from Lesotho, Mozambique or Zimbabwe, stand out as particularly interested in becoming hawkers, vendors or traders. These may be economic opportunities that respondents feel are open to foreigners who come to South Africa. But it may well indicate something of the character of those who choose to risk leaving their home country to seek a better life in another.

Shifting from the entrepreneurial spirit of those in the informal sector, the same characteristic surfaces with the more formal desire of respondents to start their own business. Those who wish to emigrate from Lesotho and Zimbabwe are very interested in starting their own businesses, a wish that requires some education and risk. Conversely, those intending to leave Mozambique are not predisposed to starting their own business, reinforcing the earlier finding that it tends to be less educated people from Mozambique who favour migrating to South Africa. Indeed, a parallel can be found for teachers: those from Lesotho and, to a modest extent, Zimbabwe have intentions to migrate, but not so teachers from Mozambique.

On the surface, then, long-term migration to South Africa is influenced by jobs, and everyone agrees that economic conditions are better in South Africa than in their own country. But even if jobs are a necessary condition for inducing long-term migration, they do not explain why so few plan to capitalise on such favourable economic conditions. For example, it might be expected that those who plan to migrate believe there is an abundance of jobs in South Africa, and they know where good employment can be obtained. The reality, however, is that those who plan to migrate do not have an especially optimistic view of the South African economy, and many do not know specifically where they

TABLE 7.8: JOB PREFERENCES OF POTENTIAL MIGRANTS TO SOUTH AFRICA			
	Lesotho	Mozambique	Zimbabwe
Venda/hawker/trader			
Intend migrating	10	36	24
Do not intend migrating	7	23	21
Miner			
Intend migrating	19	20	7
Do not intend migrating	19	18	5
Start own business			
Intend migrating	9	6	6
Do not intend migrating	4	8	3
Teacher			
Intend migrating	5	2	5
Do not intend migrating	2	3	5
Note: N = 2 300.			

might find a job. This is especially true for respondents from Mozambique, many of whom intend migrating, but who seem to lack specific information.

We gain some additional insights from the type of jobs people intend to seek. For many, it is not regular, industrial work they seek, but rather the opportunity to manage their own business. This they would do either informally through trading and hawking or, more formally, for those who have more resources.

BEYOND STEREOTYPES AND JOBS

Our analyses thus far have indicated that the prototypical migrant tends to be a young, single man, who is educated in the case of Lesotho and Zimbabwe, and less educated in the case of Mozambique. Our analysis of how those who intend migrating perceive conditions in South Africa compared with their own country, especially with respect to economic opportunities, has raised as many questions as it answered. That is, there was no widespread halo effect – ie that those who intend migrating perceive South Africa as the "land of milk and honey". Instead, positive perceptions, while recognising that South Africa offers superior economic prospects, were muted.

If those who intend migrating do not stand out as having an overly rosy perception of South Africa in the job domain, what might the critical factors be, beyond the demographic stereotype, that prompt people to consider long-term migration seriously? It may well be that the deciding factors are not to be found in the demographic mobility of the potential migrant or broadly-based economic, political and social conditions in South Africa compared to their home country. Instead, the deciding factors may well have to do with the immediate social circumstances that have an impact on the potential migrant, such as those associated with family and friends. If such were the case, policy-makers may well feel that these are factors beyond their legislative control. While true, a knowledge of such factors may reassure policy-makers that long-term migration requires a particular configuration of immediate conditions, and thus even in desperate circumstances the majority are not likely to pursue the long-term migration alternative.

In this section, we explore three immediate circumstances that might prompt an individual to contemplate long-term migration seriously. Specifically, we examine the extent to which the respondent would receive encouragement from his or her family to migrate, whether or not they have family and friends already in South Africa and, finally, whether they are actually in a position to make the decision to migrate.

Family encouragement

The role that family encouragement plays in respondents' intention to migrate is summarised in Figure 7.3. It is clear that those who intend migrating feel that they are encouraged to do so by their family. For respondents from Lesotho, family encouragement is especially critical. As we have seen, migration from Lesotho is a normal process, open to all (Chapter 1). It may well be that in the context of such freedom the deciding factor of whether or not to migrate is the extent to which an individual receives encouragement from the family. Respondents from Zimbabwe who intend migrating also judge that they receive encouragement from their family. For Mozambicans, the role of family encouragement is also important, but there is little difference between those who intend migrating and those who do not, suggesting that family encouragement is not a deciding factor either way. Again, Mozambique surfaces as unique in the sense that the usual contributing factors to migration are less influential.

Family and friends in South Africa

Another important factor that may influence the decision to migrate is the potential support of family or friends who are already in South Africa. In Table 7.9, we highlight the percentage of respondents who have family and friends in South Africa and compare this to their stated migration intentions. For respondents from Lesotho and Zimbabwe, those who intend migrating are those with family or friends already in South Africa but no such trend emerges for Mozambique. In fact, Mozambicans who intend migrating are less inclined to have family in South Africa.

Having friends and family in South Africa is supportive in two fundamental ways. Firstly, it offers the migrant immediate support in the form of housing, community, local information and interpersonal and emotional comfort. Secondly, family and friends in South Africa serve as role models providing the person at home with intimate, realistic frames of reference for contemplating the novel and risky decision to migrate. As we have seen, these forms of support do influence respondents from Lesotho and Zimbabwe. Again, for people in Mozambique the decision to migrate is based on more basic needs, and the process will be initiated and completed with or without the support of family and friends.

In order to gain a more comprehensive appreciation of the role that family and friends play in the decision to migrate, we present an analysis that combines the two questions that explore their role (the results are presented in Figure 7.4). The first bar for each country in Figure 7.4 depicts the extent to which the entire sample of respondents from that country intend migrating. As we learned earlier, for all three countries, the majority of respondents are not considering long-term migration, which is reflected in the average ratings for the entire sample being well on the "do not intend migrating" side of the scale. The next bar demonstrates the extent to which having friends in South Africa and family encouragement raise the chances for a respondent to consider long-term migration. In contrast, the third bar describes the intentions of those who do not have friends in South Africa and who do not receive encouragement to migrate from their family.

The effect of having friends in South Africa and family encouragement from family is quite dramatic for respondents from Lesotho. Those with this form of immediate support indicate that they are far more serious about long-term

TABLE 7.9: THE PRESENCE OF FRIENDS AND FAMILY IN SOUTH AFRICA						
	Respondents who have family in SA			Respondents who have friends in SA		
	Les.	Moz.	Zim.	Les.	Moz.	Zim.
Intend to migrate (%)	40	26	68	46	30	62
Do not intend to migrate (%)	37	28	57	38	30	42
Note: N = 2 300.						

migration than those without support. That the role of family and friends would play an especially important role for respondents from Lesotho is understandable. Migration to South Africa from Lesotho is relatively easy, normal, and can be contemplated by respondents who vary widely in terms of their demographic profile. Being older or married, for example, are not serious deterrents to migration for Basotho, with more immediate circumstances related to family and friends taking on greater importance.

The role of family and friends does not impact as strongly on the decision-making process of respondents from Mozambique. For respondents from Zimbabwe, friends in South Africa and family encouragement raises the intention to migrate noticeably, and those who lack support have little intention to migrate.

Who makes the decision to migrate?

Table 7.10 describes the percentage of respondents who claim that they, personally, make the decision whether or not to migrate. The most striking feature of

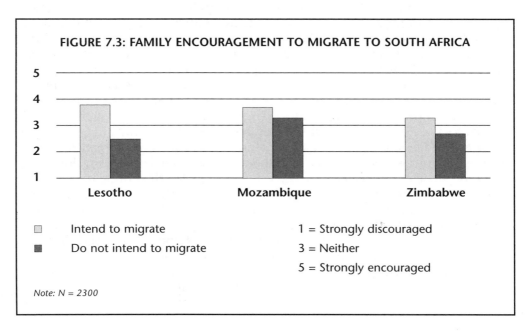

FIGURE 7.3: FAMILY ENCOURAGEMENT TO MIGRATE TO SOUTH AFRICA

Table 7.10 is the extent to which respondents from Mozambique appear to act alone. More than half the respondents from Lesotho and Zimbabwe report that the decision to migrate is not entirely up to them, and must be made in concert with other family members. The families of respondents from Mozambique seem far less involved in the decision-making process.

The ultimate question, also described in Table 7.10, asks if the respondent would actually be able to go to South Africa if she or he chose. The answer is that those who intend migrating, be they from Lesotho, Mozambique or Zimbabwe, feel the freedom to choose to migrate. Even those who do not intend migrating tend to believe they are free to migrate, but to a lesser extent. Once again Mozambique stands out, insofar as even those who choose not to migrate feel overwhelmingly that they are free to do so.

CONCLUSIONS AND POLICY CONSIDERATIONS

The challenge of this chapter has been to use survey results from a given day to make inferences about future behaviour. What needs to be emphasised is that the focus was on migration in future and on the type of migration likely to have the greatest impact on South Africa, ie long-term migration.

Having already been to South Africa and intending to migrate in the future are very different realities. Indeed, most respondents in the survey who had already been to South Africa have no intention of migrating in future, and conversely, some who have never been to South Africa are seriously contemplating long-term migration. Thus, past behaviour and intentions for the future are separate issues. From a policy perspective, then, in terms of our forward-looking question, it is clear that only a small minority of respondents from Lesotho, Mozambique or Zimbabwe have any serious intention of migrating. It would be fair to note, however, that respondents from Mozambique do indicate greater interest in migrating to South Africa than those from the other countries.

Three constellations of factors potentially related to future migration were analysed: the demographic profile of the future migrant; the role of economic opportunities in South Africa; and how support from family and having family and friends in South Africa impacts on the decision to migrate in the future.

In terms of the demographic profile of the stereotypical long-term migrant, it was clear that consistent with the stereotype, it is the young, single man who

TABLE 7.10: MAKING THE DECISION AND THE ABILITY TO MIGRATE TO SA						
	Respondents who can personally make the decision			Respondents who feel able to migrate		
	Les.	Moz.	Zim.	Les.	Moz.	Zim.
Intend migrating (%)	47	65	43	67	81	84
Do not intend migrating (%)	49	60	42	64	77	64
Note: N = 2 300.						

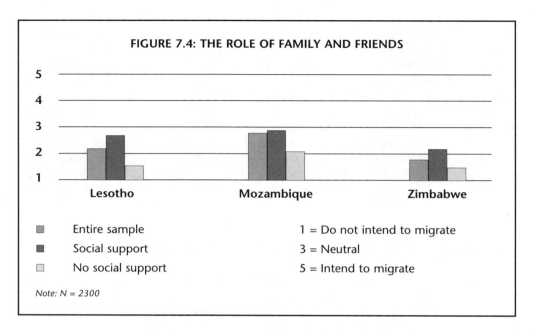

is most likely to migrate. Young, single men are by no means the only potential migrants from the three countries surveyed (there will likely be a wide demographic range of future migrants), yet this group will be most prevalent. Confirming this stereotype was to be expected since people with these characteristics are less constrained by family and community roots and obligations.

Of course, South African policy-makers are aware that the same lack of constraints will affect such migrants in terms of the stability with which they are integrated within their adopted society. Policy that can facilitate the transition for such mobile newcomers would add a constructive dimension to the migration process.

Of special interest was the role that education played in our demographic profile. For Lesotho and Zimbabwe it was the more educated respondent who conformed to the prototype of the future migrant, whereas for Mozambique it tended to be those who are less educated. Clearly, then, future migrants from Mozambique stand out in terms of "likely to be more numerous" and "likely to be less educated".

Our second theme involved respondents making a comparative analysis between conditions in their own country and South Africa. What emerged was a clear consensus that South Africa offers economic opportunity and, to some extent, progressive social programmes. However, on all other dimensions respondents preferred conditions in their own country. While everyone agreed that South Africa has jobs to offer, this was not the determining factor in terms of making the difficult decision to migrate there. Even those who do not intend migrating are aware of the economic opportunities in South Africa. Clearly then, economic opportunity is a necessary but not sufficient condition for the decision to migrate.

Our final theme focused on the immediate social circumstances surrounding the potential migrant. What emerged was that factors such as encouragement to migrate from family as well as having family and friends already in South Africa influence the decision to migrate. However, these more immediate social factors contrasted dramatically with the role of the prototypical demographic factors, and the result is a clearer portrait of the future migrant from each of the three countries. Migration is easy and normal for residents of Lesotho and thus, immediate social support factors are decisive in terms of the decision to embark on long-term migration to South Africa. Residents of Mozambique find themselves in more difficult geopolitical circumstances and thus immediate social support is less decisive in the decision-making process. Instead, the unconstraining demographic factors associated with being young, single and male assume more importance. Finally, for residents of Zimbabwe the decision to migrate involves a mixture of demographic and social support factors.

Future long-term migrants to South Africa from Lesotho and Zimbabwe are likely to engage the migration process in a normal and predictable manner. Policy designed with such prototype migrants in mind will no doubt reflect on migration as a constructive process that is sensitive to human rights. Future migration from Mozambique is likely to be more volatile, but the volatility arises from geopolitical conditions that are comprehensible. Therefore, policy should not be crafted in response to these exceptional circumstances. Rather, exceptional programmes are needed to facilitate the migration process.

Chapter Eight

The lives and times of African migrants and immigrants in post-apartheid South Africa

by David A. McDonald, Lephophotho Mashike and Celia Golden

One of the most contentious issues in the immigration debate in South Africa is the number of foreign nationals living in the country. Official figures on legal border crossings are readily available from Statistics South Africa (SSA) but it is not clear how many people are in the country "illegally". The Human Sciences Research Council (HSRC) claims the latter to be in the range of 2.5–4.1 million people, and some police estimates have gone as high as 12 million (Brunk, 1996). All of these numbers are highly suspect methodologically and probably grossly exaggerated (Crush, 1997). SSA has recently put the number as low as 500 000. Another recent study estimates the number at between 500 000 and 1 million (Crush, 1999). The truth is that there is no reliable methodology available for determining the actual number of non-citizens in South Africa. The dimensions are simply unknown and perhaps unknowable.

This lack of demographic clarity makes research on foreign nationals particularly difficult in South Africa. Without a more reliable estimate of the total number of foreigners, their country of origin, gender and other basic demographic variables, it is virtually impossible to sample reliably and to say anything conclusive about migrants as a whole. Case studies can shed light on certain aspects of migrant life in South Africa, and have indeed proven to be an extremely useful way of understanding the social and economic lives of migrants (see for example Rogerson, 1997; McDonald, 1998; Reitzes and Crawhall, 1998; Peberdy and Crush, 1998). But one cannot assume that these case studies are representative of all migrants in the country. True representivity can only be attained where reliable estimates of the overall sample population exist – both in terms of the total number of people and their demographic profile.

These sampling problems are further complicated by the fact that many non-citizens simply do not want to be interviewed due to their uncertain legal status or a fear of being harassed or deported by the South African police (these fears apply to many who are in the country legally as well). Truly "random" sampling is therefore impossible since most foreign nationals are understandably reluctant to provide detailed information about their lives to a stranger.

Regrettably, these methodological challenges do not prevent journalists, politicians and some academics from making sweeping (and often very negative) generalisations about migrants of African origin. The popular press in South Africa overflows with stereotypes about migrants, based on little more than interviews with a handful of people, second-hand evidence and/or hearsay. Even academic work on the subject tends to draw broad conclusions about migrant impacts on the basis of small and highly selective samples. The fact that a truly representative sample of migrants living in South Africa is presently impossible to achieve seems to be lost on most analysts.

This does not mean that generalisations about migrants in South Africa cannot or should not be made. Indeed, it is very important at this point in the immigration policy-making process in South Africa to have defensible statements about the character of migrants and migration in the country as a whole.[1] What is important is that researchers acknowledge these sampling constraints and develop strategies to deal with them. It may not be possible to have the "complete picture" of migration in South Africa, but it is essential to have more comprehensive, more rigorous and more transparent information that goes beyond the case study approach.

With this policy objective in mind, a research method was developed for this survey that would allow us to interview a large number of migrants (both legal and undocumented) from as many different "migrant communities" in South Africa as possible. We do not claim complete representivity here, and it is important to see this information as part of, and complementary to, the Southern African Migration Project's (SAMP's) much larger research agenda. But the research does provide the most comprehensive set of data on migrants in a post-apartheid South Africa to date and helps to identify key immigration policy issues.

In total, we interviewed 501 migrants from 10 different migrant communities in three provinces. The interviews were restricted to migrants of African origin (due to the fact that Africans make up the bulk of cross-border traffic into South Africa), representing 28 different countries and a broad cross-section of age, education, income, legal status and other basic demographics. The questionnaires were designed to elicit information on people's experiences with, and attitudes towards, cross-border migration.

This chapter provides a summary of the findings of this survey and, where applicable, makes reference to parallel surveys conducted by SAMP with residents of countries bordering South Africa (Lesotho, Mozambique, Namibia and Zimbabwe) as reported in Chapters 1–6 and in McDonald *et al* (1998). The first section of the chapter provides information on the methods used to interview migrants. This is followed by a detailed profile of the sample population (eg legal status, their modes of entry into South Africa, links with their home country). The third section of the chapter provides information on the experiences migrants have had while living in South Africa, their future plans with respect to immigration, and their attitudes towards immigration policy. The final section discusses the implications of the research for immigration policy reform in South Africa.

In general, the research reinforces the conclusions of previous SAMP research, that the majority of migrants who come to South Africa from neighbouring countries come legally, visiting temporarily to work, see friends or family, or to buy and sell goods, and are relatively well-educated, enterprising people (see Chapters 1–6). Most migrants (and potential migrants) prefer their home country to South Africa on a number of key variables and do not desire to settle in South Africa permanently.

This is not to say that there is no clandestine migration or that the South African government should simply open its borders to whoever wants to enter. What the surveys do provide is further evidence of the need to re-evaluate the popular stereotypes of migrants of African origin. Contrary to the stereotypes, migrants of African origin are not a poor and desperate lot who will do whatever it takes to get into South Africa and who can only be stopped by building a bigger fence.

A NOTE ON METHOD

Because truly random sampling of migrants living in South Africa is not possible, a "second-best" strategy of "snowball sampling" within different "communities" of migrants was developed. The selection of these communities was based on four criteria. Firstly, it was important to interview migrants from countries that have historically been a large source of cross-border migration into South Africa (eg Lesotho) since these nationals still appear to make up the bulk of the migrant population. Secondly, it was important to include migrant communities with special political and/or policy significance (eg hawkers and traders, miners, Nigerians). Thirdly, we focused on migrants in major urban areas due to the high concentration of migrants in cities and the prohibitive costs of including less densely populated rural areas in the sample. Most of the interviews were conducted in the Johannesburg area. Samples from Durban and Cape Town were also included to provide greater national representation. Finally, interviews were limited to migrants from other African countries. Africans are by far the most numerous migrants in South Africa and African migrants are the most vilified in the South African press.

Ten communities were selected (Table 8.1): 50 interviews were completed in KwaZulu-Natal (mainly in Durban); 50 in the Western Cape (mainly in Cape Town), 51 at a mine in Carletonville and 350 in Gauteng (Johannesburg and the East Rand). To gain the confidence of individuals within each of these communities, a community member was either trained to do the interviews or to facilitate the interviews for an outside researcher. Several of these community liaison people had previous involvement with SAMP research. This team of field-workers was then brought together for a two-day training workshop in Johannesburg to review the questionnaire, address translation issues and practise interview techniques.[2]

TABLE 8.1: MIGRANT COMMUNITIES SELECTED FOR INTERVIEWS	
Migrant community	Number of interviews
Basotho	50
Mozambicans	50
Zimbabweans	50
Nigerians	50
Malawians	50
Francophone Africans	50
Contract miners	51
Hawkers and traders	50
Migrants in metropolitan Durban	50
Migrants in metropolitan Cape Town	50
Total	501

A snowball sampling procedure was used to select interviewees (ie the person being interviewed was asked to give the name of someone else in that "community" who would be willing to grant an interview). This method allowed for an element of randomness and ensured that the confidence of the interviewee was maintained by the mere fact of being referred by a friend. Researchers were also asked to ensure that as broad a cross-section of people as possible within each community (ie in terms of gender, legal status, etc) was interviewed. The survey itself consisted of approximately 200 questions, the majority of which were closed-option responses due to the large sample size. The data was then entered into an Statistical Package for the Social Sciences (SPSS) database.

In total, 28 African countries were represented in the survey (Table 8.2). One respondent gave Israel as a country of citizenship but came to South Africa from Egypt and speaks Arabic as a home language. Another respondent said he was a "citizen" of South Africa (and therefore should not have been interviewed) but gave Igbo as the language spoken at home and is presumably originally from Nigeria.

A MIGRANT PROFILE

Gender

A significant portion of the sample comprised women (Table 8.3). As Belinda Dodson notes in her analysis of the SAMP surveys in Lesotho, Mozambique and Zimbabwe (see Chapter 5), women migrants are an increasingly important feature of cross-border movement in South Africa. Of the 107 women interviewed (21% of the total), the majority were from SADC countries: 49% of the interviewees from Mozambique, 18% of the interviewees from Lesotho, 25% of the interviewees from Zimbabwe and 18% of the interviewees from Malawi. The Democratic Republic of Congo (DRC) was also heavily represented by women (32%), but women for the most part made up a much lower percentage of the country profile the further one went physically (and historically) from connections with South Africa. Only three of the 21 Ivorians interviewed were women, and of the 18 Senegalese none were women. In the case of Nigerians, only six out of 61 interviewees were women (10%). As the research assistant reported,

TABLE 8.2: COUNTRY OF CITIZENSHIP OF SAMPLE POPULATION		
Country	Number of respondents	% of total
Malawi	56	11
Zambia	4	1
Zimbabwe	77	15
Mozambique	59	12
Botswana	1	–
Lesotho	101	20
DRC (formerly Zaire)	22	4
Nigeria	61	12
Congo Brazzaville	11	2
Kenya	9	2
Senegal	18	4
Ivory Coast	21	4
Rwanda	5	1
Benin	7	1
Gabon	3	1
Mali	6	1
Cameroon	7	1
Ghana	9	2
Burkina Faso	3	1
Uganda	2	–
Swaziland	3	1
Ethiopia	1	–
Burundi	6	1
Angola	1	–
Sierra Leone	1	–
Somalia	2	–
Israel	1	–
Sudan	3	1
South Africa	1	–

Notes: N = 501. Figures may not add to 100% due to rounding. A dash (–) signifies a value of less than 0.5% but greater than zero.

TABLE 8.3: GENDER BREAKDOWN OF SAMPLE		
Gender	Number	Percent
Male	394	79
Female	107	21

most of the respondents told her there were very few female Nigerians in South Africa.

The gender imbalance from West Africa appears to fit the international experience highlighted by Dodson (Chapter 5): that men tend to be more mobile than women and to move further afield and to a wider range of destinations. Dodson notes that as migration routes become more established and entrenched, women do begin to participate in greater numbers, a scenario that appears to fit Lesotho, Mozambique and Zimbabwe (see also Chapter 6 on this point). In future, we might therefore expect to see more women coming to South Africa from East and West Africa.

Age and education

One of the most enduring stereotypes of African migrants in South Africa is that they are young with little, if any, education. Our sample challenges both of these stereotypes. Although half the sample was under 30 years of age, a quarter was over 35 and the average age was 32. More importantly, only 1% of the sample had no formal education. Fully 73% had at least some secondary school education, while 22% had some tertiary education (eg university, technical college) with an average of 11.4 years of formal education among the entire sample.

Employment and income

In terms of employment, 78% of the sample was working part- or full-time in South Africa, with 38% of those employed working in the informal sector and 62% in the formal sector.[3] Of the 22% that were not employed, 8% claimed to be students and were therefore not in the job market. These high levels of employment and productive activity are not surprising given the need to support oneself in a foreign country. They are also a by-product of the varied skills that many migrants bring with them. Some 78% of respondents were employed in their home country before coming to South Africa, which suggests that foreign migrants tend to bring employable skills and/or the ability to be self-employed in both the formal and informal sectors.

Table 8.4 provides a breakdown of the types of occupations the migrants interviewed held while in South Africa. Please note that this table refers to past and present jobs in South Africa, and that only 10% of the sample have never had a job in the country (not including "students").

Although respondents were not asked about job creation, other SAMP studies have found that African migrants are not just competing for jobs with South Africans, but are also creating them, particularly in the informal sector (Rogerson,

TABLE 8.4: OCCUPATIONAL CATEGORIES OF MIGRANTS IN SOUTH AFRICA	
What is your present occupation here in SA? If currently unemployed, what was your last job in SA? [Sorted by category] (%)	
Employer/manager (formal sector)	1
Professional (lawyer, accountant, teacher, etc.)	12
Non-manual office worker	5
Skilled manual labourer	15
Semi-skilled manual labourer	4
Unskilled manual labourer	7
Miner	7
Agricultural worker (on a farm)	–
Trader, hawker, vendor	30
Member of armed forces/security personnel	3
Student	8
Never had a job in South Africa	10
Not applicable	1
Notes: N = 496. Some of the respondents from the sample of miners were classified as skilled or semi-skilled labourers.	

1997; Peberdy and Crush, 1998). With 38% of the respondents in this sample working in the informal sector it is likely that some are creating jobs for South Africans and bringing goods and skills to the country that might not otherwise be available.

Despite the low migrant unemployment rate, most of the sample is poor, with almost half (46%) of the respondents earning less than R1 000 per month, 18% having no income at present, and more than a third not being able to depend on a regular income. But not all African migrants are poor. A significant number of the respondents are earning substantial salaries as professionals and skilled tradespeople, with 13% earning over R3 000 per month and at least 5% earning over R7 000 per month (see Table 8.5).

TABLE 8.5: INCOME PER MONTH (IN RAND)[4] (%)	
No income	18
R1–R99	2
R100–R499	5
R500–R999	21
R1 000–R1 499	21
R1 500–R1 999	14
R2 000–R2 999	9
R3 000–R3 999	5
R4 000–R4 999	2
R6 000–R6 999	1
>R7 000	5
Note: N = 451.	

More research is needed to fully understand the labour-market implications of cross-border migration in South Africa. What is clear is that South Africa's current labour and immigration legislation affecting migrants is extremely *ad hoc* and inconsistent across different sectors of the economy. There is a need to both regularise and recognise the potential contributions that permanent and temporary workers from other African countries can make to a wide range of economic activity in the country (see for example Reitzes, 1998a).

Legal status and modes of entry

Another prevailing stereotype of migrants from other African countries is that most are in the country without proper or any documentation. In this sample, the overwhelming majority (93%) hold official documents allowing them to be in the country.[5] Of the only 7% who are in South Africa without documentation, the highest proportion is from Mozambique (29% of the Mozambique sample). This gives further impetus to the argument that South Africa has a "Mozambique problem", not an "illegal immigration problem" (Covane, Macaringe and Crush, 1998). Only 3% of the 101 Basotho interviewed were in the country without proper documentation while many of the countries represented had no undocumented migrants. The figures for migrants from the West African countries of Nigeria, Senegal and the Ivory Coast – countries that are increasingly perceived to be a source of criminality in South Africa – were clustered around the average at 8%, 5% and 5%, respectively. The breakdown of legal status for the sample as a whole is displayed in Table 8.6.

Consistent with the high level of legal documentation, the majority of respondents also entered South Africa using formal transport on their last trip, with more than a third of the sample arriving by plane. Only 18 respondents (less than 4% of the sample) came to the country "on foot". Some of these migrants presumably took a bus to the border and then walked through customs to catch another bus on the South African side – a common practice.

It has become very difficult for residents of most African countries to get

TABLE 8.6: LEGAL STATUS OF RESPONDENTS

Status	Number of respondents	% of total
Permanent resident of SA	67	13
Refugee permit holder	135	27
Work permit holder	113	23
Other official documentation	151	30
No official documentation	33	7
Citizen of South Africa	1	–

official documentation for South Africa. This makes the highly legalised nature of current border crossings all the more impressive. The visa situation is particularly onerous in Zimbabwe where delays and hassles in obtaining official documentation are reported regularly by residents (McDonald et al, 1998: 15). Some 25% of all respondents said that "getting the necessary documents" was the single biggest problem they had in getting to South Africa (an additional 7% mentioned "security checks/harassment by police"). Forty-three percent of respondents said they experienced "no problems" getting to South Africa, suggesting that the system can and does work for a large proportion of foreign nationals.

Clandestine border crossing clearly does occur. But if this survey (and the corresponding SAMP surveys in the source countries for migrants) is any guide, border traffic into South Africa is a highly regularised and legalised phenomenon. It is important that South Africa fosters and builds on this legality rather than makes it more difficult for people to cross, thereby forcing migrants, who will come anyway, underground.

Finally, it is important to highlight the large number of asylum seekers and refugees in the sample (27%), most of whom are from East and West Africa. South Africa has lacked a consistent and coherent refugee policy since 1994. With the adoption of a new Refugee Act by the South African parliament in November 1998, the country is finally in a position to address refugee issues as distinct from other migration traffic. A massive campaign is clearly necessary to educate the public and officials on the differences between migrants and refugees. The latter have all too often been treated as the former, a point amply demonstrated by the very similar experiences and attitudes to life in South Africa among the different migrant/refugee groups in this survey.

Deportations

Since 1994, South Africa has deported more than 600 000 people. The vast majority of these (99.5% in an average year) are to SADC countries. Only 921 people have been deported to East and West Africa in the last five years. As could be expected, then, virtually none of the non-SADC migrants in the sample have ever been deported. What is surprising, given that 60% of the sample are SADC-country citizens, is that fewer than 5% have been deported in the past (most from Malawi and Mozambique). This suggests either that deported people tend to stay at home or that there is indeed considerable "revolving door" migration involving multiple deportations of particular individuals.

Of the small group of former deportees in the sample, only 25% still did not have proper documentation on their current visit. In other words, most past deportees now have official documentation to be in South Africa. The potential for repeat deportation is therefore less than 2% of the sample (assuming people retain their legal status, have valid documentation and/or are not unjustifiably deported).

Migration histories

Southern Africa has a long history of cross-border migration. Not surprisingly, some 45% of respondents had been to South Africa before their current trip. Thirty percent claim to have at least one parent who has worked in South Africa and an additional 25% claim to have at least one grandparent who has worked in the country. These figures are consistent with the findings in the surveys of source countries (see Chapter 1, Table 1.2).

The cross-generation aspect of migration is an important part of cross-border movement and informs a wide range of economic, social and cultural activities. There are some important regional variations here. As Table 8.7 reveals, a majority of respondents from traditional source countries like Malawi, Lesotho and Mozambique had been to South Africa before their current visit. Similarly, 45% of Mozambicans and 65% of Basotho had parents who worked in South Africa. Some 44% of Mozambicans and 52% of Basotho have grandparents who have worked in South Africa.

In contrast, most migrants from West and East Africa are visiting South Africa for the first time and most are the first members of their family to come. Only a small proportion of Nigerians, Senegalese and Ivorians (the latter two being the major Francophone countries in the sample) had visited South Africa previously. Fewer than 10% of West Africans had parents who had been there before. Not a single non-SADC interviewee had grandparents who had been to South Africa.

Regional differences are also apparent in the length of time that migrants have been coming to South Africa. Mozambicans first came, on average, just more than six years ago, and Basotho almost 10 years ago.

TABLE 8.7: MIGRATION HISTORIES OF RESPONDENTS (IN SELECTED COUNTRIES OF ORIGIN)		
Have you visited SA before this trip? (%)		
Home country	Yes	No
Lesotho	80	20
Malawi	72	28
Mozambique	61	39
Zimbabwe	53	47
Ivory Coast	14	86
Nigeria	12	88
Senegal	6	94
Note: N = 393.		

Nigerians, Senegalese and Ivorians first came, on average, 2.5 years ago. Figure 8.1 displays the average lengths of stay on this current visit for several of the SADC and non-SADC source countries.

Distance and apartheid legislation have no doubt been key factors in these regional differences in migration histories and distance will most likely ensure that the bulk of African migrants continue to come from SADC countries in the foreseeable future. Nevertheless, the creation of less discriminatory immigration legislation in South Africa, the expansion of better and cheaper transportation networks and an increase of personal and familial networks in South Africa will ensure that non-SADC countries will become an increasingly important part of the migration nexus in the twenty-first century.

Migration networks also display marked regional differences (Table 8.8). A strong majority of migrants from traditional source countries had a place to stay, and friends and family in South Africa before arriving. Migrants from newer source countries like Nigeria, Senegal and the Ivory Coast were much less likely to have these networks in place. Interestingly, there were no significant differences in this respect between men and women.

Links with the home country

The majority of migrants have substantial responsibilities in their home countries. Some 90% of those interviewed own a house in their home country, 42% were either the head of the household or spouse of the head of the household, and 49% are married or co-habiting. Of this latter group, the overwhelming majority were married to a national of their home country. Fifty percent of those interviewed travel home at least once a year, but these trips are more frequent for migrants from neighbouring countries than they are for those from further afield. Some 77% of Zimbabweans, 86% of Mozambicans and 89% of Basotho said they travelled home at least once a year, while only 23% of Ivorians, 10% of Nigerians and 6% of Senegalese did the same.

More than half of the sample (55%) also said that they send money home on a regular basis (mainly to a spouse or parents), and this was equally true of migrants from SADC and non-SADC countries. The amount of money sent home was fairly even across the different source countries, with an average for the sample as a whole of R345 per month. However, men were more likely than women to send money home (55% versus 33%), and sent approximately R100 more per month on average than women, no doubt due in large part to the lower earnings of women in the sample.

Overall, then, this survey provides a very different profile of African migrants than the stereotypical image of the impoverished, illiterate and parasitical "alien" of officialdom and the popular press: 93% of the sample population are in the country legally; 49% have partners; more than a third are heads of households; more than 90% own their own home; 78% are working; and 73% have at least some secondary school education.

LIFE IN SOUTH AFRICA

Respondents were asked a series of questions about what it is like to be an African migrant living in South Africa. Given the sample size and length of the questionnaire it was not possible to use open-ended questions. Interviewees were able instead to choose responses from a range of response options and/or provide a ranking of their opinions. This section looks specifically at how migrants feel they are treated by various groups in South Africa, what they think South African attitudes are towards foreigners of African origin, their experiences with crime in the country and how they compare South Africa with their home country.

Treatment by various groups in South Africa

Xenophobic sentiment is argued to be "growing alarmingly" in South Africa (Crush and Mattes, 1998; see also Chapter 8. It is perhaps surprising, therefore, to learn that a majority of those interviewed felt that they are treated well or neutrally by most groups in South Africa. Nevertheless, there are some disturbing responses in reported treatment by black South Africans, the police and government officials.

The best treatment would appear to come from citizens of a migrant's home country who are living in South Africa (Table 8.9). Some 95% of respondents said that they were treated "well" or neutrally by this group. The rankings are somewhat lower, but still very high, when it comes to other Africans from SADC countries, with 85% saying they are treated "well" or neutrally by this group.

The figures start to slide, however, when it comes to treatment by South African nationals. White South Africans rank the best with 82% of respondents saying this group treats them "well" or neutrally, with black South Africans being ranked significantly lower at 65%. Landlords, employers, government officials and police officers fall in between these rankings with 82%, 77%, 69% and 63% of respondents, respectively, saying they are treated "well" or neutrally by these groups.

TABLE 8.8: MIGRANT NETWORKS IN SOUTH AFRICA (IN SELECTED COUNTRIES OF ORIGIN)

Did you have a place to stay in SA before arrival (% who said "yes")	
Zimbabwe	91
Mozambique	73
Lesotho	71
Nigeria	49
Ivory Coast	78
Senegal	52
Did you have at least one member of extended family in SA before arrival (% who said "yes")	
Zimbabwe	35
Mozambique	74
Lesotho	76
Nigeria	15
Ivory Coast	28
Senegal	9
Did you have at least one friend in SA before arrival (% who said "yes")	
Zimbabwe	49
Mozambique	64
Lesotho	79
Nigeria	43
Ivory Coast	61
Senegal	38

Note: N = 337.

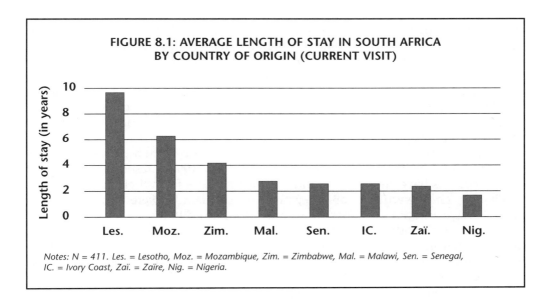

FIGURE 8.1: AVERAGE LENGTH OF STAY IN SOUTH AFRICA BY COUNTRY OF ORIGIN (CURRENT VISIT)

Notes: N = 411. Les. = Lesotho, Moz. = Mozambique, Zim. = Zimbabwe, Mal. = Malawi, Sen. = Senegal, IC. = Ivory Coast, Zaï. = Zaïre, Nig. = Nigeria.

At first glance, these figures may not appear all that alarming, and it is indeed heartening to learn that a large majority of the respondents feel that they are reasonably well treated by South African citizens. As Maxine Reitzes (1998b)

TABLE 8.9: PERCEIVED TREATMENT IN SOUTH AFRICA					
	Very good	Good (%)	Neither good nor bad	Bad (%)	Very bad (%)
Treatment by people from respondent's country of origin	29	51	15	3	2
Treatment by other people from Southern African countries	10	51	27	7	6
Treatment by white South Africans	8	37	36	15	4
Treatment by black South Africans	5	31	29	23	13
Treatment by employers	8	36	33	21	3
Treatment by landowners/landlords	9	48	25	11	7
Treatment by government officials, eg customs and immigration officials	6	29	34	21	10
Treatment by police officers	3	22	38	21	15

Note: N = 501.

points out: "Hostility to foreigners, while clearly a serious problem...may not be as universal or as undifferentiated as media reaction suggests...and this in turn implies that attempts by [South Africa's] decision- and policy-makers to reverse xenophobic attitudes have at least a reasonable prospect of success."

Nevertheless, the flipside is that one in five respondents said they are treated "badly" by South Africans, with one in three saying they are treated "badly" by black South Africans and police officers. Clearly there is a serious problem here that needs to be addressed.

Also of concern is that the majority of respondents feel that South Africans harbour very negative attitudes towards foreigners. Only 19% of respondents feel that South Africans have "positive"attitudes towards people from their home country, while 58% say the attitudes are "negative" (the remainder were either neutral or did not have an opinion). There are some important differences across countries, however, with Lesotho registering the most positive responses (47%) and only 7% of Mozambicans, 7% of Zimbabweans and 8% of Nigerians thinking they were perceived positively in South Africa. Refugees were also much more likely to say that they were perceived negatively in South Africa (see Table 8.10).

The most vulnerable migrants (ie those who have limited experience in the country are unemployed, young, refugees, or are women) have had the most negative experiences in South Africa and are the most pessimistic when it comes to their perceptions of South African attitudes towards them.

A related SAMP survey of South African attitudes to non-citizens, discussed in Chapter 8, shows that the perception of being unwelcome is not imagined. When asked about immigration policy preferences, 25% of South African citizens said they would like to "prohibit people from coming to South Africa" and a further 45% said they would want to "place strict limits on immigration". South Africans also consistently ranked different groups of foreigners in the "dislike" category. Yet it must be kept in mind that 40% of the migrants interviewed in this survey said that South Africans have a positive or neutral view of people (Table 8.11). Almost one-quarter of the sample (23%) have been "assaulted" and close to half (42%) have been robbed. Crime rates are high to begin with in South Africa, but these figures are well above the national average of 23% of people (and 21% of African South Africans) who say they have been a "victim of crime" (South African Institute for Race Relations, 1998).

Refugees were most likely to have been victims of crime (60% said they had been robbed at least once), as were respondents from West Africa (eg 67% of Senegalese said they had been robbed versus only 22% of Zimbabweans). On the gender front, men were twice as likely as women to have been assaulted and 30% more likely to have been robbed. Far from being the perpetrators of crime, therefore, migrants are disproportionately the victims of crime, made worse by inadequate redress in law and lack of protection by the police.

Our survey also found that 29% of female respondents have been "harassed" in South Africa (compared to 34% for the sample as a whole). Much of this harassment would presumably refer to over-zealous police and immigration officials looking for a bribe or simply making life difficult for migrants, but some of it may have a sexual connotation as well. In terms of sexual abuse, rape did not figure prominent-

TABLE 8.10: PERCEPTIONS OF SOUTH AFRICANS' ATTITUDES TOWARDS FOREIGNERS

South African views of people from your home country	Positive (%)	Negative (%)	Neither/ don't know (%)
Overall responses	19	58	22
By legal status			
Permanent resident	20	67	14
Refugee	12	78	10
Work permit holder	36	37	28
Other official documentation	18	54	28
No documentation	6	55	39
By country of origin (selected countries only)			
Malawi	23	68	9
Zimbabwe	7	48	46
Mozambique	7	79	14
Lesotho	47	25	28
Nigeria	8	82	10
Ivory Coast	10	76	15

Notes: N = 501, N = 375.

ly, with three of 107 of the women interviewed saying they had been raped while in the country (all from Mozambique). Women were possibly reluctant to talk about this very personal, sensitive subject with an interviewer, and the real situation may be much worse. A recent article in the Zimbabwean press (Inter Press Service, 1998) suggests that women from outside South Africa are particularly vulnerable when it comes to sexual abuse in that country, either because of their tenuous legal status or their reluctance to face the economic and social costs of legal redress:

TABLE 8.11: MIGRANTS AS VICTIMS OF CRIME

Have you been assaulted or robbed in SA? (%)	Yes	No
Assaulted	23	77
Robbed	42	68

Note: N = 501.

> A rape victim [from Zimbabwe] said many women who are raped by their employers are afraid to go to the police as they might be harassed or even killed by their employers and could be deported. 'Employers in South Africa take advantage of our desperation and abuse us. The employers become angry and violent if you try to resist. We have lost our beloved ones and every day a woman is either raped or killed,' said [the victim]. [Another victim] told of how she was raped by a police constable after she had gone to the police station to lodge an assault charge against her employer. 'The police officer raped me in broad daylight and he threatened to

kill me if I intended to report the matter. In South Africa Zimbabwean w'men are greatly at risk of being raped and there is nowhere one can report a case."

Levels of satisfaction in South Africa

Despite all the crime and the negative attitudes of South Africans, 75% of respondents said that "overall conditions" in South Africa were better than their home country, and just more than half (55%) said they were "satisfied" with their life in the country. Similarly, a slight majority (51%) said that conditions in South Africa were "better" than they expected before they arrived while only 26% said conditions were "worse" (Table 8.12). Nevertheless, these responses are hardly a ringing endorsement of life in South Africa with 45% of respondents "unsatisfied" or neutral about the quality of life in South Africa.

This ambivalence about the quality of life in South Africa is even more apparent in a series of questions that asked respondents to compare their home country to South Africa on a variety of social, economic and political issues. An analysis of these responses makes it clear that migrants have fairly strong and pervasive opinions on what they like about South Africa and what they do not like. Table 8.13 provides a summary of these findings, placed in descending order (ie topics that are the bases on which a majority of respondents prefer South Africa are placed towards the top of the table and those on which respondents prefer their home country are placed towards the bottom).

Basic services like education, water and health care, and economic opportunities, are clearly deemed to be better in South Africa than the home country. Preference for South Africa drops below the 50% mark when it comes to less tangible, but extremely important, issues like freedom, peace and a place to raise a family. Importantly, access to land is deemed to be much better in the home country. South Africa scores worst in the categories of crime and personal safety. An overwhelming 86% found the crime situation better in their own country and 73% personally felt safer there.

When asked to name the best and the worst part about being in South Africa,

TABLE 8.12: LEVELS OF SATISFACTION IN SOUTH AFRICA (%)			
	Better in SA	About the same	Better in home country
Overall conditions in SA versus home country	75	13	12
	Better	About the same	Worse
Overall conditions in SA better or worse than expected	51	24	26
	Satisfied	Neither satisfied nor unsatisfied	Unsatisfied
Level of satisfaction with SA	55	21	24
Note: N = 501.			

TABLE 8.13: COMPARISONS OF SOUTH AFRICA AND THE HOME COUNTRY			
	Better in SA (%)	Better in home country (%)	About the same (%)
Availability of decent health care	89	5	6
Availability of decent shopping	89	5	6
Availability of decent jobs	69	14	17
Opportunities for trading, buying and selling of goods	68	22	10
Availability of decent schools	68	18	14
High levels of democracy	67	25	8
Availability of clean water	61	9	30
Availability of decent houses	59	23	18
Availability of decent food	56	18	26
High levels of disease	50	19	31
High levels of freedom	47	41	12
Cost of living	27	63	10
A decent place to raise your family	23	65	12
High levels of peace	15	64	21
Safety of myself and family	13	73	14
Availability of land	11	81	8
Levels of crime	4	86	10

Note: N = 501.

a similar trend appears. "Overall living conditions" and jobs are deemed to be the best thing about living in the country (29% and 21% of respondents, respectively), while "crime" and "xenophobia" are considered to be the worst part about living in the country (55% and 8% of respondents, respectively, citing these factors as the single biggest problem). Clearly, the potential benefits of jobs and other material services are countered by very deep-seated concerns about safety and a broader quality of life.

Reasons for coming to South Africa

Why are Africans from other countries in South Africa? This particular sample covers a group that has been in South Africa for an average of four years, and 88% of the people in it plan to stay for a minimum of six months. Owing to the nature of snowball sampling methods we were more likely to get migrants who were fairly well established in the country. In other words, this sample does not include tourists and other short-term visitors who, based on evidence from other SAMP surveys, would appear to make up a sizeable portion of the cross-border traffic in the region.[6]

Despite this sampling bias, only 48% of respondents gave income-related reasons for why they came to South Africa. The majority of the respondents (52%) came to the country for non-economic reasons (Table 8.14). This challenges the stereotype that citizens of other African countries only come to South Africa for jobs.

ATTITUDES TO MIGRATION AND IMMIGRATION POLICY

Perceived impacts of migration

The bulk of previous scholarly work on cross-border migration in the region points to the negative consequences of migratory labour and apartheid-era immigration laws. From exploitative labour practices and deferred pay systems to the transmission of AIDS and the "stretching" of families, there is ample evidence to suggest that cross-border migration has served to undermine the social, cultural and economic integrity of SADC states (See for example Bundy, 1979; Lacey, 1981; Murray, 1981; First, 1983; Packard, 1989; Crush, Jeeves and Yudelman, 1992). One of the more unexpected findings from the SAMP surveys in source countries, therefore, was that the majority of respondents felt that cross-border migration had neutral or positive impacts on their families, their communities and their countries as a whole (McDonald et al, 1998: 21–24).

The findings are confirmed here with an overwhelming majority of respondents saying that migration has had a neutral or positive impact on their family, their community and their home country (Table 8.15). There are, however, important differences in the way migration is perceived by migrants from different parts of Africa. In general, respondents from traditional source countries were much more positive about the impacts of migration than those from non-traditional source countries. Only 3% of respondents from Lesotho, for example, said that migration to South Africa has a negative impact on their country, while 57% of Ivorians and 37% of respondents from DRC gave negative responses to the same question.

These differences can probably be explained in part by the fact that respondents (and their families) from countries like Lesotho and Zimbabwe have a much longer, intergenerational history of migration to South Africa and have been able

TABLE 8.14: THE PRIMARY REASON CITED FOR COMING TO SOUTH AFRICA ON CURRENT VISIT

Reason	%
Look for work	21
School/study	15
Work	14
Safety for respondent and his/her family	9
Opportunities for trade/buying and selling	8
Overall living conditions	7
Availability of decent jobs	6
Join family/friends	4
Seek political asylum	3
Visit family/friends	2
Availability of decent shopping	1
More democracy	1
Availability of decent schools	1
More peace	1
Other	7

Note: N = 501.

TABLE 8.15: PERCEIVED IMPACTS OF MIGRATION TO SOUTH AFRICA ON FAMILY, COMMUNITY, COUNTRY (%)

	Very negative	Negative	No impact	Positive	Very positive	Don't know
Your family	2	14	23	38	13	10
Your community	1	16	29	30	5	19
Your country	5	24	22	19	4	25

Note: N = 501.

to develop coping strategies. Indeed it would appear that citizens of traditional source countries have been able to make the most of an otherwise exploitative and discriminatory system of migratory labour and it is important not to represent individuals as mere "victims" of a migratory system (McDonald et al, 1998: 24).

Another similarity with previous SAMP surveys is that women were equally likely to be as positive or neutral about the effects of migration as men, despite the enormously negative effects that migration has had on family life and the disproportionate share of family work that falls on most African women as a result.

The questionnaire did not ask interviewees why they felt migration was positive or negative, but there are at least two possible explanations for why women might respond the way they did. Firstly, for women who have been restricted to a limited geographical area for most of their lives for social and/or economic reasons, the opportunity to travel out of the country, even under duress or with very few resources, may be an extremely empowering experience. And as a range of economic opportunities that were once only the domain of male migrants in South Africa begin to open up for women, migration may have an even greater appeal. Secondly, as difficult as migration into countries like South Africa may be at the personal level, many women may be "prepared to endure personal difficulties in order to secure benefits for their families and wider communities" (see Chapter 5).

One final point concerns the high proportion of respondents who did not give any response (the "don't know" column in Table 8.15). Non-answers were much lower for the effects of migration on the family (10%) than the country (25%). This is presumably because respondents did not feel that they had enough information to comment on the latter. But given the long history of migration in the region and the integral part it has played in the national psyche of most SADC states, it is surprising that 32% of Malawians, 43% of Zimbabweans and 33% of Basotho do not have an opinion on the matter.

Rights of non-citizens

The "rights" of non-citizens is a hotly contested issue in virtually every (im)migrant-receiving country, with very concrete political and economic implications. Should (im)migrants have access to state-funded education, health care and other basic services? Do (im)migrants have the same basic human rights as citizens and do these rights apply equally to legal and undocumented migrants? Who should have the right to obtain a job and who should have the right to citizenship?

In the context of South Africa, with extreme poverty, inequality and a shrinking fiscus, these questions raise some very difficult moral and economic dilemmas. Does one offer health care and education to non-citizens (even if they are prepared to pay) when there are millions of South Africans without these services? At the same time, can one deny migrants access to these resources when South African exiles were granted asylum and support in other cash-strapped African countries during the anti-apartheid struggle?

A full discussion of these questions is beyond the scope of this report but it is important to note that there is a widespread and extremely negative rhetoric in South Africa about the need to curtail the rights of non-citizens.[7] The popular press is full of stories about the "hefty burden" that "illegal aliens" place on South Africa's economy, with one study by the South African Police Services (SAPS) claiming (without any supporting evidence) that "illegal immigrants are costing the country more than R2 billion a year in housing, health, education and policing" and that an "increase in numbers could have a crippling affect on the economy" (*Saturday Argus*, 17 August 1998).

The Minister of Home Affairs, Mangosuthu Buthelezi, has recently become more cautious in this regard, arguing that "many [non-citizens] are investing and providing necessary and welcome skills" in the country, but he has also been quoted as saying it is imperative that "illegal immigrants did not have access to services paid for by the South African taxpayer" (*Sowetan*, 30 April–7 May 1997). Equally important, in the national survey of South Africans' attitudes towards immigrants (discussed in Chapter 8), a large majority of South African citizens felt that social services should be reserved for South Africans only.

It is certainly understandable that South African politicians and citizens would be concerned about the impact that increased migration might have on limited post-apartheid resources. However, the information is simply not available at this point for the kinds of statements outlined above to be made. Indeed, the research that is available suggests that non-citizens actually contribute to the South African economy and fiscus through the purchase of goods and services, the importing of skills and creation of jobs in the small, medium- and micro-enterprise sectors in particular (Rogerson, 1997; Peberdy and Crush, 1998).

More importantly, non-citizens do not necessarily expect to be granted subsidies for housing and other basic services and many say that they are willing to pay for the services they receive (McDonald, 1998). The profile of migrants that has been described in this chapter and in Chapters 1–6 would suggest that most migrants are extremely law-abiding and entrepreneurial people who make a net financial contribution to South Africa, not to mention cultural and other non-material contributions.

Nevertheless, the results of this survey do make it clear that non-citizens are very keen to use state resources and want access to employment in South Africa. Fully 96% of respondents feel that non-citizens should have the same access to health care as South Africans, while 93%, 79% and 79% feel non-citizens should have equal access to education, housing and jobs respectively (Table 8.16). One third of respondents (or a member of their family) claim to have used a school while they have been in South Africa, and 56% claim to have used a hospital or clinic. Clearly there are very real resource implications here and it is critical that new immigration legislation deal with these questions in an informed and humane manner.[8]

It also important to note the difference between political and economic rights. While a large majority of respondents expect equal economic rights like access to a job, only a small minority expects to be able to vote in a South African election. Most expect the right to be able to apply for permanent residence and citizenship and therefore to have the right to vote if they attain this status, but this right is clearly deemed to be something that should be restricted to legalised citizens. In other words, the non-citizens interviewed for this research expect to be able to participate in the social and economic affairs of the country, but do not expect the South African government "willy-nilly" to make political rights available to anyone who is in the country.

This last point is reinforced by responses to the question about amnesty in Table 8.16. When asked whether the South African government "should offer amnesty to all foreigners now living illegally inside the country", there was a

TABLE 8.16: ATTITUDES OF MIGRANTS TOWARDS THE RIGHTS OF NON-CITIZENS IN SOUTH AFRICA						
The South African government should offer people from other African countries who are in SA:						
	Strongly agree	Agree	Neither agree nor disagree	Disagree	Strongly disagree	Haven't heard enough about it/Don't know
The same chance at a job as South Africans	52	26	5	13	2	B
The same access to medical service as South Africans	61	35	1	3	B	B
The same access to a house as South Africans	49	30	8	11	1	1
The same access to education as South Africans	55	38	2	3	1	1
The right to vote in South African elections	12	12	13	31	25	7
The right to become a permanent resident of South Africa	44	38	7	5	2	5
The right to become a citizen of South Africa	33	30	13	14	6	4
Amnesty to all foreigners now living illegally inside the country	33	23	15	16	7	6
Note: N = 501.						

polarisation of attitudes with 53% of respondents agreeing that amnesty should be offered and the remainder uncertain or disagreeing. The politico-legal right to amnesty is obviously put in a different class than the more material rights of access to jobs, education and health care.

Immigration policies

Further evidence of a nuanced set of opinions on the rights of migrants came with questions directly related to immigration policy. When asked about who should be allowed into the country, 27% of respondents felt that the government should "place strict limits on the number of foreigners who can enter [the country]", with an additional 42% saying that the government should only "let people in as long as there are jobs available". Only 25% of respondents supported an "open-door" policy.

Responses to this question were virtually the same across age and gender. There were, however, important country-of-origin differences, with the highest proportion of "open-door" responses coming from Basotho (43%), a finding that fits with the research discussed in Chapter 1, which found Basotho much more willing than other neighbouring countries to want completely free movement of people across borders. Less than 20% of Nigerians, Zimbabweans and Mozambicans, on the other hand, opted for the "open-door" option.

Migrants also feel that the South African government has the right to deport people from South Africa. A majority (53%) felt that migrants who have committed crimes should be deported, with an additional 15% and 19% respectively saying that migrants not contributing to the economy and migrants who are in the country without proper documentation should be deported. Only 10% said that "no one" should be deported (Table 8.1). But once again Basotho demonstrated their relative preference for a freer movement of peoples, with 29% saying that "no one" should be deported.

Finally, it is important to note that a majority of respondents take borders seriously (see the third question in Table 8.17). Opinions are certainly polarised on the issue, with 45% of respondents saying that borders are not that important to them, but given the artificiality of borders in most of Africa it is perhaps not surprising that so many respondents would feel this way. The more important message is that 54% of respondents do think borders are important, and that notions of territoriality and sovereignty are not simply dismissed by migrants.

In sum, the migrants interviewed for this research take immigration policy seriously. As long as these policies are applied fairly and humanely, a majority of migrants and potential migrants from the continent would likely be willing to accept rules and regulations that manage the migration process.

FUTURE PLANS

How long are migrants planning to stay in the country? Popular perception in

TABLE 8.17: ATTITUDES TOWARDS IMMIGRATION POLICY	
The South African government should:	**(%)**
Let anyone in who wants to enter	25
Let people in as long as there are jobs available	42
Place strict limits on the number of foreigners who can enter South Africa	28
Prohibit people from entering from other countries	1
Don't know	5
The South Africa government should send back to their own countries:	**(%)**
Everyone	2
Only the ones that are not contributing to the economy	15
Only the ones who are here without the permission of the South African government	19
The government should not send back anyone to their own countries	10
Only those who have committed crimes	53
Don't know	2
Importance of borders between countries in Southern Africa:	**(%)**
Very important	21
Important	33
Not very important	17
Not important at all	28
Don't know	1

Note: N = 501.

South Africa would have it that once migrants get into the country they will never want to leave. The reality, however, would appear to be very different. Nine percent of the migrants interviewed said they wanted to leave as soon as possible. Another 17% say they will only stay between a "few days" and a year (Table 8.18). The most common response (37% of the total) was "a few years". Only 6% of respondents said they plan to stay "permanently" and most of those already have permanent residence.

But even the notion of "permanence" needs to be questioned. As outlined in Table 8.18, the desire to stay in South Africa decreases dramatically as the *degree of permanence* increases. Hence, while 53% of respondents would like to become "permanent residents" of South Africa, only 24% want to become "citizens", 18% would like to retire in the country and only 9% would want to be buried in South Africa. Similarly, only 17% of respondents said they "would want [their] children to think of themselves as South African", suggesting that migration is a temporary (albeit extended for some) sojourn into South Africa for well-defined social and/or economic purposes.

The overwhelming majority of the migrants interviewed for this research do not intend to stay in South Africa forever. They have mixed opinions about the

TABLE 8.18: FUTURE PLANS OF MIGRANTS			
Intended length of stay in South Africa			%
Leave as soon as possible			9
A few days/weeks			2
Up to six months			10
Six months to a year			5
A few years			37
Indefinitely			15
Permanently			6
Don't know			16
Do you want to:	Yes (%)	No (%)	Unsure (%)
Become a permanent resident of SA?	53	38	9
Become a citizen of SA?	24	66	9
Live in SA when you retire?	18	68	14
Be buried in SA?	9	80	11
Note: N = 501.			

overall quality of life in South Africa, and are obviously keen to maintain links with their home country and return there at some point in the not-too-distant future. Their responses are, of course, only stated intentions, and it is conceivable that economic, political and social conditions at "home" may continue to make South Africa an attractive and increasingly "permanent" destination point. But it is equally conceivable that a well-managed immigration system in South Africa could better facilitate short-term, circular migration and thereby alleviate the pressures that some migrants feel to stay in the country longer than they would like.

POLICY IMPLICATIONS AND CONCLUSIONS

The policy implications of this research support and confirm those based on SAMP migration surveys in Lesotho, Mozambique, Zimbabwe and Namibia. These similarities are important because they demonstrate the potential for more regularised and humane immigration legislation in South Africa, while still managing the migration process. These general policy recommendations were (and are) as follows (McDonald *et al*, 1998: 32–35; Frayne and Pendleton, 1998: 34–35):
- Migration into and out of South Africa is an eminently manageable phenomenon. The overwhelming majority of those interviewed for this research are in the country legally and take notions of sovereignty and territoriality seriously. Moreover, the demographic profile of these respondents shows relatively

high levels of education and important family and economic responsibilities at home. In short, migration would appear to be a highly regularised and legal process conducted by responsible people, and it is important that South Africa build on this process rather than forcing migrants and migration into more clandestine modes of operation.

- The *de facto* and *de jure* criminalisation of migrants as a result of media stereotyping and difficulties in obtaining official documentation have led to serious human rights abuses of foreigners by South African police, immigration authorities and the general public, tragically illustrated by the murder of three African foreigners by an angry mob at a train station in Johannesburg in September 1998. As the interviews for this research indicate, far from being the perpetrators of crime, migrants are disproportionately the victims of crime, made worse by inadequate redress in the law or lack of protection by the police. New immigration legislation should address these human rights issues and make immigration policy more consistent with the Bill of Rights in the new South African Constitution. Immigration and security authorities should also address these human rights abuses at a more practical level with their staff in terms of education and discipline.
- With jobs and other income-generating opportunities being one of the key motivating factors for migration among respondents, it is evident that regional integration and economic parity are critical aspects of any South(ern) African immigration policy regime. Integration and parity are long-term goals, of course, but it is essential that policy-makers and practitioners recognise both the immediate importance of cross-border movement for socio-economic stability in the region (and beyond) *and* the need to address the more micro-economic impacts that immigration policy can have on household opportunities and welfare outside the country.
- The bulk of the cross-border traffic in South Africa would appear to be short-term. The Draft Green Paper on Immigration Policy in South Africa makes a point of differentiating between long-term or permanent immigration and short-term migration, and, for all intents and purposes, it discusses the implications of these two different forms of cross-border movement for immigration policy and management at some length. What should be stressed, however, is that the empirical evidence from our research once again supports the need for this distinction and lends credence to the argument that managing short-term migratory flows is not only feasible but also essential.
- Once again, Basotho stand out as distinct from other African nationals in terms of their experiences with and attitudes towards migration to South Africa. Significantly more Basotho than any other nationality in this sample want to stay in South Africa permanently, have strong migrant networks in the country, expect full economic and political rights while in South Africa and would like to see a much freer movement of peoples across the border. Follow-up workshops with the research assistants confirmed these findings, with many unprompted comments from Basotho interviewees that they felt more settled in South Africa than any other group due to cultural and linguistic ties, and the fact that most have family in the country. These results bring into further focus

the need to explore the possibility of some kind of special immigration compact between South Africa and Lesotho (see Chapter 1).

There are some additional policy-relevant findings that emerge from this research:
- Migration into South Africa is now a truly pan-African phenomenon and will become increasingly so. Any casual observer would notice the enormous variety of African dress and language on the streets of Johannesburg. This observation is nothing new, but we now have data from several West African countries that allows us to compare the migration experiences and attitudes of non-SADC nationals with those from the more traditional migrant source countries. It is important that policy-makers are sensitive to these regional differences, and that they acknowledge the new role that South Africa has begun to play with respect to the movement of peoples on the continent as a whole.
- Women are an increasingly important part of the migration nexus, and their experiences and aspirations with cross-border migration are different in many respects from men. Policy-makers must pay attention to these gender dynamics when it comes to legislating and managing immigration policy in South Africa (see Chapter 5).
- Although the majority of migrants interviewed do not intend to stay in South Africa permanently, they do plan to stay for several months or several years and they expect to have access to basic social and economic services. To date, there has been little more than political rhetoric from immigration authorities in South Africa about the enormous "burden" these expectations will place on the South African budget and labour market, but there is virtually no systematic evidence to support these claims. Access to housing, education, health care and other social and welfare services needs to be addressed as part of a larger basket of immigration rights and responsibilities. It is essential that these decisions be based on reliable, empirical evidence of what is happening on the ground as well as reference to international policy experiences and treaty obligations.

And what of the moral obligations that the new South Africa arguably has towards other African countries and citizens who lent their support during the anti-apartheid struggle? In qualitative follow-up meetings with the interviewers, they stated that many respondents expressed strong and unprompted opinions to the effect that South Africa needs to "pay back" for the sacrifices made by other Africans.

Many respondents argued that during the apartheid era, the ANC-in-exile created the impression that their hosts would be welcome in a post-apartheid South Africa. One Nigerian respondent, for example, said: "At school we used to save money which we were told was going to be used to help the ANC to fight apartheid." Many of the Nigerians interviewed now feel that the South African government is not interested in addressing their employment and welfare concerns and some report being engaged in a campaign to discourage their fellow countrymen and -women from coming to South Africa because of the "bad treatment" they would receive.

These comments aside, it is clear from the survey that cross-border migration is not going to disappear in South Africa, no matter how draconian an approach to immigration policy some South African commentators might like to see. Nor is (im)migration a process that should be seen in too self-interested a light. Immigration policy is a process of "give-and-take" and South Africa must see itself as part of a larger pan-African group of nations. There are broader social, economic and cultural linkages that emerge as a result of cross-border movement and South Africa needs to prepare itself for these changes. Continued research into the qualitative and quantitative experiences that migrants have with immigration authorities and with the migration process is an essential part of this preparation, and it is important to base policy decisions on reliable information.

Acknowledgements:

Alastair Machin, Lephophotho Mashike and Celia Golden of Labour Market Alternatives (LMA) in Johannesburg co-ordinated the field work for this research and conducted the initial data analysis. Karl Gostner of LMA co-ordinated the data input. Robert Mattes and David McDonald compiled the questionnaire and John Gay oversaw the training workshop for the research assistants. Anne Mitchell produced the tables. Jonathan Crush provided editorial assistance on an earlier draft of this chapter. The research was designed and co-ordinated by David McDonald.

A special thanks is due to the research assistants. Their commitment to methodological rigour and the extraordinary efforts made to ensure the confidence of interviewees (often under very difficult circumstances) has contributed to a reliable data set. These researchers (and the "communities" of migrants they interviewed) are as follows: Emmanuel Bai (hawkers and traders); Koffi Gervais (Francophones); Zacharia Ombe (Mozambicans); Albertinah Mucavele (Mozambicans); Sharon Mlambo (migrants in Durban); Johnson Mugwaga (migrants in Cape Town); Jack Rampou (Basotho and mineworkers); Mogudi Maaba (Zimbabweans and mineworkers); Xolani Yokwe (migrants in Durban); Bitton Mwale (Malawians); Solange Lana (Nigerians).

REFERENCES

Brunk, M, 1996, "Undocumented migration to South Africa: More questions than answers". *Public Information Series*. Cape Town: Idasa.

Bundy, C, 1979, *The rise and fall of the South African peasantry*. Berkeley: University of California Press.

Covane, L, Macaringe, J, and Crush, J, 1998, "The revolving door", *Crossings*, 2(2).

Crush, J, 1997, "Covert operations: Clandestine migration, temporary work and immigration policy in South Africa", *SAMP Migration Policy Series*, No. 1. Cape Town and Kingston: Southern African Migration Project.

Crush, J, (ed), 1998, *Beyond control: Immigration and human rights in a democratic South Africa*. Cape Town: Idasa.

Crush, J, 1999, "The discourse and dimensions of irregularity in post-apartheid South Africa", *International Migration*, Vol. 37, No.1.

Crush, J and Mattes, R, 1998, "Xenophobia: Hostility growing alarmingly", *Crossings*, 2(3).

Crush, J, Jeeves, A, and Yudelman, D, 1992, *South Africa's labour empire: A history of black migrancy to the gold mines*. Cape Town/Boulder: David Philip Publishers/Westview Press.

First, R, 1983, *Black gold: The Mozambican miner, proletarian and peasant*. Brighton: St. Martin's Press.

Frayne, B and Pendleton, W, 1998. "Namibians on South Africa: Attitudes towards cross-border migration and immigration policy", *SAMP Migration Policy Series*, No. 10. Cape Town and Kingston: Southern African Migration Project.

Inter Press Service, 1998, "Zimbabwe: The tragedy of border jumpers", *Inter Press Service*, 16 November. Harare.

Lacey, M, 1981, *Working for Boroko: The origins of a coercive labour system in South Africa*. Johannesburg: Ravan Press.

McDonald, D, 1998, "Left out in the cold? Housing and immigration in the new South Africa", *SAMP Migration Policy Series*, No. 5. Cape Town and Kingston: Southern African Migration Project.

McDonald, D, Gay, J, Zinyama, L, Mattes, R, and De Vletter, F, 1998, "Challenging xenophobia: Myths and realities about cross-border migration in Southern Africa", *SAMP Migration Policy Series, No. 7*. Cape Town and Kingston: Southern African Migration Project.

Murray, C, 1981, *Families divided: The impact of migrant labour in Lesotho*. Cambridge: Cambridge University Press.

Packard, R, 1989, *White plague, black labour: Tuberculosis and the political economy of health and disease in South Africa*. Berkeley: University of California Press.

Peberdy, S and Crush, J, 1998, "Trading places: Cross-border traders and the South African informal sector", *SAMP Migration Policy Series*, No. 6. Cape Town and Kingston: Southern African Migration Project.

Reitzes, M, 1998a, "Nice work if you can get it: Foreign workers and the job market", *CPS Policy Brief*, No. 8. Johannesburg: Centre for Policy Studies.

Reitzes, M, 1998b, "The stranger within the gates: Xenophobia and public leadership", *CPS Policy Brief*, No. 9, Johannesburg: Centre for Policy Studies.

Reitzes, M and Crawhall, N, 1998, "Silenced by nation-building: African immigrants and language policy in the new South Africa", *SAMP Migration Policy Series*, No. 4. Cape Town and Kingston: Southern African Migration Project.

Rogerson, C, M, 1997, "International migration, immigrant entrepreneurs and South Africa's small enterprise economy", *SAMP Migration Policy Series*, No. 3. Cape Town and Kingston: Southern African Migration Project.

South African Institute for Race Relations, 1998, *South Africa Survey 1997–98*. Johannesburg.

ENDNOTES

1. At the time of writing (December 1998) a Draft Green Paper on International Migration had been released by the Department of Home Affairs (May 1997), and the drafting of a White Paper on Migration was in progress.
2. Due to the enormous number of languages involved in the study it was decided that translating interviews in advance was not feasible. Instead, a close review of the questionnaire at the workshop (in English) was used to highlight possible areas of translation difficulties in order to allow field workers to develop translation strategies consistent with the essence of each question.
3. This includes the 10% of the sample from the "hawkers and traders" community. The community sampling method therefore picked up an additional 28% working in the informal sector.
4. Does not include those who said "Do not know" or who "Refused to disclose amount" (3% and 7% of total sample, respectively).
5. The figure of 93% is based on interviewee responses and not on verifiable document checks. Given the sensitivity of the issue, some could have been tempted to give incorrect information. There is also the possibility that some have false documentation or that the documentation they hold allows them to be in the country for reasons other than work.
6. In our 1997 national survey of Lesotho, for example, 36% of those who said they had visited South Africa last did so to visit family or friends, or to go on a holiday. The figures for Mozambique and Zimbabwe were 17% and 16%, respectively (see McDonald *et al*, 1998: 19).
7. For a more detailed discussion see J. Crush (ed), 1998, *Beyond control: Immigration and human rights in a democratic South Africa* (Cape Town: Idasa).
8. It is beyond the scope of this report to discuss the implications and debates around access to social services on the part of legal and undocumented migrants in detail. Suffice to say, the new South African constitution makes it clear that only "juristic persons" should have access to most social services. This terminology clearly excludes undocumented migrants but does not clearly distinguish between different categories of "legal" migrants. This constitutional uncertainty about who has what rights is further complicated by different legislative interpretations. The White Paper on Housing, for example, states that housing subsidies are available to "legal RSA residents" but never explicitly states how this group is to be classified (see McDonald, 1998).

Chapter Nine

South African attitudes to immigrants and immigration

by Robert Mattes, Donald M. Taylor, David A. McDonald,

Abigail Poore and Wayne Richmond

Decision-makers in democratic societies are required to perform a delicate balancing act when it comes to articulating formal immigration policy. Immigration legislation is the basic tool by which a government resolves a fundamental question: who will be allowed to become a full participant in the nation, and on what terms? Policy-makers must balance a variety of competing considerations, ranging from the health of the economy and protecting the national interest, to safeguarding the human rights of newcomers and maintaining national harmony. Achieving the appropriate balance is a major challenge for all immigrant-receiving countries. It is especially challenging for post-apartheid South Africa whose immigration policy thus far has been driven by the dysfunctional "Aliens Control Act", an extension of the ideology of apartheid itself (Peberdy and Crush, 1998a: 18–36).

Confronted with such a daunting challenge, it is essential that policy be based on the best available information. To that end, this chapter describes the results of a national South African public opinion survey, conducted in mid-1997, that focused on South Africans' views of immigrants and immigration policy. Public opinion is not the only input that needs to be considered when formulating immigration policy, but legislators do need to be aware of public preferences and prejudices.

The chapter is divided into four sections. We begin with a brief overview of the methodology in order to establish the credibility of the research. We then describe the attitudinal profile of South Africans with respect to basic immigration policy alternatives as well as a number of more specific policy issues, including deportation, amnesty, preferential treatment for certain categories of newcomers, and rights that should be accorded newcomers.

The second section of the chapter examines the attitudes that South Africans have towards migrants from different parts of the world. In general, South Africans hold very negative views of immigrants and immigration but there are some important differences along racial lines that will be highlighted. We also explore the possible reasons for why these attitudes are so negative and isolate salient attitudinal differences within the South African population. We explore, in particular, the perceived impact of immigration, people's direct contact with foreign nationals and South African attitudes towards diversity, both in terms of how South Africans view newcomers into the country and how they view each other.

The third section attempts to begin to explain why South Africans are so hostile to immigration and immigrants. In doing so, we run a series of bivariate and multivariate correlations and multiple regression analyses in an attempt to highlight some of the factors shaping South African attitudes towards immigration policy. These cross-sectional and associational statistical methods have their limits, however. They do not, for example, provide insight into the historical origins of hostility towards (im)migrants in South Africa or how these attitudes have evolved over time. A fuller explanation of the anti-immigrant phenomenon described in this chapter would require a more historically grounded analysis of the impact of discourses of nation-building and national identity, the isolationism of the late apartheid era, the cultural superiority complex of white South Africa, and so on – tasks that are beyond the scope of this chapter. Nevertheless, the analysis presented here does point to some of the salient features of peoples' opposition to a more open immigration policy framework and suggest some likely interpretations for these attitudes.

The final section of the chapter discusses the implications of these findings for contemporary immigration policy reform and public education in South Africa.

A NOTE ON METHOD

Policy-makers often face the challenge of crafting policy in the absence of relevant information, or even worse, a glut of misinformation. Moreover, the issue of immigration is so emotionally charged that it is often difficult to distinguish myth from reality (McDonald *et al*, 1998). It is important, therefore, to briefly outline the methodology employed in this research, so the reader can better assess the credibility of the report and its significance in comparison to related research.

Two key issues are highlighted here: firstly, who was surveyed and how they were surveyed; and secondly, how people's responses to the survey were analysed. On the first point, a total of 3 500 South Africans were surveyed (a larger-than-average sample size due to over-sampling in key areas), with sample selection being made from official census data and information from national organisations that attempt to maintain population statistics. From this information a clustered, randomly stratified, nationally representative sample was drawn.

Specifically, the procedure involved randomly selecting a series of "primary sampling units" (PSUs) from a larger list of suburbs and magisterial districts, the chance of selection being weighted proportionately by the population of the suburb or the district. Once a PSU had been established, maps were used to select, at random, a place to begin interviewing. Interviewers would then be required to walk in a randomly determined direction and conduct an interview at every nth home, depending on how many interviews were required within that designated PSU. The use of such detailed sampling procedure ensures that no systematic bias affects the sampling procedure. Once the survey was completed, the 3 500 respondents were compared with existing population statistics and the data was weighted according to any discrepancies. Thus, a combination of careful sample selection and post-sample analysis correction yields a sample that accurately represents the nation of South Africa.

To further guard against potential bias, surveyors were required to follow strict rules once a household had been selected for inclusion in the sample. They were first required to list all household members over the age of 18. From this list the surveyor chose the actual person to be interviewed according to a pre-established random schedule. Once the person was selected, the interviewer made three attempts to schedule an interview. Only after three failed attempts was the interviewer allowed to replace that person following the same procedure at a predetermined randomly selected replacement household.

The logistics of preparing a nationwide survey of this type are formidable. For example, it was necessary to have the survey instrument translated from English into the other 10 official languages, and then translated back into English using the "double-blind" method to ensure that translations reliably communicated the intended meanings. In addition, co-ethnic interviewers had to be found so respondents would be interviewed by someone who could speak their language fluently.

The survey instrument was crafted so that respondents were required to answer questions in a standard format, but one that offered them a range of response alternatives. The interviewer, therefore, was required to pose a set of predetermined questions in a predetermined order. The order of questions was carefully determined to proceed from simple to more complex questions, and from non-personal questions to more socially sensitive ones.

For each question, respondents answered according to clearly defined categories. In the simplest case, the answer categories might be a simple "yes" or "no", but in most cases respondents could express their attitude using a scale with a variety of subtle category differences. For example, respondents might be asked to indicate their attitude toward undocumented immigrants by answering on an 11-point scale, ranging from a very negative attitude (the 0 end of the scale) to a more neutral attitude (the 5 position on the scale) to an extremely positive attitude (the 10 position). Such a format allows for aggregate comparisons and statistical analysis.

ATTITUDES TOWARDS IMMIGRATION POLICY

In the light of the increased reports of anti-foreigner intolerance in South Africa, and the visibility of the debate in the news media, one could be forgiven for believing that immigration has become "public issue number one". Interestingly, the results of the present survey (coupled with a series of public opinion polls conducted since 1994) reveal that compared to other national problems, migrancy and immigration issues hardly figure at all.

When asked about the three most important problems facing South Africa, not one person mentioned migration or immigration as an important issue in September–October 1994. This figure increased to 3.4% in September–November 1995 but decreased to 1% in the current South African Migration Project (SAMP) survey (June–July 1997) (Taylor and Mattes, 1998). Clearly, immigration and migration are not the national obsessions they are often made out to be. Although it is essential to develop new, more pragmatic and realistic immigration legislation in South Africa as soon as possible, policy-makers need not respond hastily to populist pressures in an area as delicate as immigration reform. Moreover, policy-makers can feel some latitude to articulate a policy that is both rational and just.

In order to assess the preferences of South Africans in terms of immigration policy, and to be able to compare their attitudes to people in other societies, care was taken to use a question asked in several other international surveys. The SAMP survey therefore asked what the government ought to do about people from other countries coming to South Africa, and offered respondents a range of options along a continuum from a totally open-door policy to a flexible policy based on labour requirements, to a rigid system of quotas, to a total ban on immigration.

It is clear from the results presented in Table 9.1 that South Africans are not open towards newcomers, with only 6% of South Africans favouring a totally open immigration policy. Seventeen percent support a flexible policy of tying immigration to the availability of jobs while almost half (45%) support placing strict limits on migrants and immigrants. Finally, an extraordinary one-quarter (25%) of the public wants a total prohibition on migration to the country.

There are three important features to these attitudes towards immigration policy. Firstly, opposition to immigration and foreign citizens is widespread. There are some noticeable differences among racial groups, with Africans and Asians adopting the most restrictive attitudes (Table 9.1), but support for a restrictionist approach is shared by all South Africans.[1] Importantly, these attitudes cut across income groups, age groups and groups with very different levels of education.[2]

TABLE 9.1: SOUTH AFRICAN ATTITUDES TO IMMIGRATION					
How about people from other countries coming to SA? Which one of the following do you think the government should do?	Total (%)	African (%)	White (%)	Coloured (%)	Asian (%)
Let anyone in who wants to enter	6	7	2	3	3
Let people come as long as there are jobs available	17	15	26	21	9
Place strict limits on the number of foreigners who can come here	45	42	49	57	46
Prohibit people coming here from other countries	25	28	8	9	33
Don't know	7	8	6	11	9

Notes: N = 3 500. Figures in tables may not add to 100% due to rounding. A dash (–) represents a value of greater than zero but less than 0.5%.

Secondly, public opinion has actually become more hostile over the past two years. Preference for a flexible policy tied to the availability of jobs has decreased by eight percentage points (from 27% to 19%), and support for total prohibition has increased by nine percentage points (from 16% to 25%). While any interpretation of these trends must remain speculative, one important factor may be the relentless (and largely negative) coverage of cross-border migration issues in the South African media, particularly as it relates to undocumented, "illegal" migration.[3]

Thirdly, South Africans are more hostile to immigration than citizens of any other country for which comparable data is available, including traditional immigrant-receiving countries. Table 9.2 compares South African responses to different policy alternatives with reactions to identical questions in two separate surveys: the 1997 surveys conducted by SAMP in Zimbabwe, Lesotho and southern Mozambique (Chapters 1–4), and the 1995 World Values Survey for which data from eighteen countries are now available. What emerges from the data is that South Africans endorse very restrictive immigration alternatives by international standards.

It is worth noting, however, that there are few countries in which the majority of the population views immigration positively. Even in countries like Canada and the United States – both with long histories of immigration and significant public education programmes emphasising the positive role that immigrants play in social, political and economic life – anti-immigration attitudes are prevalent. Nevertheless, it is clear that the negative attitudinal profile in South Africa represents a major challenge for policy-makers and for those responsible for public education on migration issues.

Having established extreme opposition to open immigration policies, we turn our attention to more specific policy issues that have been, and are currently, the focus of much debate. Specifically, we profile respondents' attitudes towards (a) the practice of deporting undocumented immigrants, (b) the idea of legalising the presence of non-citizens currently living in South Africa, (c) whether there are any categories of immigrants and migrants who deserve preferential treatment, and finally, (d) what rights immigrants should enjoy.

Attitudes towards deportation

The South African government has been actively involved in deporting foreigners living in the country "illegally". Since 1990, more than one million people have been removed; more than 99% of these deportees went to SADC states and 82% went to Mozambique alone. Policy-makers, however, disagree about the effectiveness of this policy (Covane, Macaringue and Crush, 1998: 1–2). For example, the Deputy-President feels that deportations are a waste of resources while the Minister of Home Affairs seems to favour increasing resources and policing for deportation and border control (Bernstein, Schlemmer and Simkins, 1997: 6). Regardless, thousands of undocumented migrants are routinely, and summarily, deported to their home countries every week.

TABLE 9.2: SOUTH AFRICAN ATTITUDES TOWARDS IMMIGRATION IN INTERNATIONAL PERSPECTIVE

	Let anyone in who wants to enter (%)	Let people come as long as there are jobs (%)	Place strict limits on the number of foreigners who can come here (%)	Prohibit people coming here from other countries (%)	Don't know (%)
South Africa (1997)	6	17	45	25	7
South Africa (1995)	6	29	49	16	0
Russia (1995)	6	48	28	18	2
Philippines (1995)	9	16	63	12	0
Peru (1995)	8	39	40	12	4
China (1995)	7	33	40	11	9
Argentina (1995)	8	49	31	9	3
United States (1995)	5	32	53	8	0
Finland (1995)	8	30	51	8	3
Taiwan (1995)	2	16	30	7	45
Japan (1995)	4	41	40	6	8
Chile (1995)	10	50	31	7	1
Nigeria (1995)	18	37	40	6	3
Spain (1995)	14	55	23	4	3
Zimbabwe (1997)	16	30	48	4	0
Australia (1995)	5	52	39	3	2
Southern Mozambique (1997)	12	61	23	2	0
Sweden (1995)	8	32	55	1	3
Lesotho (1997)	61	23	12	3	1

Source: 1995 World Values Study; 1997 SAMP Surveys.

The results of the present survey with respect to deportation are consistent with people's attitudes towards general immigration policy. Very few South Africans (4%) oppose the practice of returning people to their home country. Just less than half of South Africans support an expulsion policy restricted to people involved in "illegal" activity – either for being here without official permission (32%) or for committing crimes (17%). Another 17% go further and support a policy of returning those, such as the unemployed, who are not contributing to the economy. Finally, one in five (21%) favour returning all non-citizens (Table 9.3).

Thus, South Africans take a consistently restrictive position once again. With only minor differences, these attitudes are widely shared across race, income, education, and age. It should be noted, however, that the questionnaire did not

TABLE 9.3: ATTITUDES TOWARDS DEPORTATION					
How about people from other countries who are presently living in SA? Who do you think the government should send back to their countries?	Total (%)	African (%)	White (%)	Coloured (%)	Asian (%)
The government should not send back any people to their own countries	4	5	1	3	9
Only those who have committed crimes	17	17	9	23	24
Only those who are here without the permission of the South African government	32	32	29	36	34
Only those who are not contributing to the economy	17	14	36	17	13
All of these people	21	24	18	8	14
Don't know	8	8	7	13	6
Note: N = 3 500.					

ask people for their attitudes about specific methods of deportation. It is certainly possible that if South Africans were more aware of the absence of due process and reported human rights abuses that often take place during deportation, their responses might have been different.[4]

Attitudes towards legalising the status of undocumented migrants

Related to deportation is the question of what to do with people living in the country without proper documentation. One option pursued by the South African government in 1995/96 was to grant permanent residence to those who had been living or working for a given period in the country.

Two such offers have already been made and a third was pending at the time of writing. The first was for contract miners who had worked for at least 10 years in a South African mine. The second was for any Southern African Development Community (SADC) citizen who had been living in South Africa, and/or had a South African partner/child, and/or had been working in South Africa for a period of five straight years, and had no criminal record. A third amnesty for Mozambican refugees still living in South Africa was due to begin in July 1999.

It is unclear how many South Africans are aware of these "amnesties", and it was beyond the scope of the survey to explain the process in detail to each respondent. Instead, we simply asked people for their opinions about amnesty/legalisation as a policy option in the future. Only 14% of South Africans support legalisation as a general principle, while 59% are opposed. Seventeen percent neither supported nor opposed the idea (possibly because they did not know what an amnesty entailed) and 9% said they did not know or had not heard enough to have an opinion on the matter (Table 9.4). While all groups opposed amnesty, many more Africans supported the idea (18%) than representatives of other racial groups (3% to 6%).

TABLE 9.4: ATTITUDES TOWARDS AMNESTY					
Would you support or oppose the government offering amnesty to all foreigners now living illegally inside the country?	Total (%)	African (%)	White (%)	Coloured (%)	Asian (%)
Support	14	18	3	6	4
Neither support nor oppose	17	18	13	14	24
Oppose	59	55	76	58	64
Don't know/haven't heard enough	9	9	8	22	8
Note: N = 3 500.					

Attitudes towards selective immigration

Another aspect of immigration policy under debate is whether the government should adopt a selective immigration policy that chooses people by country of origin and/or skills. The survey clearly showed that South Africans do not hold an undifferentiated view of potential immigrants.

Many people were willing to give preferential treatment to particular categories of migrant or immigrant. For example, a substantial proportion supported preferences for economic reasons: 63% supported special preferences for skilled workers, 50% supported a policy favouring those with mining contracts. Only one-third (34%) supported preferences for refugees, however. In terms of place of origin, 31% supported preferences for Europeans or North Americans, 27% for Southern Africans, and 22% for Africans from outside the region.

There were marked differences between African and white respondents on this question. Africans stood out in two respects. Firstly, they were much more willing than other South Africans to make exceptions for miners and those with needed skills. Secondly, they were no more likely to support preferences for African foreigners than their white counterparts. Thus, African respondents appeared more attuned to the needs of the South African economy when it came to distinguishing non-citizens from one another.

Whites clearly distinguished between non-citizens on the basis of where they come from. Specifically, whites were much less willing to countenance a policy that favoured African immigrants over those from Europe or North America. Whites were also much less willing to accept refugees (most of whom would presumably be black).

What is perhaps more surprising is that black South Africans also favoured immigrants from Europe and North America over those from Southern Africa and the rest of Africa. The reasons for this are unclear, but most likely relate to the perception that African immigrants are a drain on the country and compete directly for scarce resources. This sentiment is arguably less pronounced when white immigrants are considered.

Attitudes towards rights for resident non-citizens

A final aspect of immigration policy concerns the legal rights of resident non-citizens. The South African constitution grants certain categories of rights to all residents of the country. Moreover, the South African Constitutional Court has recently applied the equality provisions of the Constitution to foreign citizens, striking down regulations that prohibited foreign citizens from being permanently employed as teachers in state schools. It is therefore of interest to see what ordinary people feel about the question of rights for non-citizens from elsewhere in Africa.

Despite steps designed to offer rights to established immigrants, the attitudes of South Africans remained negative. Large percentages of respondents in the survey oppose offering African non-citizens the same access to a house as a South African (54%), the right to vote (53%) or the right to citizenship (44%). Opinion is more divided with respect to granting foreign children equal access to education (39% opposed, 37% supported) and equal access to medical service (39% opposed, 38% supported). Moreover, while all South Africans stand in clear opposition to granting rights to non-citizens, whites, and to a lesser extent Asians, are consistently less willing to grant legal and socio-economic rights, as the results in Table 9.5 illustrate.

TABLE 9.5: ATTITUDES TOWARDS RIGHTS FOR IMMIGRANTS					
What about government policy toward people from other African countries who are in SA? Would you support or oppose giving them:	Percent "opposed"				
	Total	African	White	Coloured	Asian
The same access to medical service as South Africans	39	34	61	41	38
The same access to a house as South Africans	54	50	69	59	75
The same access to education as South Africans	39	36	57	38	44
The right to vote in South African elections	53	49	74	58	53
The right to become a citizen of South Africa	44	44	51	34	47

Note: N = 3 500.

Potential anti-migrant behaviour

Thus far, the results have detailed a strong strain of opposition to immigration. It is relevant, therefore, to ask how South Africans are likely to treat foreigners living in the country, and whether intolerant attitudes would lead to anti-social behaviour. More specifically, to what extent might opposition to immigration turn into actual anti-immigrant action?

The news media has been filled with reports from various places around the country where foreign citizens have been the target of a range of different forms of abuse at the hands of South Africans. It is unclear how widespread this abuse is, and one must be careful not to exaggerate this violence because of sensational reporting in the press. But there is nonetheless a disturbing level of violent activity aimed specifically at foreign nationals.[6] The killings of two Senegalese and a Mozambican by a mob of angry South Africans at a train station in Johannesburg is a tragic example.

When asked "How likely is it that you would take part in action to prevent people who have come to South Africa from other countries in Southern Africa from engaging in a variety of activities?" approximately one-third of South Africans said that it was "likely" or "very likely" (Table 9.6). Thirty-four percent said it was likely they would try to prevent a foreign national from moving into their neighbourhood or operating a business in their community, and 31% and 32% respectively said it was likely that they would try to prevent foreign nationals from sitting in a class with their child or becoming co-workers.

Four points need to be elaborated with respect to Table 9.6. Firstly, it must be remembered that attitudes do not always translate into action. These responses represent predispositions to act in a certain way, not intentions. The fact that a respondent says he or she would act does not mean they would actually do it when the time came or when they had met the actual person against whom this act would be taken (ie once the abstract concept of "foreigner" had been concretised into an actual, and perhaps likeable, person).

Secondly, people may never be in the position to act on these attitudes in this manner. Thirdly, the percentages reported in Table 9.6 are all slightly lower than the proportions of respondents who said that they were willing to take part in similar actions against their "least liked group" within South Africa. In other words, if someone identified Afrikaners or Muslims as the "group" that they least liked in the country, they were slightly more willing to take action against that group than against foreign nationals. This is not a particularly encouraging finding, given the high levels of violence in South Africa today, but it does place people's attitudes towards foreigners in context.

Finally, two-thirds of respondents either had no opinion on the issue or said that it was "unlikely" that they would ever take action against non-citizens, suggesting that a clear majority of respondents would not take part in such activities. Nevertheless, the fact that a third of South Africans said that it was likely that they would take some kind of collective action against foreigners is a real cause for concern.

TABLE 9.6: LIKELIHOOD OF TAKING ACTION AGAINST FOREIGNERS					
How likely is it that you would take part in action to prevent people who have come to SA from other countries in Southern Africa from doing the following activities:	Percent who said "likely" or "very likely"				
	Total	African	White	Coloured	Asian
Moving into your neighbourhood	34	36	32	27	25
Operating a business in your area	34	35	32	26	23
Sitting in a class with your child	31	34	27	22	17
Becoming one of your co-workers	32	35	27	24	18
Note: N = 3 500.					

In a more direct question, respondents were asked what they would do if they found out about someone who was in South Africa "illegally". Almost half of our sample (48%) said they would do nothing. Thirty-five percent said they would report them to the police and another 12% said they would report them to their local community association or street committee. Only 3% said they would get people together to force them to leave.

Once again, the responses to this series of questions were remarkably similar across racial groups. Africans were the most willing to take part in some form of collective action against foreigners, but they were less likely to report an "illegal" migrant to the police. Even more interesting is the fact that women are just as likely to take action against foreign nationals as are men, and people with university degrees are just as likely (and in some cases more likely) to participate in these activities as South Africans with little or no formal education. Thus, willingness to take action against non-citizens is virtually uniform across all relevant demographic groups.

Conclusions

Based on these results, we now have a clear profile of people's attitudes towards immigrants and immigration. Simply stated, South Africans do not like foreign nationals regardless of where they come from and they prefer highly restrictive immigration policies. Consistent with this negative profile are responses to specific immigration issues. In general, people support deportation, they do not endorse legalisation, and they are particular about who they would let into the country and about offering rights to non-citizens.

Despite this consistently negative profile, policy-makers and public educators can still count on some latent support should they decide to instigate a campaign designed to create a more favourable immigration climate. On each of the questions about immigration policy there was a sizeable minority who expressed relatively positive attitudes towards more open policy alternatives, and who expressed a neutral and/or positive attitude towards immigrants themselves. While clearly in the minority, these respondents nevertheless provide a base from which to launch a public education campaign to make people more aware of the contributions that foreign nationals make to South Africa and/or to stimulate a more informed debate on immigration issues.

ATTITUDES TOWARDS IMMIGRANTS

We now turn to an assessment of what South Africans think about (im)migrants themselves and where these attitudes might come from. Due to space restrictions we limit ourselves here to a discussion of African and white respondents only.

Attitudes towards migrants from different countries

Respondents were asked about their attitudes towards people living in South Africa from neighbouring countries in Southern Africa, West Africa, Europe and North America, as well as people who have come to South Africa without proper documentation (so-called "illegal immigrants"). They indicated their attitudes towards these different groups on an 11-point scale ranging from 0 (completely unfavourable) to 10 (completely favourable), with 5 representing the neutral point. The mean scores for these questions are presented in Figure 9.1.

Figure 9.1 clearly shows that all non-citizens, regardless of their country of origin or legal status, fall into the "unfavourable" category. Foreign citizens who are in the country "illegally" are certainly the most disliked; people from Europe and North America are the least disliked. Generally, dislike is widespread and very strong.

This dislike of non-citizens is all the more apparent when set against attitudes towards other groups within the country. As Figure 9.1 suggests, whites and Africans rank their own racial group, and even each other's racial group, much more favourably than the various categories of foreigners (with the notable exception of people from Europe and North America). In this respect, whites and Africans are strikingly similar in their disapproval of non-South Africans.

The key difference between white and African respondents is that whites rank foreigners from Europe and North America (most of whom would presumably be white) higher than they rank their fellow Africans. Africans, on the other hand, rank white South Africans higher than any category of foreigner, including those

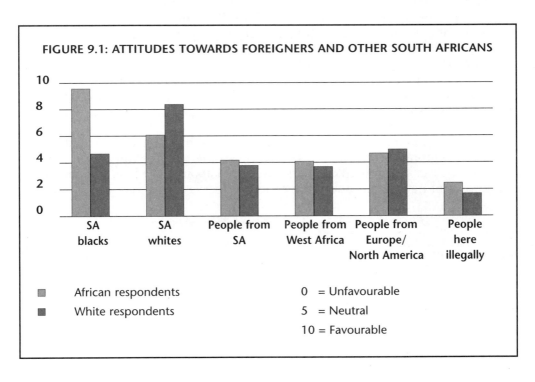

from neighbouring Southern Africa countries (the vast majority of whom would be African). We will return to this point in more detail later in the chapter.

Perceived impacts and threats of foreigners

Most South Africans clearly believe that immigration has negative consequences for the social and economic health of the country. Only 18% of respondents agreed when asked if they thought immigrants make South African society stronger (60% disagreed), only 30% agreed that immigrants bring needed skills to the country (43% disagreed) and only 20% agreed that immigrants make the economy stronger (59% disagreed) (Table 9.7). Finally, 61% felt that immigrants put additional strains on the country's resources (19% disagreed). Here, too, there are significant racial differences, with whites having particularly negative attitudes and Africans being much more willing to agree that immigrants bring needed skills to the country.

People were also asked what, if anything, they had to fear from Southern Africans living in South Africa. In order to determine these perceptions of threat, respondents were given the freedom to reveal their beliefs without any suggestions from the interviewer. Responses were then categorised by grouping together those spontaneously generated beliefs that referred to the same theme but with slightly different wording. Table 9.8 lists all the threats cited by at least 1% of the total sample.

Significantly, one-quarter of the sample (24%) said that they had "nothing" to fear from foreigners living in South Africa. Even more striking is the strong consensus about what there is to fear. Forty-eight percent of the total sample mentioned crime, 37% mentioned threats to jobs or the economy in general and 29% cited diseases (predominantly HIV and other STDs). In contrast, only 3% mentioned competition for housing, 2% a fear of their land or the country being overrun and 1% cultural or linguistic differences. The repetitive character of the spontaneous responses suggests that there are widespread stereotypes about the negative impact of newcomers.

Whites are much more likely to cite fears about jobs, the economy and crime, and are less prone to mention fears that newcomers might import disease. In contrast, African respondents are less concerned about the economic and criminal impact of newcomers and more concerned about health issues.

TABLE 9.7: PERCEIVED IMPACTS OF IMMIGRATION			
Do you agree or disagree that when people come here from other African countries they:	Total	Africans	Whites
Make South African society stronger (% who "disagree")	59	57	76
Make the South African economy stronger (% who "disagree")	58	56	75
Bring needed skills to SA (% who "disagree")	42	38	65
Put a strain on South African resources (% who "agree")	61	57	72
Note: N = 3 500.			

TABLE 9.8: PERCEIVED THREATS FROM IMMIGRATION			
What, if anything, do you have to fear from people living here from neighbouring countries?	Total sample (%)	Africans (%)	Whites (%)
Nothing to fear	24	26	24
Threat to jobs and economy	37	37	56
Criminal threat	48	40	45
Threat of disease	29	30	16
Overpopulation	9	9	8
Worsen housing shortages	3	3	6
Threat to land	1	2	2
Cultural differences	1	2	0

Notes: N = 3 500. Columns add to more than 100% due to the fact that respondents gave more than one response.

Nevertheless, the slightly different profile for African and white respondents is overshadowed by an overriding consensus. Issues of the economy, crime and health clearly represent widely held beliefs that are salient for all South Africans, and these beliefs are decidedly negative. Thus, South Africans not only hold negative attitudes towards foreigners, but they also have a readily accessible set of stereotypes with which to justify or rationalise their negative attitudes. Like any stereotype, its legitimacy is less important than the fact that most people believe it to be true.

Contact with foreigners

Are the negative attitudes, and in particular the well defined stereotypes, that South Africans have of foreigners based on personal experience and interaction with foreigners? To address this question, respondents were asked to indicate the extent of their contact with people from neighbouring countries (the group of non-citizens clearly in South Africa in the greatest numbers).

The results (see Table 9.9) indicate that respondents' attitudes and stereotypes are not based on direct personal experience. Only 4% of the national sample reported that they had "a great deal" of contact with people from Southern Africa. Another 15% said they had "some" contact, but most claimed to have had "hardly any" contact (20%) or absolutely "no" contact (60%). Perhaps surprisingly, Africans are slightly less likely to have had contact with non-citizens than white respondents.

In general, it seems safe to conclude that South Africans' attitudes towards and stereotypes about foreigners are not the result of direct personal experience. This has important implications for public policy and education. Most importantly, the lack of first hand contact suggests that the widely shared stereotypes concerning negative impacts on the economy, crime and health are being propagated through indirect means (eg media, schools, interpersonal communications). Thus, it may be possible to counteract such stereotypes with a well-devised public education programme.

TABLE 9.9: PERSONAL CONTACT WITH NON-CITIZENS			
How much contact do you have with people from neighbouring countries in Southern Africa?	Total	African	White
A great deal	4	4	5
Some	15	16	20
Hardly any	20	21	17
None	60	58	57
Don't know	1	1	1
Note: N = 3 500.			

Xenophobia

Since 1994, there has been a growing tendency in popular and academic writing to use the term "xenophobia" to explain opposition to immigrants and immigration in South Africa. Unfortunately, the term has been used loosely and is rarely defined. A recent HSRC/Institute for Security Studies report, for example, suggests that there are "high levels of xenophobia" in South Africa based on the fact that 65% of a national sample said that "illegal immigration" was a "bad thing" or a "very bad thing" (Schutte, Shaw and Solomon, 1996). This is an extremely narrow use of the term xenophobia, and does little to help our understanding of the extent and causes of the phenomenon.

The conventional dictionary definition of xenophobia is "a dislike of foreigners". Using this definition, it is clear from our earlier discussion that South Africans are indeed extremely xenophobic (see Figure 9.1). The fact that South Africans rank their own and other racial groups in the country significantly higher than they rank every category of foreigner suggests that South Africans do indeed dislike foreigners, simply because they are foreigners.

However, the etymological roots of xenophobia are actually much broader, referring to a "fear of the unknown" or anything that is "different". It is to this broader definition of xenophobia that we must turn in an attempt to gauge more systematically South Africans' supposed intolerance for people, ideas and cultures that are different from their own, and to try to relate this intolerance to their attitudes towards immigration.

We began by asking a series of eight questions that measure people's "acceptance of diversity". In these questions respondents were asked whether it was easy for them to like and trust people with different ideas or people from different cultures, whether exposure to different cultures was enriching, whether it was useful to listen to differing viewpoints, and whether different viewpoints should be allowed. These items are listed in Table 9.10. The percentage indicates the proportion of respondents who gave an answer that demonstrates an acceptance of diversity and the rows are arranged in descending order.

The results were somewhat surprising. Contrary to what one might expect, given the emotionally charged and disjointed history of social interaction within South Africa, South Africans tend to accept diversity and difference. As many

TABLE 9.10: ATTITUDES TOWARDS DIVERSITY		
	African (%)	White (%)
One should listen to various points of view before making a judgement about what's going on (agree)	85	88
You can usually accept people from other cultures, even when they are very different from you (agree)	72	63
Exposure to different cultures enriches one's life (agree).	67	61
It is easy for you to like people who have different views from your own (agree)	66	64
Listening to viewpoints which differ from your own is usually a waste of time (disagree)	52	57
A group should not allow members to hold opinions different from those of the group (disagree)	40	60
You dislike having to interact with people who are different from you (Disagree)	47	55
You can't trust a person if they come from a culture different from yours (Disagree)	41	49

Note: N = 3 184.

as 85% of Africans and 88% of whites, for example, agreed that "one should listen to various points of view before making a judgement about what's going on". Not all of the results from Table 9.10 are this positive, however, and one does not need a survey of this type to know that South Africans of all racial groups still exhibit a great deal of discrimination towards one another. Nevertheless, the results are largely in the positive range and are encouraging for those who advocate tolerance and understanding in the new South Africa. Most important for our discussion is that "xenophobia" in South Africa is not an all-encompassing fear of anything new or different. South Africans are at least modestly accepting of diversity and difference.

Further evidence of some acceptance of diversity among South Africans was found in response to a question about whether people from other countries in Southern Africa could be "part of the South African nation". A majority of respondents (57%) said that people from the region *could not* readily integrate into the country and become full citizens, but a sizeable minority (42%) said that people from the region *could* integrate (see Table 9.11), suggesting once again that South Africans are not blindly opposed to immigration and newcomers in the country.

Xenophobia, therefore, is a more complex phenomenon than is typically portrayed in the media and in many academic and policy papers. Researchers and policy-makers would do well to try to better understand the dynamics behind this dislike for foreigners, while at the same time try to build on the apparent willingness of South Africans to accept to a certain degree new ideas, people and cultures.

TABLE 9.11: ATTITUDES TOWARDS INTEGRATION OF NEWCOMERS IN SOUTH AFRICA			
What about people from other countries in Southern Africa who move here? Can they become part of the South African nation?	Total (%)	Africans (%)	Whites (%)
Yes	41	42	39
No	58	57	61
Don't know	1	1	0
Note: N = 3 500.			

STATISTICAL ANALYSIS OF SOUTH AFRICAN ATTITUDES TOWARDS IMMIGRATION

Having detailed the attitudes of South Africans towards immigrants and immigration, we now turn to the question of why they seem so hostile. Is it simply because they dislike foreigners? Is racism a factor? Is it the perceived threats that create such a strong preference for a restrictive immigration policy?

As noted in the introduction, a full analysis of these questions would require a broad historical survey of the impact of discourses of nation-building and national identity, the isolationism of the late apartheid era, the ideology of cultural superiority of white South Africa under apartheid, and so on. The analysis here is limited to statistical associations between opposition to immigration and other attitudinal responses from the survey. Nevertheless, the data does offer some important insights into the relationships between opposition to immigration and other attitudinal characteristics, and will hopefully contribute towards a better understanding of what can be done to address these attitudes.

We began the analysis by running a series of bivariate correlations examining the relationship between immigration policy preferences (from Table 9.1) and a range of possible explanatory variables (eg racism). We then ran a series of multiple regression analyses to determine which factors have the most direct impact on South Africans' opposition to immigration. We conducted separate multiple regression analyses for Africans and whites to see if the reasons for opposition differed. This proved to be the case.

Explaining African opposition to immigration

A large number of the factors that might be expected to explain African attitudes to immigration are indeed correlated with it at the bivariate level (eg a dislike of foreigners). Most of these relationships disappear once we statistically control for the simultaneous impact of other variables with multiple regression analysis. In the end, a relatively limited number of factors explain a large proportion of African opposition to immigration ($R^2=.24$). The following list outlines the most important associations (in order of statistical significance):[7]

- *Beliefs about immigrants = social impact.* Those who disagreed with the statement that newcomers "make our society stronger" were much more likely to oppose immigration (beta=.21).[8] This item had the strongest multivariate correlation in the final model.
- *Beliefs about integration.* Those who believe that newcomers are unable to become "part of South Africa" were much more likely to oppose immigration (beta=-.16).
- *Perceived job threat.* Those who spontaneously said in open-ended questions that immigrants are a threat to jobs and the economy in South Africa were more likely to oppose immigration (beta=.13).
- *Dislike of black foreigners.* Those who showed a strong dislike of African immigrants (a composite measure of ratings of West Africans and Southern Africans) are significantly more likely to oppose immigration (beta=.12).
- *Beliefs about immigrants = negative economic impact.* The more a person is inclined to think that migrants are a drag on the South African economy (ie those who said "disagree" to the last three questions in Table 9.7) the more likely they are to oppose immigration (beta=.11)
- *Perceived health threats.* Those who spontaneously volunteered in open-ended questions that they fear immigrants spread or carry disease are more likely to oppose immigration (beta=.09).
- *Contact with foreigners.* Although very few South Africans said they have a lot of contact with non-citizens, those who did have a lot of contact were much less likely to oppose immigration (beta=-.09).
- *Acceptance of diversity.* The more one is able to accept diversity in ideas and culture the less likely they are to oppose immigration (beta=.08).

African opposition to immigration is therefore primarily a function of beliefs about what immigrants do while they are in the country with respect to health and social interaction as well as a simple dislike of (black) immigrants. In other words, what seems to characterise African opposition to immigration is a perceived threat to society posed by a group of disliked people who are deemed to be unassimilable into South Africa.

The particular dislike of African non-citizens is linked to a broader racism: African South Africans who hold racist views of whites, coloureds and Asians within the country are also more likely to dislike African foreigners (beta=-.28).[9] This result is interesting because it is counter-intuitive. One might think that the more African South Africans reject white, Asian and coloured South Africans, the more they would embrace fellow Africans from outside the country due to some kind of pan-Africanist, pro-black sentiment. But the data reveals that the relationship goes in precisely the opposite direction.

As one might expect, the fear of job loss and a perceived negative impact on the economy also have strong associational links with opposition to immigration. Dissatisfaction with immigration is therefore linked to beliefs about the impact of immigrants on the economy, the belief that they "work for less" and "steal" jobs, houses and other benefits they are not entitled to.

Explaining white opposition to immigration

As was the case for Africans, most of the bivariate correlations between the various potential explanatory factors and immigration policy for whites disappear once we control for simultaneous interrelationships among all the factors. Only three variables retain an independent impact on opposition to immigration:

- *Preference for white immigrants*. Whites generally have low opinions of black newcomers and "illegal immigrants" (most of whom would presumably be black). Yet like or dislike of black foreigners does not, in statistical terms, determine their opposition to immigration. Views of black foreigners are certainly linked to opposition to immigration, but this bivariate relationship only explains 14% of the variance on views on immigration. The more significant factor is whether they happen to like white foreigners. In other words, if white South Africans like white foreigners they support immigration, but if they dislike white foreigners they oppose immigration. Whether or not white South Africans have favourable views of white newcomers (ie people from North America or Europe) is therefore the single strongest predictor of whites' opposition to immigration (beta=.23).
- *Relative deprivation*. South African whites who believe that their self-defined group[10] is doing worse economically and politically than other groups in the country are significantly more likely to oppose immigration (beta=.22).
- *Beliefs about integration*. The less whites believe that Southern African immigrants can become members of the South African nation, the more likely they are to oppose immigration (beta=-.19).

White opposition to immigration would appear to be a function of beliefs about assimilation, a dislike of (white) foreigners and perceived economic deprivation. Thus, as we saw with African respondents, while whites often complain that foreigners take jobs and cause crime, the impact of these beliefs on opposition to immigration or dislike of foreigners is glaringly absent. Economic fears of immigration are related to a person's own economic situation rather than to the perceived impacts of immigration on the economy.

What is more, as we also saw with African respondents, those whites who are negative towards other racial groups in South Africa are less likely to have positive views of foreign whites, not more. Racists are not looking outwards for racial allies. *Racists dislike foreigners even if they are racially similar.*

POLICY IMPLICATIONS

The policy and public education implications of this research are considerable. On the public education front, we have uncovered an attitudinal profile that will not be easily overcome. South Africans are unlikely to be quickly persuaded to support immigration, or view immigrants more favourably, simply by providing more accurate and more positive information about what immigrants actually do, or about their true impact on the country. They may not be persuaded at all if that education effort focuses only on economic data. As we have seen, it is quite likely that public outcry over immigration's effect on unemployment and housing may simply cover a more affective dislike of foreigners. People may be moved to more sympathetic positions if they could be convinced that immigrants pose less of a public health threat, but that would depend in part on what the actual health statistics have to say.

Nevertheless, creating a better public awareness about the actual experiences and intentions of non-citizens living in South Africa (permanently and temporarily) must be a policy priority of the South African government. If South Africa is to adequately address xenophobia in the country and develop a more pragmatic approach to cross-border movements in the region, it is essential to have public support – or at least a softening of public opposition – for these policies on the ground.

Parallel surveys of migrants by SAMP have clearly demonstrated that the large majority of people who come to South Africa have no desire to stay in the country permanently. Migrants from other African countries generally contribute to the social and economic fabric of the country, and are responsible, relatively well-educated and law-abiding citizens of their own nation (see Chapters 1–7). Information like this could help to ameliorate the anxiety that South Africans appear to have about the impacts of trying to accommodate culturally different and "unassimilable" people. The fact that a sizeable minority of respondents (42%) felt that Africans from neighbouring countries could in fact integrate into South Africa, and 23% would like to see more open or flexible immigration policies, are grounds for optimism in this respect.

The lack of contact that South Africans have with immigrants is also noteworthy, particularly when those few who have had contact are significantly less inclined to oppose immigration. One response to this would be to try and engineer more direct and positive contact between citizens and non-citizens (eg community forums, sporting events) and to try and build a more personal public awareness of the roles, interests and future plans of migrants.

This need for public education is all the more important in the light of the South African government's recent suggestion that the best way to enforce and monitor immigration legislation is to have civil society act as watchdogs in conjunction with local police and immigration officials (Republic of South Africa, 1999: 22):

> The Immigration Service should enforce immigration laws within each community and co-operate with police structures and community interests to ensure that illegal aliens are not harboured within the community....By checking, in cooperation with the community, whether illegal aliens are receiving services from banks, hospitals, schools and providers of water supply or electricity, they should contribute to creating the perception that South Africa is not a good receptacle of illegal immigration, thereby reducing the "pull" factors...[This] programme should be advertised in foreign countries to create, at the point of origin, the perception that South Africa does not offer the answers that foreigners are looking for when they immigrate illegally.

The dangers of such a shift in policy enforcement could hardly be more disconcerting, given the extremely negative and ill-informed profile of South African attitudes towards foreigners outlined in this chapter. The potential for vigilantism and grievous human rights abuses is enormous and could very easily outweigh any potential benefit from community participation.

The South African government is aware of these attitudinal challenges. It also states in the White Paper on International Migration (released in March 1999) that the immigration service should ensure that "the community does not perpetrate crimes against aliens or display xenophobic behaviour", and there are calls for the "training and education of broad segments of the public service and of the public" (Republic of South Africa, 1999: 22, 42). However, there is no indication of how this education might take place and no budgetary commitment to implementing an educational campaign. If the government of South Africa is serious in its shift to a broader notion of immigration "governance", then it must commit itself to a broad-based educational programme to combat xenophobia and address the widespread negative stereotypes of immigrants and immigration.

Finally, public education should also concentrate on raising the curtain of ignorance that South Africans have about neighbouring countries not just information about what people from other Africans countries do while they are in South Africa, but more and better information about *Africa* itself, that great void in the South African public's mind about life north of the Limpopo.

ACKNOWLEDGEMENTS

The authors would like to thank the following people for their input into survey design and/or for comments on earlier drafts of this chapter: Jonathan Crush, John Gay, Wilmot James, Douglas Palmer and Lovemore Zinyama. Additional funding for the survey was provided by the United States Agency for International Development (USAID) and the United States Institute for Peace (USIP).

REFERENCES

Bernstein, A, Schlemmer, L and Simkins, C, 1997, "Migrants: Is 'get tough' the way?" *Cape Times*, 27 October.

Covane, L, Macaringue, J and Crush, J, 1998, "The revolving door", *Crossings*, 2(2).

McDonald, D, 1998, "Left out in the cold? Housing and immigration in the new South Africa", *SAMP Migration Policy Series*, No. 5. Cape Town and Kingston: Southern African Migration Project.

McDonald, D, Gay, J, Zinyama, L, Mattes, R and De Vletter, F, 1998, "Challenging xenophobia: Myths and realities about cross-border migration in Southern Africa", *SAMP Migration Policy Series*, No. 7. Cape Town and Kingston: Southern African Migration Project.

Peberdy, S, and Crush, J, 1998a, "Rooted in racism: The origins of the Aliens Control Act", in J. Crush (ed), *Beyond control: Immigration and human rights in a democratic South Africa*. Cape Town: Idasa.

Peberdy, S and Crush, J, 1998b, "Trading places: Cross-border traders and the South African informal sector", *SAMP Migration Policy Series*, No. 6. Cape Town and Kingston: Southern African Migration Project.

Republic of South Africa, 1999, *White Paper on International Migration*. Pretoria: Government Printers.

Schutte, C, Shaw, M and Solomon, H, 1997, "Public attitudes regarding undocumented migration and policing/crime", *African Security Review*: A working paper series, 6(4). Johannesburg: Institute for Defence Policy.

Taylor, H, and Mattes, R, 1998, "The public agenda: Public priorities for government action, 1994–1997", *POS Reports*, Cape Town: Idasa's Public Opinion Service.

ENDNOTES

1. We have opted to use racial categories as the primary variable in the data tables in this section of the chapter, not because race itself determines attitudes but because race is so closely correlated to other important socio-economic variables in South Africa (eg income, education, living conditions) and continues to play an important part in any socio-economic analysis of the country.
2. A study by the Human Sciences Research Council (HSRC) and the Institute for Security Studies found that what they called "anti-immigrant sentiment" increased with education. However, this finding was based on a survey item that asked people simply whether they thought "illegal immigration was a bad thing for the country". Respondents were not given an opportunity to offer an opinion on different policy options, and the results are therefore non-comparable to the SAMP data (see Schutte, Shaw and Solomon, 1996).
3. The role of the media in the development of a negative discourse on immigrants and immigration is clearly an important issue. A more thorough discussion of this issue is beyond the scope of this report. A more detailed analysis of this issue will be the subject of a forthcoming SAMP report on print media in Southern Africa.
4. See for example "Abuse of undocumented migrants, asylum seekers and refugees in South Africa", *Human Rights Watch* report, released in March 1998.
5. The term "illegal" is pejorative and implies criminal activity and is therefore no longer used by progressive academics and NGOs or by the United Nations. The term was used in this survey simply because it is the most commonly used term in the public discourse about "undocumented migrants", and respondents would be familiar with it. Nevertheless, it is possible that the term itself may have contributed to people's negative responses to the question.
6. For an overview of violence perpetrated against foreign hawkers and traders in the Johannesburg area, see Peberdy and Crush (1998b). For a discussion of two communities with large numbers of foreign nationals where violence has occurred in the past but is no longer a major issue, see McDonald (1998).
7. It should also be noted that these factors had impacts on support for immigration that were independent of one another. For example, among those who equally dislike immigrants, those who are dissatisfied with economic conditions are still more likely to oppose immigration.

8. Beta is a standardised multiple correlation coefficient.
9. In order to measure "racism", we used a variety of factors. Firstly, we examined the favourability ratings people give to their own race group (racial in-group rating). As we saw in Figure 9.1, whites and Africans ranked their own group much more favourably than the other's group. We then created an average measure of each person's rating of all three race groups different than their own to create a mean racial out-group rating. Finally, we subtracted a person's mean *out-group* score from their *in-group* rating to create a scale of Racial In-Group Favouritism that measures the distance between a person's rating of their own racial group and their ranking of all others. This variable is on an 11-point scale where higher scores indicate greater racism.
10. The exact wording of the question asking people for a "self-defined group" was as follows: *We have spoken to many people and they have all described themselves in different ways. Some people describe themselves in terms of their language, for example Swazi, Venda or Ndebele. Other people describe themselves according to their religion such as Methodist or Jewish. Still other people describe themselves in terms of their race, for example Asian or black, and some people describe themselves as working class, middle- or upper-class. Thinking about yourself, which specific group do you feel you belong to first and foremost?*

Appendix A

Research methodology for the surveys in Lesotho, Mozambique, Zimbabwe and Namibia

This appendix describes the methodologies employed in the surveys conducted in Lesotho, Mozambique, Zimbabwe and Namibia in 1997 and 1998 (as discussed in Chapters 2–5, respectively). The purpose of the appendix is two-fold: firstly, to provide additional credibility to the surveys in terms of methodological rigour; and secondly, to provide researchers with a detailed account of how the surveys were conducted for future research activities.

PLANNING WORKSHOP

Planning for the surveys began at a three-day workshop in Harare, Zimbabwe, in October of 1996. In addition to the project co-ordinator and the principal researchers from Lesotho, Mozambique and Zimbabwe (Namibia was not brought on as a participant until March 1998), there were also survey design experts from South Africa and Canada and a research associate from SAMP. This workshop established the conceptual framework for the survey instrument, sampling and translation strategies, training programmes for field workers, and time lines and publication objectives. Initial planning for the surveys of South African citizens (Chapter 9) and African migrants living in South Africa (Chapter 8) also took place at this workshop.

SURVEY DESIGN AND TRANSLATIONS

The survey instrument was developed (in English) in a repetitive process over several months with each of the researchers having input on question design, order and priority. After four drafts of the questionnaire pilot tests were run in each country, culminating in a final draft. This final draft then went through translations and back-translations in each of the relevant languages to identify any translation problems. A final English draft was done and translations were made in each of the relevant languages.

SELECTION AND TRAINING OF FIELD WORKERS

In Lesotho, a dedicated team of field workers at the offices of the Lesotho research partner (Sechaba Consultants) were used to conduct the surveys. These researchers conducted the pilot tests and worked on the translations with the primary researcher. A training session was conducted before the interviewers went into the field with the final survey.

In Zimbabwe, graduate students from the University of Zimbabwe conducted the interviews. These students were selected on the basis of their residence in each of the districts of the country selected for interviews (see "sample selection" below) and their ability to speak the language of that district. A two-day training session was held at the university before the students went out into the field.

In Mozambique, field workers were a combination of students from the national university and staff of the primary researcher. The two-day training session was conducted by the South African research partner in collaboration with a local Mozambican supervisor.

In Namibia, interviews were conducted by students from the University of Namibia who spoke the languages of the areas selected for the survey. Interviewer training was done in conjunction with the Lesotho research partner to ensure compatibility with the surveys in the other three countries that had been conducted one year earlier.

In all four countries, the training consisted of the following: role playing; reviewing the conceptual purpose of the survey and each of the individual questions; explaining sample selection procedures (both within and across households); explaining the recording of responses (both open- and closed-ended response options); and answering queries. The same training programme was used in each country.

SAMPLING STRATEGIES

In Lesotho and Zimbabwe, surveys were conducted with a random, nationally representative sample. In Mozambique and Namibia, surveys were conducted in selected geographical and demographic areas for logistical and budgetary reasons. In all four countries sample lists were initially compiled using census data and/or aerial maps (depending on what was available and reliable) to form a list of enumerated areas.

Once a random list of enumerated areas was drawn, interviewers would go to every nth dwelling in a given direction starting at a certain point. A card selection procedure was then used to select household members, by which each member of the household older than 15 that was going to be at home that evening was eligible for selection (ie including those members who were not currently present in the household but would return later that day). Household members then selected a card from the researcher, and the person who randomly selected the card with the mark on the back was the person who would be interviewed. If the card belonged to the person who was not at home the researcher would return later in the day for the interview. If the person was not at home that evening, a new interview point would be selected using a predetermined selection procedure. Random field visits by the principal researchers in each country served to ensure further that these procedures were being followed by field staff.

Needless to say, this random selection procedure was an enormous undertaking (particularly so given the dearth of reliable census material in some areas and the logistics of sending researchers to remote parts of each country), and we cannot over-emphasise the importance attached to ensuring that sample selection was as representative and random as possible under the circumstances. The following paragraphs provide additional sampling details for each of the four countries.

In Lesotho, the locations of households included in the sample were based on the population distributions given by recent national censuses. Census data were used to weight the probability of drawing an interview point (from which five interviews were done) from given geographical areas (using the smallest geographical unit for which we had reliable data). Some sampling points in remote areas were substituted with a point chosen from a geographical unit taken from a second, randomly selected list. A cut-off age of 65 years was also used, while in the other countries there was no upper age limit. Research assistants in Lesotho also alternated between choosing males and females in successive households, while no such restriction was in place in the other countries. These inter-country differences are not believed to have brought about any serious distortion in comparing results.

In Zimbabwe, 32 survey areas were randomly selected from a list of national population census enumeration areas compiled by the Central Statistical Office; 17 in rural areas and 15 in urban areas. A research assistant was assigned to conduct interviews in each of the 32 survey sites with adult members of randomly selected households. Each research assistant was required to complete approximately 30 interviews over a two-week period.

In Mozambique, only the southern half of the country was randomly surveyed due to the exorbitant costs of a national survey and the apparent lack of migration to South Africa from the more remote, northern provinces. Census data in Mozambique is very dated and therefore had to be assessed in conjunction with aerial maps to weight the probability of drawing an interview point (from which five interviews were done). As with Lesotho, some sampling points in remote or dangerous areas were substituted with a point chosen from a geographical unit taken from a second, randomly selected list. Mozambique posed the most serious challenges to random sampling strategies, and research was made all the more difficult due to poor transport and communication networks, but the sample can be considered as reliable as possible under the circumstances.

In Namibia, budgetary and logistical constraints necessitated a more selective sampling strategy. The northern regions of Namibia are home to about 65% of the Namibian population, but this part of Namibia is remote from the border with South Africa and it is relatively unlikely that many people from this area have visited South Africa. Therefore, this area was under-sampled in terms of national population, but included to provide information and opinions about South Africa from populations that are unlikely to have first-hand experience of the country. In these northern regions, 100 interviews were conducted with rural communal dwellers (Caprivi and north-central Namibia) and 150 interviews were conducted with residents of northern communal area towns (Katima Mulilo, Rundu and Oshakati). These 250 interviews comprise 42% of the sample (of the interviewees only 12% had been to South Africa).

The remaining 58% of the sample (350 interviews) were collected in central and southern towns (including Luderitz and Walvis Bay), with 100 interviews in the capital city of Windhoek. The population in these towns comprises about 25% of the national population. The urban bias of the sample is intentional in order to capture those segments of the population that are mobile and more likely to have visited South Africa.

Data was not collected from the rural communal areas of the central and southern parts of Namibia because of the relatively sparse population in these areas (especially in the southern part of the country). Together the population in these areas makes up only 7% of the total Namibian population. In addition, no large-scale labour migration to South Africa to work on the mines or on farms takes place today or did in the past from the central, southern or northern communal areas of the country, which would have required these areas to be surveyed more intensively. The only exception to this pattern was limited labour migration to South African mines by people in the Kavango region. However, this was discontinued more than 20 years ago. Thus, the Namibian situation regarding labour migration is quite different from that in Lesotho and Mozambique. Today, as in the past, undocumented border crossings to South Africa were not part of the migration history of Namibians going to South Africa. The Namibian-South African border is remote from the majority of the Namibian population, is located in a dry and rugged part of the country, and not easily accessible by foot.

It should also be noted that the method of sampling was different for rural and urban areas. The rural area selection was based on a cluster/stratified method that consisted of designating three enumerator areas within each rural area that had been identified. The list of enumerator areas was obtained from the Central Statistics Office (CSO) of Namibia, and demarcated on a regional map for the various sample areas selected for the survey. Using a table of random numbers, the three enumerator areas and substitute areas were selected from the maps within each rural sample area across Namibia. The subsequent selection of households and individual respondents within these sample areas was consistent with methods used in the other countries.

Urban area sampling was based on a systematic\stratified method using data on urban population size provided by the CSO and local authorities. Using a sample interval determined by dividing the total number of questionnaires to be administered by the number of households in the selected urban area, the field supervisors selected an arbitrary starting point and identified every nth dwelling. The only areas where this method was not followed were Windhoek suburbs other than Katutura. Respondents for these suburbs were selected proportionally according to population size by drawing names from the Windhoek telephone directory systematically. Potential respondents were called and appointments made for interviews. This was necessary because of the difficulty of gaining personal access to dwellings due to high walls and guard dogs. As with the rural areas, the individual respondents were selected using a random card method.

DATA ANALYSIS

Once collected, the data from Lesotho, Mozambique and Zimbabwe were entered on computer using the Statistical Package for the Social Sciences (SPSS), compiled into a single data set, and shared among the researchers. A three-day workshop was then held in Pretoria, South Africa, in June 1997. The principal researchers from these countries and other migration experts from the region, Canada and the United States were at the workshop to evaluate the aggregate data. This workshop was the start of a repetitive process of data evaluation across these three countries as well as an evaluation of the data along gender lines (Chapter 6) and in terms of its implications for future migration trends (Chapter 7). The research in Namibia was not conducted until mid-1998 and was evaluated independently, using data from the other three countries and a previous *SAMP Migration Policy Series* report (McDonald et al, 1998).

With approximately 200 survey questions and 2 900 interviews, the amount of data is formidable, translating to more than half a million responses. Recodes, bivariate and multivariate correlations, factor analysis and multiple regressions complicate the picture even further. Researchers have made every effort to highlight the most salient results from the survey data and have attempted to highlight the most important demographic and geographical variables related to migration attitudes and experiences. Inevitably, however, important data is "left on the cutting room floor" and the analyses in Chapters 2–7 are no exception. The reproduction of the aggregate survey results in Appendix B is an attempt to make more of this data available to readers, but ultimately it is the manipulation of the data-set itself that reveals much of the intricacies of the surveys.

COMMUNICATIONS

With researchers based in six different countries it was essential to have an effective mode of communication. Face-to-face meetings are undeniably the most effective and productive way of planning and evaluating research, and the two workshops described above were invaluable to the success of this research project. But the costs of these meetings made it necessary to rely on alternative modes of regular communication.

Telecommunication facilities (fax, phone) are reasonably reliable in Southern Africa, but are prohibitively expensive to use on a regular basis. The advent of e-mail, however, has revolutionised the communication process in terms of costs, speed and ease of communication, and proved to be an indispensable tool for this research project. Not only was it possible to communicate on a daily basis if necessary (service interruptions in Mozambique notwithstanding), it also allowed for the instantaneous transfer of large data files and reports, making an interactive and repetitive evaluation process reality and not just rhetoric.

REFERENCE

McDonald, D, Gay, J, Zinyama, L, Mattes, R. and De Vletter, F, 1998, "Challenging xenophobia: Myths and realities about cross-border migration in Southern Africa", *SAMP Migration Policy Series*, No. 7. Cape Town and Kingston: Southern African Migration Project.

Appendix B

Aggregate summary of results from surveys in Lesotho, Mozambique, Zimbabwe and Namibia

The tables below are a summary of the results from surveys conducted in Lesotho (Les), Mozambique (Moz), Zimbabwe (Zim) and Namibia (Nam). The surveys in the first three countries were conducted at approximately the same time in 1997, while the survey in Namibia was conducted a year later in 1998.

The statistics are presented here to provide readers and researchers with a record of the questionnaire used as well as a summary of the aggregate results. Aggregate results, in and of themselves, only provide a superficial presentation of the survey findings, however. The real analytical challenge comes from a deeper cross-sectional analysis of the data as presented in chapters 2-7. Nevertheless, the following tables do provide an overview of the main trends and allow for a comparison of aggregate data across the four countries.

NOTES FOR TABLES

1. A dash (–) signifies a value of greater than 0 and <0.5%;
2. Unless otherwise noted, all figures represent percentages;
3. Columns may not add to 100% due to rounding;
4. LMZN refers to Lesotho, Mozambique, Zimbabwe and Namibia. SA refers to South Africa;
5. Unless otherwise noted, statistics refer to the entire sample for each country.

	Les	Moz	Zim	Nam
Number of completed interviews	692	661	947	601
Date of interviews	Feb–Mar 1997	Mar–Apr 1997	Mar–Apr 1997	June–July 1998

What was your age as of your last birthday (in years)?	Les	Moz	Zim	Nam
Minimum	15	16	15	15
Maximum	66	81	95	86
Mean	36	33	35	36

What language do you speak mostly at home?	Les	Moz	Zim	Nam
Shangaan, Tsonga, Ronga, Tswana	0	75	3	0
Sesotho	99	–	1	0
Ndebele	0	0	9	0
Shona	0	0	76	0
Venda	0	0	5	0
Chewa	0	0	2	0
Xhosa	1	0	0	0
English	–	–	0	3
Ndau	0	0	2	0
Portuguese	0	23	0	1
Afrikaans	0	1	0	31
Otjiherero	0	0	0	2
Nama/Damara	0	0	0	12
Oshiwambo	0	0	0	24
Kwangari	0	0	0	8
Lozi	0	0	0	17
German	0	0	0	1
Other	0	–	1	1

Have either of your parents ever gone to work in SA?	Les	Moz	Zim	Nam
Yes	81	53	24	26
No	17	46	75	75
Don't know (DO NOT READ)	3	1	1	–

Have any of your grandparents ever gone to work in SA?	Les	Moz	Zim	Nam
Yes	51	32	23	23
No	20	54	70	70
Don't know (DO NOT READ)	29	14	7	8

How many people from your immediate family live or work in SA (this excludes cousins, etc)?	Les	Moz	Zim	Nam
None	39	27	66	62
A few, some	56	60	27	31
Most	4	10	4	4
Almost all	–	2	1	2
Entire family except myself	–	–	–	–
Don't know (DO NOT READ)	–	2	1	1

Survey results in Lesotho, Mozambique, Zimbabwe and Namibia

How many of your friends live or work in SA?	Les	Moz	Zim	Nam
None	44	31	58	62
A few, some	49	38	34	32
Most	7	26	6	4
Almost all	–	2	2	2
Don't know (DO NOT READ)	0	2	–	1

How many people from the community where you stay, live or work in SA?	Les	Moz	Zim	Nam
None	1	8	33	50
A few, some	45	28	40	33
Most	46	36	10	4
Almost all	1	15	4	–
Don't know (DO NOT READ)	7	1	14	13

Many people from this country are going to SA to stay or work. Has this had any impact on you personally?	Les	Moz	Zim	Nam
Very positive	11	22	13	4
Positive	41	46	35	13
No impact	12	20	46	63
Negative	27	8	4	15
Very negative	8	0	1	2
Don't know (DO NOT READ)	2	3	2	3

Many people from this country are going to SA to stay or work. Has this had any impact on your family?	Les	Moz	Zim	Nam
Very positive	10	19	12	2
Positive	37	50	34	13
No impact	13	17	46	63
Negative	27	17	5	15
Very negative	6	–	1	3
Don't know (DO NOT READ)	7	4	3	5

Many people from this country are going to SA to stay or work. Has this had any impact on your community?	Les	Moz	Zim	Nam
Very positive	9	9	10	1
Positive	41	51	40	10
No impact	4	15	25	48
Negative	24	12	6	19
Very negative	9	1	1	4
Don't know (DO NOT READ)	12	11	19	18

Many people from this country are going to SA to stay or work. Has this had any impact on LMZN?	Les	Moz	Zim	Nam
Very positive	10	11	11	3
Positive	36	47	36	12
No impact	3	7	14	30
Negative	28	17	12	24
Very negative	12	2	3	10
Don't know (DO NOT READ)	10	15	24	22

If someone close to you went to SA, what would be your main concerns or worries? (Which of the worries you mentioned concerns you most)	Les	Moz	Zim	Nam
Becoming involved in an affair in SA	3	4	2	1
Get injured	63	9	20	25
Become a victim of crime	8	23	24	29
Become involved in crime	2	9	5	5
Get a disease	4	6	14	5
Have a second family	3	7	3	1
Never come back	8	33	13	17
Lose own language and culture	–	2	1	2
Lose religious or moral values	–	1	–	1
Nothing would worry me	3	0	3	2
Might get killed there	0	0	8	2
Other	5	7	5	8

Here are some statements about what happens when people from this country go to stay or work in SA. Please tell me whether you agree or disagree? (PROBE FOR STRENGTH OF OPINION.)

Become involved in crime	Les	Moz	Zim	Nam
Strongly agree	29	5	16	13
Agree	32	22	43	32
Neither agree nor disagree	4	16	10	13
Disagree	20	41	17	31
Strongly disagree	7	12	5	8
Don't know (DO NOT READ)	9	5	8	4

Become victim of crime	Les	Moz	Zim	Nam
Strongly agree	40	10	29	21
Agree	42	41	52	54
Neither agree nor disagree	1	14	6	10
Disagree	11	23	6	9
Strongly disagree	2	9	1	1
Don't know (DO NOT READ)	7	4	6	4

Carry diseases to SA	Les	Moz	Zim	Nam
Strongly agree	10	2	14	7
Agree	16	8	38	26
Neither agree nor disagree	2	23	19	22
Disagree	38	42	16	27
Strongly disagree	26	14	4	7
Don't know (DO NOT READ)	9	10	8	11

Get diseases in SA	Les	Moz	Zim	Nam
Strongly agree	46	6	25	14
Agree	40	28	44	44
Neither agree nor disagree	2	23	14	21
Disagree	5	26	7	11
Strongly disagree	2	9	1	2
Don't know (DO NOT READ)	6	9	8	8

Take jobs from South Africans	Les	Moz	Zim	Nam
Strongly agree	18	4	10	5
Agree	34	14	36	31
Neither agree nor disagree	1	17	14	24
Disagree	32	44	21	25
Strongly disagree	9	11	5	6
Don't know (DO NOT READ)	6	10	14	10

Lose jobs to South Africans	Les	Moz	Zim	Nam
Strongly agree	21	1	5	6
Agree	32	10	26	23
Neither agree nor disagree	1	19	21	25
Disagree	31	43	24	23
Strongly disagree	8	11	5	5
Don't know (DO NOT READ)	8	15	19	10

Please tell me whether you agree or disagree with the following statements. (ASK RESPONDENT FOR OPINION AND THEN PROBE FOR STRENGTH OF OPINION.)

It is basic human right for people to be able to cross from one country into another without obstacles	Les	Moz	Zim	Nam
Strongly agree	61	16	23	13
Agree	20	33	40	28
Neither agree nor disagree	0	6	4	2
Disagree	16	27	25	42
Strongly disagree	1	10	5	15
Don't know (DO NOT READ)	2	6	4	2

It is ridiculous that people from this country cannot freely go to another country, all because of some artificial border	Les	Moz	Zim	Nam
Strongly agree	56	10	12	12
Agree	20	28	27	27
Neither agree nor disagree	0	14	12	7
Disagree	20	33	34	39
Strongly disagree	2	9	7	13
Don't know (DO NOT READ)	2	6	8	3

People who live on different sides of borders between two countries are very different from one another	Les	Moz	Zim	Nam
Strongly agree	33	11	11	12
Agree	35	32	30	40
Neither agree nor disagree	1	15	10	8
Disagree	25	29	36	26
Strongly disagree	3	4	7	11
Don't know (DO NOT READ)	4	8	5	4

It is very important for LMZN to have a border that clearly differentiates it from other countries	Les	Moz	Zim	Nam
Strongly agree	24	25	29	35
Agree	20	41	41	45
Neither agree nor disagree	1	8	7	4
Disagree	46	14	11	9
Strongly disagree	8	2	5	7
Don't know (DO NOT READ)	2	10	6	1

What about the relationship between LMZN and SA. Which of the following would you like to see happen?	Les	Moz	Zim	Nam
The two countries joining together under one government	41	7	9	13
Both countries keeping their own government, but there being complete freedom of movement of people and goods across the border	40	67	71	56
Total independence between the two countries	19	22	16	29
Don't know (DO NOT READ)	1	5	4	2

If you chose the first option, go to the next question, otherwise skip it.

Q16B You said that you would prefer the two countries joining together. Would you prefer to have (based on those who would prefer the two countries joining together):	Les	Moz	Zim	Nam
LMZN becoming a new province within SA?	45	43	28	31
LMZN becoming part of [nearest province in SA]	12	7	16	13
[nearest province in SA] becoming part of LMZN	40	14	25	30
Don't Know (DO NOT READ)	4	36	31	27

Have you ever been to SA?	Les	Moz	Zim	Nam
Yes	81	29	23	38
No	19	71	76	62
Don't Know (DO NOT READ)	0	0	1	0

How many times in your lifetime?	Les	Moz	Zim	Nam
Minimum	0	0	1	1
Maximum	1 000	38	50	200
Mean	68	5	6	14
Median	26	3	3	6

How many times in the past 5 years?	Les	Moz	Zim	Nam
Minimum	0	0	0	0
Maximum	720	26	71	100
Mean	21	2	6	4
Median	5	1	2	2

How frequent were your visits in the past 5 years (of those who have been to SA)?	Les	Moz	Zim	Nam
More than once a month	19	10	6	1
Once a month	13	1	18	0
Once every few months	21	12	12	9
Once or twice a year	18	25	26	25
Less than once or twice a year	17	19	18	38
I have been just once	12	33	21	27

In general, how long do you tend to stay (in weeks) (of those who have been to SA)?	Les	Moz	Zim	Nam
Minimum	0	0	1	0
Maximum	1 872	484	288	104
Mean	55	59	17	6
Less than 1 month	66	20	71	87
Between 1 and 3 months	9	9	9	6
Between 3 and 6 months	5	9	2	3
Between 6 months and 1 year	4	20	10	2
> than 1 year	11	42	7	3

What was the purpose of your most recent visit (of those who have been to SA)?	Les	Moz	Zim	Nam
To look for work	8	22	14	2
To work	17	45	15	11
Buy and sell goods	3	2	21	2
School	1	1	1	1
Study at university/tecknikon	–	0	1	2
Shopping	19	4	21	1
Business	2	2	8	7
Visit family or friends	34	12	13	39
Holiday, tourism	2	5	3	19
Medical treatment	6	4	2	4
Other	8	2	3	12

Have you ever been to [the closest neighbouring country other than SA]?	Les	Moz	Zim	Nam
Yes	1	3	13	14
No	99	97	86	86
Don't know (DO NOT READ)	0	1	1	0

How many times in your lifetime (of those who answered "yes" to the previous question)?	Les	Moz	Zim	Nam
Minimum	–	1	1	1
Maximum	–	4	12	100
Mean	–	2	2	6

Let's talk about your most recent visit to SA.

How did you get there (of those who have been to SA)?	Les	Moz	Zim	Nam
Foot	4	14	14	1
Bus	17	20	35	19
Plane	0	3	5	9
Car	6	19	8	58
Horse or donkey	–	1	1	0
Train	5	38	19	9
Combi or taxi	68	4	16	3
Other	1	1	2	1

Survey results in Lesotho, Mozambique, Zimbabwe and Namibia

Were you able to obtain a passport before you went (of those who have been to SA)?	Les	Moz	Zim	Nam
Yes	98	75	77	86
No	2	23	23	15
Don't know (DO NOT READ)	0	3	0	0

Were you able to obtain an entry visa/permit before you went (of those who have been to SA)?	Les	Moz	Zim	Nam
Yes	88	73	70	58
No	12	23	30	42
Don't know (DO NOT READ)	0	4	0	0

Did you have a place to stay before you left, or did you find one once you were there (of those who have been to SA)?	Les	Moz	Zim	Nam
Had a place to stay	67	62	60	87
Found one once I was there	32	37	40	14
Don't know (DO NOT READ)	1	1	0	0

Did you have family or friends in SA before you left home (of those who have been to SA)?	Les	Moz	Zim	Nam
Yes	74	60	64	78
No	26	39	36	22
Don't know (DO NOT READ)	0	1	0	0

If so, how many?	Les	Moz	Zim	Nam
Minimum	0	0	1	1
Maximum	50	30	50	100
Mean	4	4	5	12

Did you work in SA (of those who have been to SA)?	Les	Moz	Zim	Nam
Yes	41	71	36	20
No	60	29	64	80
Don't know (DO NOT READ)	0	0	0	0

[If yes] Did you have a job before you went or did you find it once you were there (of those who have been to SA and had a job in SA)?	Les	Moz	Zim	Nam
Had a job before I went	69	43	22	51
Found a job once I was there	31	57	64	49
Other	0	0	14	0

What kind of job? (only frequencies > 5%) (of those who have been to SA and had a job in SA)	Les	Moz	Zim	Nam
Miner	63	44	9	18
Housework	7	0	3	11
Farm work	3	6	2	5
Driver	3	4	2	0
Factory worker	2	–	8	2
Builder	–	–	11	7
Buying and selling goods	–	–	11	5
Gardener	–	–	6	2
General Hand	–	–	6	2
Bricklayer	–	8	–	0
Mechanic	–	7	–	2
Business owner	–	7	–	0
Other	18	21	40	46

How long were you employed (in months) (of those who have been to SA and had a job in SA)?	Les	Moz	Zim	Nam
Minimum	1	0	1	0
Maximum	2 050	199	168	286
Mean	145	47	28	28

How much did you earn (per month in Rand) (of those who have been to SA and had a job in SA)?	Les	Moz	Zim	Nam
Minimum	6	1	1	2
Maximum	4 650	7 500	2 500	5 000
Mean	547	724	602	806

Did you send money back to LMZN (of those who have been to SA and had a job in SA)?	Les	Moz	Zim	Nam
Yes	89	71	70	21
No	11	29	30	79

If sent money back, how much (per month in Rand) (of those who have been to SA and had a job in SA)?	Les	Moz	Zim	Nam
Minimum	2	2	1	1
Maximum	2 000	5 000	600	800
Mean	315	369	188	345

Overall, how would you rate your experience in SA (of those who have been to SA)? Was it:	Les	Moz	Zim	Nam
Very positive	29	32	37	27
Positive	46	51	48	54
No impact	3	4	6	10
Negative	12	6	5	5
Very negative	9	4	2	4
Don't know (DO NOT READ)	1	1	1	–

Why have you returned to LMZN (of those who have been to SA)?	Les	Moz	Zim	Nam
Returned after holiday or visit ended	35	15	26	24
Wanted to come back home	15	22	25	44
Family reasons	8	9	7	14
Sick/injured	5	3	1	0
Contract ended	2	18	9	4
Retired from job	2	3	3	2
Lost job or retrenched	11	10	2	2
Found job at home	1	1	1	1
Travel documents expired	4	2	5	1
Expelled or deported from SA	1	11	4	0
Studies ended	–	0	1	1
Goods sold out	–	2	9	1
Other	18	5	9	6

Where do you get most of your information about SA? (DO NOT READ OPTIONS) (entire sample)	Les	Moz	Zim	Nam
I don't know anything about SA	6	5	4	7
From my own experiences in SA	48	13	13	16
From meeting SA in LMZN	1	3	3	4
Hear from others who have been to SA	14	35	60	20
Hear from others about SA	1	13	5	10
Television	2	6	4	15
Newspapers	–	4	5	7
Magazines	1	2	2	4
Radio	25	18	9	13
Other	1	1	2	4

Do you have a favourable or an unfavourable impression of SA?	Les	Moz	Zim	Nam
Very favourable	33	20	23	21
Favourable	37	48	44	42
Neither favourable nor unfavourable	6	17	12	16
Unfavourable	16	7	10	10
Very unfavourable	8	6	3	6
Don't know (DO NOT READ)	1	1	6	6

With regard to each of the following, do you think that things are better in LMZN, would they be better in SA, or would there not be much of a difference?

Cost of living	Les	Moz	Zim	Nam
Much better in LMZN	22	6	7	18
Better in LMZN	27	8	14	27
About the same	7	14	12	12
Better in South Africa	21	36	34	26
Much better in South Africa	18	29	20	10
Don't know (DO NOT READ)	5	6	13	7

Availability of land	Les	Moz	Zim	Nam
Much better in LMZN	35	27	18	20
Better in LMZN	42	40	31	40
About the same	4	7	9	15
Better in South Africa	5	10	8	9
Much better in South Africa	11	4	3	3
Don't know (DO NOT READ)	3	11	31	12

Availability of decent water	Les	Moz	Zim	Nam
Much better in LMZN	35	27	18	20
Better in LMZN	42	40	31	40
About the same	4	7	9	15
Better in South Africa	5	10	8	9
Much better in South Africa	11	4	3	3
Don't know (DO NOT READ)	3	11	31	12

Availability of decent food	Les	Moz	Zim	Nam
Much better in LMZN	17	9	10	6
Better in LMZN	22	14	24	21
About the same	11	11	17	26
Better in South Africa	24	37	17	26
Much better in South Africa	22	25	10	14
Don't know (DO NOT READ)	5	4	21	7

Survey results in Lesotho, Mozambique, Zimbabwe and Namibia

Availability of decent houses	Les	Moz	Zim	Nam
Much better in LMZN	42	16	8	7
Better in LMZN	35	26	21	27
About the same	4	10	15	26
Better in South Africa	8	27	18	20
Much better in South Africa	8	13	11	12
Don't know (DO NOT READ)	3	7	26	8

Availability of decent jobs	Les	Moz	Zim	Nam
Much better in LMZN	3	2	4	5
Better in LMZN	3	7	8	21
About the same	4	8	7	23
Better in South Africa	34	38	30	30
Much better in South Africa	53	40	33	14
Don't know (DO NOT READ)	3	5	17	8

Treatment by employers	Les	Moz	Zim	Nam
Much better in LMZN	10	8	6	8
Better in LMZN	13	12	13	25
About the same	17	22	15	26
Better in South Africa	26	21	19	14
Much better in South Africa	19	18	10	4
Don't know (DO NOT READ)	15	17	38	24

Opportunities for trade, buying and selling of goods	Les	Moz	Zim	Nam
Much better in LMZN	20	7	5	5
Better in LMZN	20	11	12	18
About the same	8	9	9	12
Better in South Africa	27	36	28	35
Much better in South Africa	20	28	25	17
Don't know (DO NOT READ)	7	9	21	12

Overall living conditions	Les	Moz	Zim	Nam
Much better in LMZN	24	6	16	17
Better in LMZN	28	13	22	36
About the same	9	13	15	18
Better in South Africa	20	35	20	15
Much better in South Africa	15	27	11	8
Don't know (DO NOT READ)	4	6	16	7

Safety of myself and family	Les	Moz	Zim	Nam
Much better in LMZN	34	30	36	42
Better in LMZN	37	49	42	45
About the same	10	7	6	4
Better in South Africa	8	7	3	2
Much better in South Africa	8	3	2	1
Don't know (DO NOT READ)	4	5	11	4

Level of crime	Les	Moz	Zim	Nam
Much better in LMZN	30	23	36	34
Better in LMZN	37	48	37	43
About the same	18	15	9	9
Better in South Africa	7	5	4	6
Much better in South Africa	5	3	3	2
Don't know (DO NOT READ)	3	5	10	6

Peace	Les	Moz	Zim	Nam
Much better in LMZN	28	29	43	37
Better in LMZN	41	46	37	47
About the same	18	15	6	9
Better in South Africa	5	2	6	2
Much better in South Africa	4	1	2	1
Don't know (DO NOT READ)	5	7	2	4

Availability of decent schools	Les	Moz	Zim	Nam
Much better in LMZN	11	7	14	5
Better in LMZN	17	12	27	18
About the same	5	7	17	18
Better in South Africa	29	34	13	28
Much better in South Africa	31	30	5	26
Don't know (DO NOT READ)	7	11	25	6

Availability of decent health care	Les	Moz	Zim	Nam
Much better in LMZN	5	3	11	5
Better in LMZN	12	5	20	17
About the same	7	5	15	19
Better in South Africa	28	38	20	34
Much better in South Africa	42	42	12	17
Don't know (DO NOT READ)	5	6	23	8

A decent place to raise your family	Les	Moz	Zim	Nam
Much better in LMZN	32	17	26	33
Better in LMZN	32	42	41	46
About the same	5	13	10	9
Better in South Africa	14	11	6	5
Much better in South Africa	13	8	3	2
Don't know (DO NOT READ)	4	8	13	5

Prevalence of disease	Les	Moz	Zim	Nam
Much better in LMZN	33	5	9	6
Better in LMZN	46	16	19	23
About the same	9	34	33	38
Better in South Africa	5	17	11	14
Much better in South Africa	3	9	6	3
Don't know (DO NOT READ)	4	19	21	16

Prevalence of HIV/AIDS	Les	Moz	Zim	Nam
Much better in LMZN	41	5	9	5
Better in LMZN	39	19	18	17
About the same	7	25	32	38
Better in South Africa	4	10	11	17
Much better in South Africa	3	5	6	6
Don't know (DO NOT READ)	7	36	23	18

Freedom	Les	Moz	Zim	Nam
Much better in LMZN	33	22	28	26
Better in LMZN	35	45	37	47
About the same	13	19	13	18
Better in South Africa	9	2	5	3
Much better in South Africa	6	2	3	1
Don't know (DO NOT READ)	4	9	14	6

Democracy	Les	Moz	Zim	Nam
Much better in LMZN	14	17	15	23
Better in LMZN	23	38	30	43
About the same	19	17	16	20
Better in South Africa	20	7	8	5
Much better in South Africa	14	3	4	3
Don't know (DO NOT READ)	10	17	26	7

Availability of decent shopping	Les	Moz	Zim	Nam
Much better in LMZN	4	2	4	3
Better in LMZN	11	5	10	13
About the same	7	5	8	9
Better in South Africa	30	29	23	35
Much better in South Africa	45	53	42	34
Don't know (DO NOT READ)	3	5	13	6

Ultimately, which of these things we have just discussed, or any others, would cause you to go to SA? (DO NOT READ OPTIONS. CIRCLE REASONS MENTIONED IN TABLE BELOW. ACCEPT UP TO 3)

Which of these is most important to you?	Les	Moz	Zim	Nam
Land	–	1	2	0
Water	–	–	1	–
Food	1	2	–	–
Houses	–	0	1	2
Jobs	53	40	35	24
Treatment by employers	–	1	1	1
Trade	1	4	8	7
Overall living conditions	2	14	5	7
Safety of myself and family	1	1	–	1
Crime	0	1	–	1
Peace	0	–	1	1
Education, schools	9	7	2	21
Health care	10	14	3	9
Place to raise your family	0	–	–	1
Diseases/HIV/AIDS	0	1	0	–
Freedom	–	0	1	1
Democracy	0	–	–	0
Getting necessary travel documents	–	1	1	–
Shopping	18	9	26	7
Nothing	0	0	8	8
Other	4	5	4	6

Survey results in Lesotho, Mozambique, Zimbabwe and Namibia

Ultimately, which of these things we have just discussed would cause you to stay in LMZN? (DO NOT READ OPTIONS. CIRCLE REASONS MENTIONED IN TABLE BELOW. ACCEPT UP TO 3)

Which of these is most important to you?	Les	Moz	Zim	Nam
Land	42	17	14	6
Water	2	2	1	1
Food	1	2	2	–
Houses	6	6	2	2
Jobs	2	3	1	2
Treatment by employers	–	1	–	–
Trade	1	–	–	–
Overall living conditions	7	5	5	5
Safety of myself and family	1	13	12	19
Crime	5	4	6	7
Peace	10	18	23	23
Education, schools	1	1	2	2
Health care	–	–	1	1
Place to raise your family	1	5	5	4
Diseases/HIV/AIDS	1	–	1	0
Freedom	10	3	6	8
Democracy	1	1	1	2
Getting necessary travel documents	–	6	1	–
Shopping	–	–	–	–
I grew up in LMZN	3	0	11	12
Other	5	12	6	6

Would your family tend to encourage or discourage you from going to SA?	Les	Moz	Zim	Nam
Strongly encourage	25	18	17	9
Encourage	19	30	23	21
Neither encourage or discourage	2	16	12	16
Discourage	15	20	22	29
Strongly discourage	33	7	21	22
Don't know (DO NOT READ)	7	9	4	3

Regardless of whether or not you want to leave this country, who would make the final decision as to whether you would go or not?	Les	Moz	Zim	Nam
My spouse	32	19	31	17
My parents	20	19	23	22
Myself	46	54	39	54
Other family members	2	6	2	–
Others, non-family (i.e. friends)	–	1	–	–
Don't know (DO NOT READ)	–	2	1	2
Other	–	0	4	5

What about you personally? Would you be able to go to SA if you wanted to?	Les	Moz	Zim	Nam
Yes	64	76	68	62
No	35	17	30	37
Don't know (DO NOT READ)	–	8	1	1

To what extent do you want to leave LMZN to go and live in SA permanently?	Les	Moz	Zim	Nam
A great extent	17	14	8	6
Some extent	8	18	11	11
Not much	10	14	11	15
Not at all	66	46	66	67
Don't know (DO NOT READ)	–	7	2	1

To what extent do you want to leave Mozambique to go and live in SA for a short period (up to 2 years)?	Les	Moz	Zim	Nam
A great extent	15	15	22	12
Some extent	35	42	27	31
Not much	10	19	15	15
Not at all	39	19	33	41
Don't know (DO NOT READ)	1	5	2	2

How likely or unlikely is it that you would ever actually leave LMZN to go and live permanently in SA in the foreseeable future?	Les	Moz	Zim	Nam
Very likely	11	3	4	4
Likely	14	10	8	8
Neither likely nor unlikely	3	12	7	6
Unlikely	5	36	19	19
Very unlikely	64	33	58	61
Don't know (DO NOT READ)	4	5	3	3

How likely or unlikely is it that you would ever actually leave LMZN to go and live for a short period in SA in the foreseeable future? (PROBE)	Les	Moz	Zim	Nam
Very likely	16	6	13	7
Likely	42	34	26	28
Neither likely nor unlikely	2	20	7	6
Unlikely	5	20	16	18
Very unlikely	32	15	32	40
Don't know (DO NOT READ)	4	6	5	2

If you were deciding to leave for SA, how would you describe the state of your knowledge about the following things?

A place to go where there were people who could take care of you when you first arrive	Les	Moz	Zim	Nam
I know about this	72	51	34	44
I do not know about this, but I know how I could find out	5	8	16	16
I do not know about his, but I might be able to find out	3	13	13	8
I do not know about this, and I do not know how to find out about it	20	12	14	14
Don't know (DO NOT READ)	1	16	22	17

How to get travel documents	Les	Moz	Zim	Nam
I know about this	92	63	59	68
I do not know about this, but I know how I could find out	2	10	13	13
I do not know about his, but I might be able to find out	1	6	9	3
I do not know about this, and I do not know how to find out about it	5	6	6	6
Don't know (DO NOT READ)	–	15	12	10

The safest way to get there	Les	Moz	Zim	Nam
I know about this	74	60	51	54
I do not know about this, but I know how I could find out	7	8	16	14
I do not know about his, but I might be able to find out	5	6	10	6
I do not know about this, and I do not know how to find out about it	13	7	7	11
Don't know (DO NOT READ)	2	19	16	15

The cheapest way to get there	Les	Moz	Zim	Nam
I know about this	70	48	52	55
I do not know about this, but I know how I could find out	8	8	15	13
I do not know about his, but I might be able to find out	6	10	9	6
I do not know about this, and I do not know how to find out about it	16	10	7	10
Don't know (DO NOT READ)	2	25	17	15

Where you could get a job	Les	Moz	Zim	Nam
I know about this	37	19	17	18
I do not know about this, but I know how I could find out	13	14	18	20
I do not know about his, but I might be able to find out	15	25	14	13
I do not know about this, and I do not know how to find out about it	33	15	18	22
Don't know (DO NOT READ)	3	27	32	27

If you could not get travel documents, how to get there without being caught by the police	Les	Moz	Zim	Nam
I know about this	12	10	9	5
I do not know about this, but I know how I could find out	3	6	7	4
I do not know about his, but I might be able to find out	3	13	6	4
I do not know about this, and I do not know how to find out about it	80	31	35	54
Don't know (DO NOT READ)	3	40	43	33

If you could not get travel documents, how to stay there without being returned by the police	Les	Moz	Zim	Nam
I know about this	12	9	8	6
I do not know about this, but I know how I could find out	2	6	5	2
I do not know about his, but I might be able to find out	3	11	6	4
I do not know about this, and I do not know how to find out about it	80	32	34	55
Don't know (DO NOT READ)	3	42	46	33

If you decided to go without travel documents, how likely is it that you:

Would get across the border without being caught by the police?	Les	Moz	Zim	Nam
Very likely	4	4	7	8
Likely	6	13	7	5
Not very likely	15	20	11	11
Not at all likely	72	35	43	57
Don't know (DO NOT READ)	4	29	30	19

Would be able to stay in SA without being returned by the police?	Les	Moz	Zim	Nam
Very likely	4	4	7	6
Likely	7	13	8	6
Not very likely	14	21	11	11
Not at all likely	71	34	43	58
Don't know (DO NOT READ)	5	29	31	19

What about these matters? How much would each of these things discourage you from going to SA?

Leaving assets in LMZN	Les	Moz	Zim	Nam
A great deal	60	27	40	54
To some extent	8	32	17	15
Not very much	7	19	12	10
Not at all	25	18	28	20
Don't know (DO NOT READ)	–	5	2	1

Leaving family in LMZN	Les	Moz	Zim	Nam
A great deal	71	35	57	60
To some extent	4	35	15	18
Not very much	5	17	8	9
Not at all	19	12	18	13
Don't know (DO NOT READ)	–	1	1	1

The expense of going	Les	Moz	Zim	Nam
A great deal	36	13	25	35
To some extent	16	25	25	25
Not very much	15	35	18	19
Not at all	33	25	28	20
Don't know (DO NOT READ)	1	3	2	1

Not having friends or family in SA	Les	Moz	Zim	Nam
A great deal	58	14	25	36
To some extent	8	23	21	20
Not very much	9	29	15	14
Not at all	24	32	36	29
Don't know (DO NOT READ)	–	3	2	2

Not having a confirmed job in SA	Les	Moz	Zim	Nam
A great deal	56	17	26	49
To some extent	15	25	21	21
Not very much	9	26	15	12
Not at all	18	27	36	16
Don't know (DO NOT READ)	1	4	4	3

Not having affordable transport to SA	Les	Moz	Zim	Nam
A great deal	63	16	25	41
To some extent	13	22	22	23
Not very much	10	29	20	16
Not at all	13	28	30	19
Don't know (DO NOT READ)	–	4	3	2

Getting the necessary travel documents	Les	Moz	Zim	Nam
A great deal	83	27	40	49
To some extent	7	27	20	20
Not very much	3	21	13	7
Not at all	7	17	23	22
Don't know (DO NOT READ)	–	7	4	2

Not being sure whether you could get into SA legally?	Les	Moz	Zim	Nam
A great deal	82	31	39	53
To some extent	11	28	22	19
Not very much	2	20	15	9
Not at all	5	13	18	16
Don't know (DO NOT READ)	1	8	6	3

If you could not get a permit, not being sure that you could get across without being caught?	Les	Moz	Zim	Nam
A great deal	84	34	49	64
To some extent	10	29	23	19
Not very much	1	17	10	4
Not at all	5	9	11	9
Don't know (DO NOT READ)	–	11	7	4

If you could not get a permit, not being sure that you could stay without being returned	Les	Moz	Zim	Nam
A great deal	83	32	47	65
To some extent	8	33	25	19
Not very much	2	14	10	4
Not at all	7	9	11	8
Don't know (DO NOT READ)	–	12	8	5

Survey results in Lesotho, Mozambique, Zimbabwe and Namibia

Not being sure of a place to stay	Les	Moz	Zim	Nam
A great deal	77	19	28	47
To some extent	9	26	23	22
Not very much	5	28	17	13
Not at all	9	22	30	17
Don't know (DO NOT READ)	0	6	3	2

Your age	Les	Moz	Zim	Nam
A great deal	12	10	14	19
To some extent	5	25	9	11
Not very much	10	28	11	11
Not at all	73	35	63	59
Don't know (DO NOT READ)	1	3	2	1

Your health	Les	Moz	Zim	Nam
A great deal	17	16	14	22
To some extent	13	22	13	11
Not very much	11	25	10	12
Not at all	59	35	60	53
Don't know (DO NOT READ)	1	2	2	2

Your family responsibilities	Les	Moz	Zim	Nam
A great deal	30	25	34	51
To some extent	12	32	23	20
Not very much	9	19	11	9
Not at all	49	21	29	19
Don't know (DO NOT READ)	–	2	2	2

Do you think that South Africans have a positive or negative view of LMZNs who go to live or work in that country? (PROBE)	Les	Moz	Zim	Nam
Very positive	13	10	6	8
Positive	31	37	25	29
Neither positive nor negative	4	16	12	17
Negative	19	23	25	22
Very negative	23	5	14	12
Don't know (DO NOT READ)	10	9	16	12

If you were to go and live in South Africa, would you expect good or bad treatment from.....? (PROBE FOR STRENGTH OF OPINION)

Fellow LMZNs living in SA	Les	Moz	Zim	Nam
Very good	56	30	38	34
Good	39	60	42	50
Neither good nor bad	1	4	7	7
Bad	3	2	6	4
Very bad	–	–	1	1
Don't know (DO NOT READ)	–	3	4	5

Other people from Southern African countries living in SA	Les	Moz	Zim	Nam
Very good	35	5	7	14
Good	46	52	38	51
Neither good nor bad	3	22	23	15
Bad	12	7	13	9
Very bad	–	0	2	3
Don't know (DO NOT READ)	4	14	15	8

White South Africans	Les	Moz	Zim	Nam
Very good	32	5	5	10
Good	43	29	22	31
Neither good nor bad	2	25	18	18
Bad	16	25	19	16
Very bad	3	5	20	16
Don't know (DO NOT READ)	5	11	15	9

Black South Africans	Les	Moz	Zim	Nam
Very good	36	4	5	17
Good	51	41	32	43
Neither good nor bad	3	25	19	21
Bad	7	19	18	10
Very bad	7	3	10	3
Don't know (DO NOT READ)	1	10	15	7

Trade unions in SA	Les	Moz	Zim	Nam
Very good	37	4	3	21
Good	51	28	17	35
Neither good nor bad	2	29	17	19
Bad	5	13	12	9
Very bad	–	2	5	2
Don't know (DO NOT READ)	4	24	47	24

Employers in SA	Les	Moz	Zim	Nam
Very good	36	7	9	15
Good	50	40	34	35
Neither good nor bad	3	27	17	20
Bad	7	7	8	10
Very bad	–	1	5	3
Don't know (DO NOT READ)	4	15	28	17

SA government officials, e.g. customs and immigration officials	Les	Moz	Zim	Nam
Very good	36	2	8	19
Good	51	26	29	43
Neither good nor bad	1	19	17	17
Bad	7	20	12	9
Very bad	1	7	10	2
Don't know (DO NOT READ)	4	27	23	11

SA police officers	Les	Moz	Zim	Nam
Very good	36	2	8	17
Good	52	23	25	45
Neither good nor bad	1	15	14	16
Bad	7	23	15	11
Very bad	1	14	18	2
Don't know (DO NOT READ)	3	23	18	1

Of the places you've mentioned you'd like to go in SA, where would you like to go most?	Les	Moz	Zim	Nam
PWV area	16	45	44	18
Cape Town	–	–	11	38
Durban	4	9	9	4
Welkom, FS	16	–	–	0
Bloemfontein, FS	7	–	–	–
Qwaqwa	7	–	–	0
Upington	0	0	0	7
Other	50	46	46	33

What is it particularly about this place, compared to the rest of the country, that would make you want to go there (first response)?	Les	Moz	Zim	Nam
Availability of jobs	17	21	15	12
Good treatment – peace	13	3	5	–
Close to LMZN	13	1	6	2
The only place I know	7	–	–	0
I used to stay there	4	–	–	2
Relatives	12	25	5	12
Shopping	–	3	5	3
Other	34	47	64	69

What sort of work would you want to do if you went to SA?	Les	Moz	Zim	Nam
Vendor, hawker	3	16	15	4
Trader	6	13	9	7
Miner	19	19	6	2
Mechanic	–	7	7	5
Industrial or factory worker	20	7	7	9
Farm work	1	3	3	5
Start own business	6	7	3	15
Teacher	3	3	6	8
Doctor	1	2	1	2
Nurse	2	1	2	6
Accountant	2	2	2	6
Engineer	2	1	1	3
Lawyer	1	1	0	2
Shop assistant	4	0	–	1
Driver	3	0	–	1
Domestic work	6	0	1	1
Don't want to work	4	2	1	–
Don't know	5	9	6	5
Other	12	7	30	18

How many people would you take with you?	Les	Moz	Zim	Nam
Minimum	0	0	0	0
Maximum	100	20	213	14
Mean	2	2	2	2

Would you send for others once you were there?	Les	Moz	Zim	Nam
Yes	57	40	48	52
No	32	50	48	48
Don't know (DO NOT READ)	11	10	4	0

If yes, how many?	Les	Moz	Zim	Nam
Minimum	0	1	0	1
Maximum	40	30	50	20
Mean	3	2	3	3

Would you send money back to LMZN?	Les	Moz	Zim	Nam
Yes	79	87	85	74
No	10	8	11	19
Don't know (DO NOT READ)	10	5	4	3

If yes, to whom? (DO NOT READ OPTIONS)	Les	Moz	Zim	Nam
Parents	41	42	51	61
Grandparents	1	2	2	2
Spouse	25	33	21	7
Children	21	12	20	13
Sister, brother	3	6	3	8
Other family, specify	2	3	2	8
Other non-family, specify	6	1	3	–

How long would you want to stay?	Les	Moz	Zim	Nam
A few days	–	2	8	5
A few weeks	–	6	9	3
One month	1	1	4	3
A few months	2	12	10	9
Half a year, six months	2	11	6	7
Six months to a year	12	21	15	10
A few years	34	37	27	40
Indefinitely	38	4	12	18
Don't know (DO NOT READ)	10	5	9	5

During your stay in SA, how often would you want to return to [LMZN]?	Les	Moz	Zim	Nam
Never	3	3	12	4
Once or twice	6	19	26	27
A few times	8	23	10	12
Occasionally	16	12	16	19
Frequently	33	30	23	22
Very frequently	24	8	8	11
Don't know (DO NOT READ)	9	5	6	5

During your stay in SA, how often would you want to return to [LMZN]?	Les	Moz	Zim	Nam
Never	3	3	12	4
Once or twice	6	19	26	27
A few times	8	23	10	12
Occasionally	16	12	16	19
Frequently	33	30	23	22
Very frequently	24	8	8	11
Don't know (DO NOT READ)	9	5	6	5

Would you want to become a permanent resident of SA?	Les	Moz	Zim	Nam
Yes	33	14	13	17
No	61	83	85	81
Don't know (DO NOT READ)	6	3	2	2

Would you want to become a citizen of SA?	Les	Moz	Zim	Nam
Yes	34	7	15	12
No	60	90	83	86
Don't know (DO NOT READ)	6	3	1	2

Would you like to live in SA when you retire?	Les	Moz	Zim	Nam
Yes	27	4	7	11
No	67	95	90	82
Don't know (DO NOT READ)	6	—	3	2

Would you like to be buried in SA?	Les	Moz	Zim	Nam
Yes	17	1	4	7
No	76	96	93	91
Don't know (DO NOT READ)	6	3	3	3

Currently, there is a good deal of discussion over how governments should deal with people who cross from one country to another. Please tell me whether you agree or disagree with the following statements, or whether you have not yet heard enough about it to have an opinion?

The South African government should offer people from other African countries who are in South Africa: (PROBE FOR STRENGTH OF OPINION)

The same rights as South Africans	Les	Moz	Zim	Nam
Strongly disagree	4	6	9	7
Disagree	8	17	21	23
Neither agree nor disagree	–	6	4	2
Agree	31	52	45	47
Strongly agree	55	14	14	16
Haven't heard enough about it/Don't know	1	5	7	5

Survey results in Lesotho, Mozambique, Zimbabwe and Namibia

The same chance at a job as South Africans	Les	Moz	Zim	Nam
Strongly disagree	1	5	6	3
Disagree	5	9	14	18
Neither agree nor disagree	–	5	6	5
Agree	32	61	52	56
Strongly agree	62	18	16	16
Haven't heard enough about it/Don't know	–	3	5	2

The same access to medical services as South Africans	Les	Moz	Zim	Nam
Strongly disagree	1	5	6	2
Disagree	1	5	5	3
Neither agree nor disagree	–	3	4	3
Agree	33	61	60	61
Strongly agree	65	23	20	28
Haven't heard enough about it/Don't know	–	3	5	2

The same access to a house as South Africans	Les	Moz	Zim	Nam
Strongly disagree	4	5	6	3
Disagree	6	8	11	13
Neither agree nor disagree	–	10	6	4
Agree	38	59	57	60
Strongly agree	52	14	13	17
Haven't heard enough about it/Don't know	–	3	6	4

The same access to education as South Africans	Les	Moz	Zim	Nam
Strongly disagree	1	6	6	1
Disagree	2	6	7	5
Neither agree nor disagree	–	5	6	2
Agree	33	61	58	55
Strongly agree	65	18	17	34
Haven't heard enough about it/Don't know	0	4	6	3

The right to vote in South African elections	Les	Moz	Zim	Nam
Strongly disagree	15	30	24	29
Disagree	18	35	31	31
Neither agree nor disagree	1	10	6	8
Agree	33	12	20	21
Strongly agree	32	3	7	6
Haven't heard enough about it/Don't know	2	9	12	6

The right to become a permanent resident of SA	Les	Moz	Zim	Nam
Strongly disagree	7	15	13	6
Disagree	10	33	26	20
Neither agree nor disagree	2	18	12	10
Agree	44	23	30	49
Strongly agree	36	5	8	9
Haven't heard enough about it/Don't know	1	5	10	6

The right to become a citizen of SA	Les	Moz	Zim	Nam
Strongly disagree	6	19	13	9
Disagree	9	35	26	19
Neither agree nor disagree	2	18	12	10
Agree	46	20	29	47
Strongly agree	35	3	8	10
Haven't heard enough about it/Don't know	—	5	11	5

The South African government should offer amnesty to all foreigners now living illegally inside the country?	Les	Moz	Zim	Nam
Strongly disagree	10	11	21	14
Disagree	18	20	21	31
Neither agree nor disagree	1	17	7	11
Agree	32	39	26	22
Strongly agree	37	5	15	15
Haven't heard enough about it/Don't know	2	9	9	8

Do you agree or disagree that SA should give people from: (PROBE FOR STRENGTH OF OPINION)

Countries in Southern Africa special treatment (compared to people from the rest of Africa or elsewhere)?	Les	Moz	Zim	Nam
Strongly disagree	21	5	16	12
Disagree	45	20	33	36
Neither agree nor disagree	3	17	10	9
Agree	20	38	25	27
Strongly agree	10	5	7	12
Haven't heard enough about it/Don't know	3	16	9	5

LMZN special treatment (compared to people from all other countries)?	Les	Moz	Zim	Nam
Strongly disagree	20	5	16	11
Disagree	43	24	35	34
Neither agree nor disagree	3	16	11	11
Agree	19	31	20	20
Strongly agree	15	16	10	20
Haven't heard enough about it/Don't know	1	9	7	4

Survey results in Lesotho, Mozambique, Zimbabwe and Namibia

How about people from other countries going to SA? Which one of the following do you think the South African government should do?	Les	Moz	Zim	Nam
Let anyone into SA who wants to enter	68	13	22	19
Let people into SA as long as there are jobs available	25	67	35	21
Please strict limits on the number of foreigners who can enter SA	6	15	36	54
Prohibit all people entering into SA from other countries	–	1	4	4
Don't know (DO NOT READ)	1	4	4	2

How about people from other Southern African countries who are presently in SA? Which one of the following do you think the South African government should do?	Les	Moz	Zim	Nam
Send them all back to their own countries	2	2	11	5
Send back only those who are not contributing to the economic well-being/livelihood of SA	12	27	32	11
Send back only those who have committed serious criminal offences	68	57	30	41
Send back only those who are here without the permission of the SA government	10	8	27	36
The government should not send back any people to their own countries	6	3	8	5
Don't know (DO NOT READ)	1	2	1	3

How about people from other countries coming here to LMZN? Do you agree or disagree with the following statements, or haven't you heard enough yet to have an opinion? The government of LMZN should: (PROBE FOR STRENGTH OF OPINION)

Allow people from other Southern African countries to come and sell goods in this country?	Les	Moz	Zim	Nam
Strongly agree	36	30	25	13
Agree	33	49	49	42
Neither agree nor disagree	1	7	5	5
Disagree	15	9	11	27
Strongly disagree	14	2	4	12
Haven't heard enough about it/Don't know	1	3	5	3

Encourage people from SA to invest here?	Les	Moz	Zim	Nam
Strongly agree	48	42	32	34
Agree	27	46	45	43
Neither agree nor disagree	1	3	5	2
Disagree	12	6	8	14
Strongly disagree	12	1	4	5
Haven't heard enough about it/Don't know	–	2	5	4

Encourage people from SA to come and farm crops and/or livestock here?	Les	Moz	Zim	Nam
Strongly agree	12	28	10	2
Agree	11	39	18	12
Neither agree nor disagree	1	11	7	5
Disagree	24	13	25	40
Strongly disagree	51	5	32	39
Haven't heard enough about it/Don't know	1	4	8	3

Which of the following do you think the government of LMZN should do?	Les	Moz	Zim	Nam
Let anyone into this country who wants to enter	61	12	16	14
Let people into this country as long as there are jobs available	23	61	30	18
Place strict limits on the number of foreigners who can enter this country	12	23	48	58
Prohibit people entering into this country from other countries	3	2	4	9
Don't know (DO NOT READ)	1	2	3	1

People in all the countries in Southern Africa should be able to move freely between those countries (PROBE)?	Les	Moz	Zim	Nam
Strongly agree	49	23	28	15
Agree	21	39	27	23
Neither agree nor disagree	1	15	10	10
Disagree	14	11	18	25
Strongly disagree	14	6	12	26
Don't know (DO NOT READ)	1	6	4	1

Apart from calling yourself a citizen of LMZN what group would you consider yourself as belonging to first and foremost?	Les	Moz	Zim	Nam
No group	4	3	21	–
Christian	37	–	12	4
Farmer	14	–	–	0
Traditionalist	5	–	–	0
Soccer player/sports	8	–	–	1
Ethnic/linguistic group	0	97	40	73
Racial group	0	0	6	20

Note: The term "group" in the Mozambican version of the survey was mistakenly translated as "language group" but was not discovered until after the surveys were in the field. The preponderance of ethnic/linguistic responses relative to the other countries can be attributed, in large part, to this translation error.

Survey results in Lesotho, Mozambique, Zimbabwe and Namibia

Being a [response to the previous question] is a very important part of how I see myself	Les	Moz	Zim	Nam
Strongly agree	76	45	57	59
Agree	15	44	31	36
Neither agree nor disagree	1	4	5	2
Disagree	6	4	3	3
Strongly disagree	1	1	2	0
Don't know (DO NOT READ)	1	1	2	1

It makes me proud to be a [response to same question]	Les	Moz	Zim	Nam
Strongly agree	77	46	57	59
Agree	15	43	31	34
Neither agree nor disagree	1	5	4	2
Disagree	7	4	4	4
Strongly disagree	1	1	1	1
Don't know (DO NOT READ)	1	1	2	2

The government of LMZN does not represent the interests and ideals of people like me	Les	Moz	Zim	Nam
Strongly agree	27	5	11	21
Agree	17	18	24	29
Neither agree nor disagree	2	21	14	11
Disagree	29	35	30	26
Strongly disagree	15	12	16	11
Don't know (DO NOT READ)	10	9	5	3

How is the present situation of people who call themselves [response to earlier question] compared to that of other groups in LMZN?	Les	Moz	Zim	Nam
Much better	25	11	13	12
Better	37	32	25	22
About the same	10	40	42	36
Worse	19	9	11	20
Much worse	5	2	4	6
Don't know (DO NOT READ)	4	6	5	4

It makes me feel very proud to be called a citizen of LMZN	Les	Moz	Zim	Nam
Strongly agree	81	58	61	61
Agree	14	40	34	35
Neither agree nor disagree	1	1	2	1
Disagree	3	2	3	2
Strongly disagree	1	—	—	—
Don't know (DO NOT READ)	—	—	—	—

Being a citizen of LMZN is a very important part of how I see myself	Les	Moz	Zim	Nam
Strongly agree	79	47	52	53
Agree	13	45	40	42
Neither agree nor disagree	1	6	3	1
Disagree	5	3	3	1
Strongly disagree	2	0	1	–
Don't know (DO NOT READ)	–	–	1	1

I feel equally strong ties to people who live in other countries in Southern Africa, as I do to other citizens of LMZN	Les	Moz	Zim	Nam
Strongly agree	44	13	21	23
Agree	24	39	38	34
Neither agree nor disagree	1	25	17	15
Disagree	20	13	17	19
Strongly disagree	9	1	3	4
Don't know (DO NOT READ)	2	10	5	5

We would like to know whether you disapprove or approve of the way that the national government has performed its job over the past year. Do you:	Les	Moz	Zim	Nam
Strongly disapprove	27	8	9	9
Disapprove	17	49	19	22
Approve	33	21	50	51
Strongly approve	12	4	12	16
Don't know (DO NOT READ)	10	17	10	3

About how much of the time do you think you can trust the national government to do what is right?	Les	Moz	Zim	Nam
Just about always	21	17	11	15
Most of the time	12	17	36	36
Only some of the time	40	48	34	37
Never	23	8	8	6
Don't know (DO NOT READ)	4	9	9	5

On the whole, are you dissatisfied or satisfied with the way democracy works in LMZN? Are you:	Les	Moz	Zim	Nam
Very dissatisfied	32	8	10	8
Dissatisfied	24	20	17	18
Satisfied	27	45	44	49
Very satisfied	13	7	10	19
LMZN is not a democracy (DO NOT READ)	1	4	4	3
Don't know (DO NOT READ)	4	16	15	2

Survey results in Lesotho, Mozambique, Zimbabwe and Namibia

Do you agree or disagree that traditional leaders should have effective powers (rather than advisory) at all levels of government (PROBE)?	Les	Moz	Zim	Nam
Strongly agree	27	22	37	33
Agree	17	32	32	33
Neither agree nor disagree	3	12	8	3
Disagree	27	13	8	16
Strongly disagree	24	9	6	11
Don't know (DO NOT READ)	2	12	1	4

For each of the following, please tell me whether you have this, have applied for it, or do not have it

LMZN passport?	Les	Moz	Zim	Nam
Have	87	29	30	37
Applied for	1	4	8	11
Do not have	11	66	61	51

South African travel work/study permit?	Les	Moz	Zim	Nam
Have	9	13	5	3
Applied for	0	4	6	3
Do not have	91	83	89	95

South African entry visa (holiday/business)?	Les	Moz	Zim	Nam
Have	6	9	6	3
Applied for	0	3	7	5
Do not have	94	87	87	95

South Africa permanent residence permit?	Les	Moz	Zim	Nam
Have	2	2	2	1
Applied for	–	1	3	2
Do not have	97	98	95	97

Passport from some other country in Southern Africa?	Les	Moz	Zim	Nam
Have	1	2	3	1
Applied for	0	1	3	2
Do not have	99	98	94	97

How often do you listen to news on the radio?	Les	Moz	Zim	Nam
One or more times a day	39	23	52	59
Several times a week	24	41	21	22
Once a week	11	12	6	6
Less than once a week	10	10	10	5
Never	15	14	10	7
Don't know (DO NOT READ)	–	2	–	1

How often do you read newspapers?	Les	Moz	Zim	Nam
One or more times a day	5	5	16	19
Several times a week	6	17	20	21
Once a week	8	15	11	17
Less than once a week	20	14	22	13
Never	60	47	30	30
Don't know (DO NOT READ)	1	2	–	1

How often do you watch news programmes on television?	Les	Moz	Zim	Nam
One or more times a day	10	7	27	40
Several times a week	8	15	16	18
Once a week	4	5	5	6
Less than once a week	17	7	12	6
Never	61	65	39	29
Don't know (DO NOT READ)	1	1	1	1

What about your present marital status? Are you:	Les	Moz	Zim	Nam
Married	63	30	64	46
Co-habitating/living together	1	24	2	6
Separated	3	3	2	2
Divorced	1	1	3	2
Abandoned	1	1	1	—
Widowed	9	5	3	5
Unmarried	22	36	25	40

Survey results in Lesotho, Mozambique, Zimbabwe and Namibia

What is your status in this household? Are you:	Les	Moz	Zim	Nam
Head of household	47	40	34	36
Spouse (husband/wife) of head of household	26	17	26	24
Child of head of household	21	32	20	21
Parent of head of household	–	3	1	1
Brother/sister of head of household	2	3	2	10
Grandparent of head of household/elder	–	2	–	–
Other family member of head of household	–	1	2	4
Visitor	1	1	2	–
Lodger	1	1	7	1
Other	1	1	4	3

How many years of formal education have you completed?	Les	Moz	Zim	Nam
Minimum	0	0	0	0
Maximum	18	20	20	23
Mean	7	6	9	9

What is your highest educational qualification?	Les	Moz	Zim	Nam
No schooling	8	15	9	7
Some primary school	36	27	18	15
Primary school completed	19	14	19	6
Some high school	26	31	40	39
High school completed	8	8	9	21
Some university	–	3	–	3
University completed	–	1	1	5
Postgraduate	–	–	1	1
Other post-secondary qualification other than university	–	1	4	3

How would you describe your present work situation? (DO NOT READ OUT OPTIONS)	Les	Moz	Zim	Nam
Unemployed (not looking for work)	8	7	29	12
Unemployed (looking for work)	32	20	22	22
Housewife (not looking for work)	9	13	12	5
Housewife (looking for work)	11	10	4	4
Student/scholar	8	17	3	11
Pensioner	1	1	2	6
Total unemployed	69	68	72	59
Self-employed formal sector (part time)	2	2	1	–
Self-employed formal sector (full time)	5	5	2	2
Self-employed informal sector (part time)	4	2	2	2
Self-employed informal sector (full time)	4	5	2	3
Work in informal sector for others (looking for formal work)	1	1	1	1
Work in informal sector for others (not looking for formal work)	–	1	1	1
Employed (part time)	1	3	3	5
Employed (full time)	14	9	15	26
National service	–	5	2	1
Other	1	–	0	–
Total employed	31	33	29	41

Purely for statistical purposes, we would like to know the total income of your household, counting all wages, salaries, pensions and other incomes that come in. Could you please give us the amount of money you receive and the number of times per year you receive it (before taxes and other deductions)

Total annual household income (in Rand)	Les	Moz	Zim	Nam
Minimum	0	8	15	0
Maximum	60 000	132 000	88 000	600 000
Mean	5 705	3 349	3 550	27 327

When it comes to making important decisions about financial matters, who is the key decision-maker in your family?	Les	Moz	Zim	Nam
Myself	53	43	50	43
My spouse	25	18	25	20
My parents	19	28	17	19
Other family members	3	9	2	14
Others, non-family	–	–	7	4
Don't know (DO NOT READ)	0	–	0	1

Survey results in Lesotho, Mozambique, Zimbabwe and Namibia

Which of the following best describes your present housing situation? Do you:	Les	Moz	Zim	Nam
Own this dwelling (Formal/traditional)	80	45	59	57
Own this dwelling (Temporary/informal/shack)	2	9	3	5
Rent/lease this dwelling from other people or companies	15	2	9	6
Rent/lease this dwelling from the government or town council	–	9	3	6
Receive this dwelling as part of your job (eg live on farm, domestic with room)	–	2	5	4
Owner-built shack	–	4	–	5
Live with your family	2	24	15	14
Live with others	–	2	5	4
Illegally occupy this dwelling	0	1	0	0
Homeless	0	0	–	0

How many rooms are there in this dwelling in total?	Les	Moz	Zim	Nam
Minimum	1	1	1	1
Maximum	9	15	30	30
Mean	3	4	4	5

How many people usually share the main meal at this household?	Les	Moz	Zim	Nam
Minimum	1	1	1	1
Maximum	17	20	42	28
Mean	5	6	6	6

What about the land on which this household is located? Is it:	Les	Moz	Zim	Nam
Owned by head of household/99-year leasehold	28	43	21	44
Communal land/land allocated by chief or land allocation committee	57	21	48	22
Employer's property	4	2	8	5
Land allocated by state	—	27	11	24
Rented from others	12	2	6	5
Occupied without permission of authorities — illegally occupied	0	5	2	1
Owned by council	0	0	4	0
Other	—	1	4	—

What type of toilet does this household use?	Les	Moz	Zim	Nam
Flush	1	20	41	61
Improved or VIP pit, latrine	19	18	13	5
Other or ordinary pit, latrine	49	53	28	9
Bucket toilet/chemical toilet	—	1	1	5
None	31	9	17	21

How do you get your drinking water?	Les	Moz	Zim	Nam
Piped — internal	1	16	25	52
Piped — yard tap	14	16	19	13
Piped — free public tap	57	9	—	19
Piped — paid for public tap	0	8	3	5
Borehole/well	16	36	51	10
Rainwater tank	—	4	1	0
Flowing river/stream	2	11	2	—
Dam/roof catchment	—	1	0	1
Stagnant water	1	—	0	0
Buy water	6	0	0	—
Other	—	1	0	1

INTERVIEWER QUESTIONS

In what type of shelter does the respondent live?	Les	Moz	Zim	Nam
Permanent — non-traditional (formal house)	72	46	57	62
Permanent — traditional hut/rondavel	16	33	33	21
Temporary structure (squatter/shack)	1	6	1	10
Flat in bloc of flats/apartment building	2	2	–	3
Flat in line of flats/townhouse	9	5	–	2
Room in house	–	2	6	2
Room in backyard	–	5	1	1
Room in hostel	0	0	0	0
Room in hotel/residential hotel	0	0	–	0
Other	0	1	1	–

Type of area in which interview conducted?	Les	Moz	Zim	Nam
Urban/city (formal)	11	16	16	12
Suburban/area on edge of town (formal)	14	26	12	16
Township/town	12	—	17	42
Rural township/town/growth centre	41	6	2	8
Rural village (cluster/kraal/communal)	22	42	46	17
Urban non-permanent shack camp	—	9	—	6
Rural non-permanent shack camp	0	2	0	0
Other	0	0	6	0

Survey results in Lesotho, Mozambique, Zimbabwe and Namibia

Respondent's race	Les	Moz	Zim	Nam
African	99	95	99	72
White	–	–	–	7
Coloured	0	4	–	20
Asian	0	–	0	–

Respondent's gender	Les	Moz	Zim	Nam
Male	51	61	56	49
Female	49	39	43	51

How would you rate the respondent's understanding of the questions?	Les	Moz	Zim	Nam
Good	43	40	45	64
Fair	40	47	42	30
Poor	16	13	12	6

How would you compare this respondent to most other respondents with regard to their:

Nervousness/anxiousness?	Les	Moz	Zim	Nam
A great deal less than others	23	17	30	28
Somewhat less than others	10	40	19	25
About the same as others	55	34	37	36
Somewhat more than others	9	8	11	8
Missing	3	1	3	3

Dishonesty/lack of openness?	Les	Moz	Zim	Nam
A great deal less than others	22	10	25	26
Somewhat less than others	10	42	22	17
About the same as others	56	38	38	38
Somewhat more than others	6	9	10	10
Missing	6	1	6	9

What was the respondent's attitude towards the interview?	Les	Moz	Zim	Nam
Angry and hostile	1	4	3	1
Impatient and restless	4	14	10	4
Co-operative, but not particularly interested	19	30	32	21
Friendly and interested	76	51	56	74

Were there any other people immediately present who might be listening during the interview?	Les	Moz	Zim	Nam
No one	53	39	61	52
Spouse	9	9	8	10
Children	10	16	12	13
A few others	24	33	17	22
Small crowd	5	3	1	3

Were there any other people immediately present who prompted the respondent during the interview?	Les	Moz	Zim	Nam
No one	89	83	84	67
Spouse	3	4	4	6
Children	1	4	4	7
A few others	7	8	7	17
Small crowd	1	1	—	2

Appendix C

Aggregate summary of results from surveys of African migrants living in South Africa

The tables below are a summary of the results from the surveys conducted with migrants from other African countries living in South Africa. The surveys were conducted in May–June 1998.

The statistics are presented here to provide readers and researchers with a summary of the aggregate results. Aggregate results, in and of themselves, only provide a superficial presentation of the survey findings, however. The real analytical challenge comes from a deeper cross-sectional analysis of the data as is presented in Chapter 8. Nevertheless, the following tables do provide an overview of the main trends and a record of the questionnaire used.

NOTES

1. A dash (—) signifies a value of greater than 0 and <0.5%;
2. Unless otherwise noted, all figures represent percentages;
3. Columns may not add to 100% due to rounding;
4. Unless otherwise noted, the N value for each table is 501;

Number of interviews completed	501

I would like to start off by asking you some questions about yourself. Please tell me which of the following categories best describes your status in SA.	
Permanent resident of SA	13
Citizen of SA	—
Refugee permit holder	27
Work permit holder	23
Other official documentation	30
Do not have any official documentation	7

Survey results of African migrants living in South Africa

Province of residence	
Gauteng	80
Eastern Cape	0
Free State	0
KwaZulu-Natal	10
Mpumalanga	0
North West Province	–
Northern Cape	0
Northern Province	0
Western Cape	10

Town (or nearest town) of residence	
Cape Town	10
Johannesburg	70
Durban	6
Boksburg	–
Alberton	–
Pietermaritzburg	4
Carlton	10

Gender	
Male	79
Female	21

Area and dwelling of residence	
Metropolitan: formal	64
Metropolitan: backyard	16
Metropolitan: hostel	11
Metropolitan: informal	4
Small urban: formal	3
Small urban: informal	1
Rural: informal	–
Metropolitan: street people	1

Where the respondent is living	
Township	13
Suburb	72
Inner city	12
Informal settlement (non-serviced)	2
Informal settlement (site and serviced)	1
Rural: settlement/village	–
Rural: farm	0

How old you are?	
Minimum	17
Maximum	61
Mean	32
Median	30

Let's think for a moment about the languages that you might use. What language do you speak mostly with your family? DO NOT PROMPT – SINGLE MENTION ONLY	
Afrikaans	1
English	7
Ndebele South Africa	1
Ndebele Zimbabwean	5
Ronga	2
Shangaan	2
Shona	9
Sotho/South Sotho	21
Chewa/Tsonga	5
Chisena/Tswana	1
Zulu	1
Swahili	2
Portuguese	5
French	11
Madingo	8
Tumbuka	3
Yao	1
Tonga	–
Ngoni	–
Wollof	1
Kinyarwanda	1
Yuroba	2
Lingala	1
Bosso	–
Kikuyu	1
Kirundi	–
Swati	1
Creole	–
Igbo	6
Somalian	–
Arabic	1
Chiganda	–
Edo	–
Agbor	–

What country(ies) other than SA are you a citizen of?	
Malawi	11
Zimbabwe	15
Mozambique	12
Lesotho	20
Zaire	4
Nigeria	12
Congo Brazzaville	2
Kenya	2
Senegal	4
Ivory Coast	4
Rwanda	1
Benin	1
Gabon	1
Mali	1
Cameroon	1
Ghana	2
Burkina Faso	1
Swaziland	1
Burundi	1
Sudan	1
Other	3

If you are married, what country is your husband/wife a citizen of? INTERVIEWER: PLEASE SPECIFY IF NOT MARRIED.	
Not married	51
Divorced	1
Widow/widower	1
Malawi	8
Zambia	1
Zimbabwe	6
Mozambique	3
Lesotho	9
Zaire	1
Nigeria	3
Congo Brazzaville	1
South Africa	3
Senegal	1
Ivory Coast	2
Benin	1
Swaziland	1
Cameroon	1
Ghana	1
Other	4

What was the last country you lived in before you came to SA?	
Malawi	10
Zimbabwe	15
Mozambique	15
Botswana	2
Lesotho	20
Zaire	4
Nigeria	7
Congo Brazzaville	3
Swaziland	3
Senegal	3
Ivory Coast	4
Other	20

Where did you stay there (town/city)?	
Town	41
City	50
Village	9

What work were you doing there?	
Employer/manager: more than ten employees	1
Employer/manager: less than ten employers	1
Professional worker	16
Supervisory office work	–
Non-manual office worker	5
Skilled manual worker	23
Miner	–
Unskilled manual worker	1
Farmer (own commercial farm)	–
Farmer (own subsistence farm)	1
Agricultural worker (on the farm)	2
Trader/hawker/vendor	17
Informal sector producer	–
Armed forces/security personnel	1
Student	16
Never had a job	13
Seeking refugee status	1
Holiday	1

Survey results of African migrants living in South Africa

How long have you been in SA (in months)	
Minimum	1
Maximum	312
Mean	45
Median	24

How long have you been in SA (in years)	
1 year	29
2 years	18
3 years	14
4 years	11
5 years	6
>5 years	22

Have you lived in any other province in SA before living in this province?	
Yes	26
No	74

IF YES What town did you live in before you came to this one?	
Johannesburg	17
Durban	13
Cape Town	7
Pretoria	1
Mafikeng/Mmabatho	4
Witbank	6
Motherwell	2
Pietersburg/Seshego	8
Bloemfontein/Mangaung	24
Welkom	6
Botshabelo	1
Ficksburg	2
Bloemfontein/Mangaung	2
Fouriesburg	2
Sebokeng	1
Virginia	1
Ladybrand	1
Wepenaar	2
Malleleketla	1
Phuthaditjhaba	1
Middleburg	1
Note: N = 126.	

IF YES, What province did you live in before you came to this one?	
Gauteng	16
KwaZulu-Natal	13
Western Cape	8
Gauteng/Pretoria	1
North West	5
Mpumalanga	6
Eastern Cape	2
Northern Province	9
Free State	41
Note: N = 128.	

We have spoken to many different people and they have all described themselves in different ways. Some people describe themselves in terms of their language such as English, Shona or Zulu. Other people describe themselves according to their religion such as Methodist or Jewish. Still other people describe themselves in terms of their race, for example Asian or black, and some people describe themselves as working class, middle or upper class. Thinking about yourself, which specific group [in respondent's country of citizenship] besides political parties, do you feel you belong to first and foremost?	
Religion	20
Nationality	9
Race	16
Language/ethnic group	31
Educational	3
Gender	–
Marital status	–
Class	15
Nature	3
Political	1
Sports	–
Don't know	1

271

For the following statement, please tell me whether you agree or disagree. The government of [respondent's country of citizenship] does not represent the interests and ideals of people like you.	
Strongly agree	29
Agree	30
Neither agree nor disagree	14
Disagree	18
Strongly disagree	6
Don't know (DON'T READ)	3

How is the present situation of people who call themselves ... (SEE Q.14) compared to that of other groups in [Respondent's country of citizenship] READ OUT. SINGLE MENTION.	
Much better	11
Better	28
About the same	31
Worse	16
Much worse	9
Don't know (DO NOT READ)	5

Here are some things people often say about the country in which they live. For each of the following, please tell me whether you agree or disagree.	Strongly agree	Agree	Neither agree nor disagree	Disagree	Strongly disagree	Don't know (Do NOT READ)
You are very proud to be called a citizen of [respondent's country of citizenship]	63	31	4	3	–	0
Being a citizen of [respondent's country of citizenship] is a very important part of how you see yourself.	49	32	8	8	2	1
It is important to you that your child is a citizen of [respondent's country of citizenship]	40	24	20	12	2	5
You feel very close to other citizens of [respondent's country of citizenship]	40	44	9	6	1	1

For each of the following statements, please tell me whether you agree or disagree.	Strongly agree	Agree	Neither agree nor disgaree	Disagree	Strongly disagree	Don't know (DO NOT READ)
You feel very close to people who call themselves South African	12	34	21	23	8	1
You think of yourself as a South African	4	10	14	39	33	—
Thinking of yourself as a South African is a very important part of how you see yourself.	3	7	15	43	32	1
You feel closer to people who live in SA than you do to citizens of [respondent's country of citizenship]	5	13	25	38	18	1

Survey results of African migrants living in South Africa

How important do you think it is for there to be borders between countries in Southern Africa?	
Very important	21
Important	33
Not very important	17
Not at all important	28
Don't know (DO NOT READ)	1

19a(ii). How important do you think it is for there to be borders between countries in the world?	
Very important	21
Important	39
Not very important	16
Not at all important	21
Don't know (DO NOT READ)	3

19b(i). What are the reasons for your answer in 19a(i)? [open-ended question categorised into most common responses].	
To prevent crime/for security reasons	30
To preserve people's identity	16
To allow for migration control	11
Borders distinguish one country from another	–
Freedom	10
To enable the nation-state to manage its economy	6
Borders are products of colonisation	6
Relationships	2
To unite people within a particular country	14
They restrict movements of people seeking refugee	1
They divide people	1
National identity	1
Other	2

Now we would like to ask you about your life in [respondent's country of citizenship] before you came to SA. Do you still have a home in [respondent's country of citizenship] to which you can return?	
Yes	93
No	5
Don't know (DO NOT READ)	2

Can you return to your home if you want to?	
Yes	83
No	15
Don't know (DO NOT READ)	3

When you think of the type of area you lived in, in [respondent's country of citizenship], would you say it was urban or rural?	
Urban/city (formal)	73
Rural	27

What was your status in your household? Were you:	
Head of household	33
Spouse (husband/wife) of head of household	8
Child of head of household	47
Parent of head of household	1
Brother/sister of head of household	3
Grandparent of head of household/elder	–
Grandchild of head of household	2
Other family member of head of household	2
Visitor	0
Lodger	2
Other	2

What type of work did you do there? DO NOT READ OPTIONS. ASK FOR MOST RECENT OCCUPATION IF UNEMPLOYED. ASK FOR MOST IMPORTANT, IF MORE THAN ONE. IF RESPONDENT WAS EMPLOYER/MANAGER, ASK HOW MANY EMPLOYEES IN COMPANY.	
Employer/manager of establishment with ten or more employees	1
Employer/manager of establishment with less than ten employees	1
Professional worker/lawyer/accountant/teacher etc	16
Supervisory office worker (supervises others)	–
Non-manual office worker (non-supervisory)	5
Foreman/supervisor	
Skilled manual worker	18
Semi-skilled manual worker	2
Miner	1
Unskilled manual worker	1
Farm (has own commercial farm)	0
Farm (has own subsistence farm)	2
Agricultural worker (works on a farm)	3
Services worker (eg hotels, taxi-driver)	3
Domestic worker	1
Trader, hawker, vendor	18
Informal sector producer	–
Member of armed forces/security personnel	–
Not applicable — student/disabled/etc	20
Never had a job	9

What was your work situation just before you left? Were you …? READ OUT. SINGLE MENTION.	
Employed	38
Unemployed	18
Student/scholar	18
Pensioner	0
Self-employed	24
National service	–
Other	1

IF EMPLOYED: Do you still have a job to return to in [respondent's country of citizenship]? If yes please specify.	
Yes	23
No	61
Don't know (DO NOT READ)	16
Note: N = 190.	

Thinking back to before you came here. How much information would you say you had about SA? READ OUT. SINGLE MENTION.	
A great deal	47
Some	34
Not very much	12
None at all	8
Don't know (DO NOT READ)	0

Where would you say you received most of your information about SA?	
I didn't know anything about SA	–
I had previous experiences in SA	10
From meeting South Africans in my own country	6
Hear from others who have been to SA	21
Hear from others about SA	32
Televisions	4
Newspapers	6
Magazines	2
Radio	4
Media (combination of all types)	10
Learning and other institutions	5
Other	–

Would you say that you had a favourable or unfavourable impression of SA? PROBE FOR STRENGTH OF OPINION.	
Very favourable	17
Favourable	55
Neither favourable nor unfavourable	14
Unfavourable	10
Very unfavourable	1
Don't know (DO NOT READ)	3

Survey results of African migrants living in South Africa

Have you ever been to SA before this current trip?	
Yes	46
No	55

Did either of your parents ever work in SA?	
Yes	30
No	69
Don't know	1

Have any of your grandparents ever worked in SA?	
Yes	25
No	66
Don't know	9

From what you know or have heard, where do most people from [respondent's country of citizenship] go to in SA? (In order of importance). PROBE FOR SPECIFIC CITIES OR REGIONS.	
Gauteng/Johannesburg	80
Western Cape/Cape Town	5
KwaZulu-Natal/Durban	2
Northern Province	–
Mpumalanga	–
Free State	1
Don't know	12

How difficult was it to get to SA?	
Very difficult	14
Difficult	13
Not very difficult	25
Not difficult at all	48
Don't know (DO NOT READ)	–

What were the worst problems you experienced in getting to SA? DO NOT PROMPT. ACCEPT UP TO THREE ANSWERS. [First answer]	
None	33
Getting the necessary documents	33
Getting money for the trip	11
Transportation (careless driving, overload, etc)	6
Did not like crossing so many borders	2
Security checks/harassment by police officers	10
Criminals	3
Language	1
Accommodation	1
Parents did not approve of my visit to SA	1
Jobs	1
Racism	1
Paying duties	

Were you able to obtain the necessary travel documents before you came to SA?	
Yes	81
No	19
Don't know (DO NOT READ)	–

How did you get to SA on your most recent trip? DO NOT PROMPT. MULTIPLE MENTION POSSIBLE.	First mention*	Second mention**	Third mention***
Foot	4	3	6
Bus	18	25	14
Plane	35	8	7
Car	10	19	18
Horse or donkey	0	1	1
Train	9	11	8
Combi or taxi	22	27	39
Ship	2	3	1
Other	1	4	7

*Notes: *N = 497. **N = 226. ***N = 171.*

If you could *not* get travel documents, did you know how to get here without being caught by the police?	
Yes	17
No	56
Don't know (DO NOT READ)	9
NOT APPLICABLE	18
Note: N = 95.	

Did you have a place to stay in SA before you left?	
Yes	70
No	30
Don't know (DO NOT READ)	–

How many of your extended family members were in SA before you left home? (exact number or best estimate)	
Minimum	0
Maximum	50
Mean	3
Median	0

How many of your friends were in SA before you left home? (Exact number or best estimate)	
Minimum	0
Maximum	99
Mean	4
Median	1

How many people from your community in [respondent's country of citizenship] were in SA before you left home? READ OUT. SINGLE MENTION.	
All	2
Greater than 50%	1
Between 25% and 50%	8
Less than 25%	34
None	18
Don't know (DO NOT READ)	38

How many family members came with you on your most recent trip?	
Minimum	0
Maximum	9
Mean	–
Median	0

How many other people came with you on your most recent trip?	
Minimum	0
Maximum	20
Mean	1
Median	0

How many other family members have come to live with you since you first came to SA?	
Minimum	0
Maximum	10
Mean	–
Median	0

How many other people have come to live with you since you first came to SA?	
Minimum	0
Maximum	50
Mean	1
Median	0

How many people from your immediate family now live or work in SA? (Exact number or best estimate)	
Minimum	0
Maximum	80
Mean	2
Median	0

What about now? How many friends from your home country do you have in SA? (Not family)	
Minimum	0
Maximum	99
Mean	8
Median	4

How many family members do you live with at present?	
Minimum	0
Maximum	20
Mean	1
Median	0

Survey results of African migrants living in South Africa

What was the main reason you came to SA?	First mention*	Second mention**	Third mention***
Work	14	6	2
Look for work	21	8	4
Cost of living	–	–	0
Availability of land	0	0	0
Availability of decent water	0	0	0
Availability of decent food	0	0	1
Availability of decent houses	–	1	1
Availability of decent jobs	6	10	6
Treatment by employers	0	1	1
Opportunities for trade/buying and selling of goods	8	7	7
School/study	15	16	9
Overall living conditions	7	18	35
Safety of myself and family	9	4	2
Lower crime	0	0	0
More peace	1	3	2
Availability of decent schools	1	1	5
Availability of decent health care	–	0	0
A decent place to raise your family	–	1	7
Prevalence of disease	0	0	0
Prevalence of HIV/AIDS	0	0	0
More freedom	–	5	7
More democracy	1	3	6
Availability of decent shopping	1	2	2
Visit family/friends	2	7	8
Join family/friends	4	4	2
To seek political asylum	3	–	0
To seek refugee status	6	1	0
Other	–	3	3

Notes: *N = 493. **N = 259. ***N = 124.

Did your family tend to encourage or discourage you from coming to SA? PROBE FOR STRENGTH OF OPINION	
Strongly encourage	18
Encourage	29
Neither encourage nor discourage	29
Discourage	11
Strongly discourage	3
My family did not know	9
Don't know (DO NOT READ)	1

Who made the final decision as to whether you should come to SA?	
My spouse	4
My parents	13
Myself	78
Other family members	4
Others, non-family (eg friends)	1
Don't know (DO NOT READ)	0

Before you left, how much did you know about the following statements? ASK FOR EACH OF THE FOLLOWING STATEMENTS:		None	Some	A great deal	Don't know (DO NOT READ)
a.	A place to go where there were people who could take care of you when you first arrived	36	27	36	1
b.	How to get travel documents	11	33	56	–
c	The safest way to get here	12	35	49	4
d	The cheapest way to get here	25	28	41	6
e	Where you could get a job	65	18	9	7

How often do you return home?	
More than once a month	2
Once a month	4
Once every few months	22
Once or twice a year	21
Less than once or twice a year	8
I have been just once	6
I have not been home yet, but would like to in the future	28
Never – I cannot return home	5
Never – I have no desire to return home	3
Don't know (DO NOT READ)	1

How would you describe your present work situation here in SA? PLEASE PROBE.	
Unemployed (not looking for work)	2
Unemployed (looking for work)	11
Housewife (not looking for work)	–
Housewife (looking for work)	0
Student/scholar	8
Pensioner	0
Self-employed formal sector (part-time)	–
Self-employed formal sector (full-time)	0
Self-employed informal sector (part-time)	2
Self-employed informal sector (full-time)	30
Work in informal sector for other (looking for permanent work)	–
Work in informal sector for other (not looking for permanent work)	1
Employed (part-time)	6
Employed (full-time)	38
National service	1
Other	–

Now we would like to ask you some questions about your life here in SA. Has your experience in SA been positive or negative? PROBE FOR STRENGTH OF OPINION.	
Very positive	10
Positive	54
Neither positive nor negative (in between)	16
Negative	14
Very negative	6
Don't know (DO NOT READ)	1

If currently employed: How long have you been employed (in months)?	
Minimum	1
Maximum	312
Mean	45
Median	24

Survey results of African migrants living in South Africa

Irrespective of whether you are now working in SA, did you have a job arranged before you came to SA?	
Yes, I had a job arranged	15
No, I did not have a job arranged	81
Came to study (not applicable)	4
Don't know (DO NOT READ)	–

What is your present occupation here in SA? LAST JOBS IN SA IF CURRENTLY UNEMPLOYED. IF RESPONDENT IS EMPLOYER/MANAGER, ASK HOW MANY EMPLOYEES ARE IN ESTABLISHMENT. (More than one answer possible)	
Employer/manager of establishment with ten or more employees	1
Employer/manager of establishment with less than ten employees	—
Professional worker/lawyer/accountant/teacher etc	12
Supervisory office worker (supervises others)	1
Non-manual office worker (non-supervisory)	4
Foreman/supervisor	0
Skilled manual worker	15
Semi-skilled manual worker	4
Miner	7
Unskilled manual worker	7
Farmer (has own commercial farm)	0
Farmer (has own subsistence farm)	0
Agricultural worker (works on a farm)	–
Trader, hawker, vendor	30
Informal sector producer	0
Member of armed forces/security personnel	3
Student	8
Disabled	0
Never had a job in SA	10
Other	0

Which of these jobs is your important source of income?	
Employer/manager of establishment with ten or more employees	1
Employer/manager of establishment with less than ten employees	1
Professional worker/lawyer/accountant/teacher etc	12
Supervisory office worker (supervises others)	–
Non-manual office worker (non-supervisory)	4
Foreman/supervisor	0
Skilled manual worker	15
Semi-skilled manual worker	3
Miner	6
Unskilled manual worker	6
Farmer (has own commercial farm)	-
Farmer (has own subsistence farm)	0
Agricultural worker (works on a farm)	0
Trader, hawker, vendor	0
Informal sector producer	30
Member of armed forces/security personnel	3
Student	7
Disabled	0
Never had a job in SA	7
Other (not applicable)	6

Note: N = 495.

Which of these jobs is your second most important source of income?	
Employer/manager of establishment with ten or more employees	1
Employer/manager of establishment with less than ten employees	0
Professional worker/lawyer/accountant/teacher etc.	9
Supervisory office worker (supervises others)	0
Non-manual office worker (non-supervisory)	6
Foreman/supervisor	0
Skilled manual worker	21
Semi-skilled manual worker	4
Miner	0
Unskilled manual worker	9
Farmer (has own commercial farm)	0
Farmer (has own subsistence farm)	0
Agricultural worker (works on a farm)	0
Trader, hawker, vendor	38
Informal sector producer	0
Member of armed forces/security personnel	1
Student	8
Disabled	0
Never had a job in SA	2

Note: N = 90.

Have you or a member of your family used:	Yes	No
Schools in SA?	34	66
A hospital or clinic in SA?	57	43

ASK FOR EACH STATEMENT LISTED BELOW. To what extent are:	Always	To a large extent	To some extent	Hardly at all	Never	Don't know
a. People from [respondent's country of citizenship] treated unfairly by South African people	13	16	46	16	3	6
b. People from [respondent's country of citizenship] treated unfairly by the South African government	5	13	38	20	16	9
c. You personally, as a [respondent's country of citizenship], treated unfairly by South Africans	9	14	38	17	22	–
d. You personally, as a [respondent's country of citizenship] treated unfairly by the South African government?	4	9	31	19	36	2

Survey results of African migrants living in South Africa

Since you have been in SA, have you received good or bad treatment from ... ASK FOR EACH GROUP. LISTED BELOW. PROBE FOR STRENGTH OF OPINION.	Very good	Good	Neither good nor bad	Bad	Very bad	Not applic.	Don't know (DO NOT READ)
a. Other people from ... [respondent's country of citizenship]	29	50	14	3	2	1	1
b. Other people from Southern African countries	9	47	24	6	5	8	1
c. White South Africans	7	34	33	13	4	6	3
d. Black South Africans	5	30	28	22	12	2	1
e. Employers	5	20	18	12	2	41	3
f. Landowners/landlords	7	37	20	9	5	20	2
g. Government officials, eg customs and immigration officials	5	28	32	20	9	4	2
h. Police officers	3	20	35	19	14	8	1

Since being in SA, have you been? ASK FOR EACH STATEMENT LISTED BELOW.	Yes	No
a. Assaulted	23	77
b. Robbed	42	58
c. Raped	1	99
d. Arrested	16	84
e. Deported/sent back to your own country	5	95
f. Harassed	34	66

Do you think that South Africans have a positive or negative view of people from [respondent's country of citizenship] who come to stay or work in this country? PROBE FOR STRENGTH OF OPINION	
Very positive	1
Positive	18
Neither positive nor negative	19
Negative	35
Very negative	23
Don't know (DO NOT READ)	3

If you went back to [respondent's country of citizenship] now, do you think that each of the following things would be better in [respondent's country of citizenship], or would they be better in SA, or would there not be much of a difference? ASK FOR EACH STATEMENT LISTED BELOW.	Much better in your home country	Better in your home country	About the same	Better in SA	Much better in SA	Don't know (DO NOT READ)
a. Cost of living	14	12	10	35	26	2
b. Availability of land	44	31	8	5	6	7
c. Availability of decent water	5	4	29	33	27	2
d. Availability of decent food	10	7	25	33	23	2
e. Availability of decent houses	8	15	17	31	26	4
f. Availability of decent jobs	4	8	15	33	32	8
g. Good treatment by employers	11	14	29	16	6	25
h. Opportunities for trade/buying and selling of goods	10	10	10	24	41	5
i. Overall living conditions	17	12	8	36	25	2
j. Safety of myself and family	53	19	14	8	5	1
k. Low level of crime	61	25	10	2	2	–
l. High level of peace	39	21	20	8	6	6
m. Availability of decent schools	7	9	13	34	30	7
n. Availability of decent health care	2	3	6	36	51	2
o. A decent place to raise your family	44	18	12	14	7	4
p. Low level/amount of disease	6	10	25	21	20	17
q. Low level/amount of HIV/AIDS	23	15	28	3	2	29
r. High level of freedom	31	13	12	19	23	2
s. High level of democracy	17	6	8	24	40	4
t. Availability of decent shopping	3	2	6	28	59	1

Would you say that overall conditions in SA are better or worse than what you expected to find when you came to SA, or are they about the same? PROBE FOR STRENGTH OF OPINION.	
Much better	8
Better	38
About the same	23
Worse	23
Much worse	5
Don't know (DO NOT READ)	3

Do you expect overall conditions in SA to be better or worse in twelve months time than they are now, or about the same? PROBE FOR STRENGTH OF OPINION.	
Much better	6
Better	34
About the same	20
Worse	19
Much worse	6
Don't know (DO NOT READ)	15

Survey results of African migrants living in South Africa

Would you say that the overall conditions in SA are better or worse than those in [respondent's country of citizenship], or are they about the same? PROBE FOR STRENGTH OF OPINION.	
Much better	14
Better	59
About the same	12
Worse	12
Much worse	1
Don't know (DO NOT READ)	3

Would you say that your overall personal conditions to be better or worse than those within your occupation, or about the same? PROBE FOR STRENGTH OF OPINION.	
Much better	4
Better	28
About the same	37
Worse	7
Much worse	2
Don't know (DO NOT READ)	22

At the moment, are you satisfied or dissatisfied with overall conditions in SA? PROBE FOR STRENGTH OF OPINION.	
Very satisfied	5
Satisfied	49
Neither satisfied nor dissatisfied	21
Dissatisfied	20
Very dissatisfied	4
Don't know (DO NOT READ)	1

Would you say that your overall personal conditions are better or worse than those of people back in [respondent's country of citizenship], or are they about the same?	
Much better	10
Better	55
About the same	14
Worse	10
Much worse	4
Don't know (DO NOT READ)	7

Would you say that your overall personal conditions are better or worse now than what you expected them to be when you came to SA, or are they about the same? PROBE FOR STRENGTH OF OPINION.	
Much better	6
Better	45
About the same	22
Worse	19
Much worse	5
Don't know (DO NOT READ)	2

At the moment, are you satisfied or dissatisfied with your overall personal conditions? READ OUT – SINGLE MENTION	
Very satisfied	66
Satisfied	52
Neither satisfied nor dissatisfied	17
Dissatisfied	18
Very dissatisfied	7
Don't know (DO NOT READ)	0

Do you expect your personal conditions to be better or worse in twelve months than they are now, or about the same? PROBE FOR STRENGTH OF OPINION.	
Much better	10
Better	51
About the same	17
Worse	6
Much worse	2
Don't know (DO NOT READ)	15

In general, would you say that your life today is better, about the same, or worse than it was in [respondent's country of citizenship]? PROBE FOR STRENGTH OF OPINION.	
Much worse	6
Worse	15
About the same	17
Better	50
Much better	11
Don't know (DO NOT READ)	2

Many people from [respondent's country of citizenship] are coming to SA to stay or work. Has this had a positive impact, a negative impact, or no impact at all, on ...? ASK FOR EACH GROUP LISTED BELOW. IF NO, CIRCLE CODE 3. IF YES, PROBE FOR STRENGTH OF IMPACT.	Very positive	Positive	No impact	Negative	Very negative	Don't know (DO NOT READ)
Your family in [respondent's country of citizenship]	13	38	23	14	2	10
Your community in [respondent's country of citizenship]	5	30	29	16	1	19
[Respondent's country of citizenship]	4	19	22	24	5	25

What is it particularly about this place, compared to the rest of the country, that makes you want to stay here/go there? ACCEPT UP TO THREE REASONS. (In order of importance)	First mention*	Second mention**	Third mention***
Land	–	0	0
Water	0	0	0
Food	0	1	1
Houses	12	6	9
Jobs	10	7	9
Treatment by employers	–	2	2
Trade	7	8	5
Overall living conditions	21	30	27
Safety of myself and family	11	9	10
Crime	1	1	1
Peace	15	11	6
Education, schools	2	2	3
Health care	0	1	1
Place to raise your family	–	–	1
Diseases	0	0	0
HIV/AIDS	0	0	0
Freedom	1	1	3
Democracy	1	0	0
Shopping	1	1	4
Relations	6	8	7
Other	7	8	9
Not applicable	4	4	6
Notes: *N = 486. **N = 365. ***N = 212.			

Ultimately, what are the best things about being in SA? (DO NOT READ OPTIONS). ACCEPT UP TO THREE REASONS. (In order of importance)	First mention*	Second mention**	Third mention***
Land	0	0	0
Water	0	–	0
Food	2	4	3
Houses	1	5	2
Jobs	21	8	8
Treatment by employers	2	1	1
Trade	9	6	7
Overall living conditions	32	36	44
Safety of myself and family	3	1	0
Crime	–	1	0
Peace	1	2	0
Education, schools	9	9	0
Health care	2	2	0
Place to raise your family	–	–	0
Diseases	0	–	5
HIV/AIDS	0	–	0
Freedom	5	7	10
Democracy	2	4	3
Shopping	2	8	10
Exposure	1	1	1
Relations	1	2	2
Other	5	3	4

Notes: *N = 490. **N = 359. ***N = 208.

What are the worst things about being in SA? (DO NOT READ OPTIONS). ACCEPT UP TO THREE REASONS. (In order of importance)	First mention*	Second mention**	Third mention***
Land	0	0	1
Water	0	0	0
Food	0	–	1
Houses	1	5	5
Jobs	5	8	10
Treatment by employers	3	4	4
Trade	–	1	1
Overall living conditions	8	10	14
Safety of myself and family	3	7	6
Crime (including corruption)	57	27	21
Peace	–	1	1
Education, schools	1	2	1
Health care	0	1	0
Place to raise your family	0	-	0
Diseases	0	0	1
HIV/AIDS	0	-	2
Freedom	4	5	9
Democracy	2	5	6
Shopping	0	1	1
Isolation from loved ones	5	5	6
Xenophobia	8	16	13
None	2	–	1
Don't Know	1	1	1
Other	0	1	1

Notes: *N = 493. **N = 368. ***N = 222.

How long do you want to stay in SA? READ OUT. SINGLE MENTION	
A few days	1
A few weeks	2
One month	1
A few months	8
Half a year, six months	–
Six months to a year	5
A few years	37
Indefinitely	15
Permanently	6
I want to leave as soon as possible	9
Don't know (DO NOT READ)	16

How often would you want to return to [respondent's country of citizenship] READ OUT. SINGLE MENTION	
Very frequently	9
Frequently	33
Occasionally	23
A few times	4
Once or twice	19
Never	5
Don't know (DO NOT READ)	6

Survey results of African migrants living in South Africa

For each of the following, please tell me whether you have this, have applied for it, or do not have it?	Have	Applied for	Do not have
a. [Respondent's country of citizenship] passport	86	1	13
b. South African travel/work/ study permit	35	3	61
c. South African entry visa (holiday/business)	30	-	69
d. South African permanent residence permit	14	6	80
e. South African temporary residence permit	16	1	83
f. Refugee status	28	2	70
g. Passport from some other country in Southern Africa	3	1	96
h. Passport from SA	2	1	97
i. Visa to another country	4	1	95

Currently, there is a good deal of discussion over how governments should deal with people who cross from one country to another. Please tell me whether you agree or disagree with the following statements, or whether you have not yet heard enough about it to have an opinion? The South African government should offer people from other African countries who are in SA: PROBE FOR STRENGTH OF OPINION. ASK FOR EACH STATEMENT LISTED BELOW	Strongly agree	Agree	Neither agree nor disagree	Disagree	Strongly disagree	Haven't heard enough about it	Don't know (DO NOT READ)
The same chance at a job as South Africans	52	26	5	13	2	–	1
The same access to medical service as South Africans	61	35	1	3	–	0	–
The same access to a house as South Africans	49	30	8	11	1	0	1
The same access to education as South Africans	55	38	2	3	1	–	1
The right to vote in South African elections	12	12	13	31	25	2	48
The right to become a permanent resident of South Africa	44	38	7	5	2	3	2
The right to become a citizen of South Africa	33	30	13	14	6	1	3
The South African government should offer amnesty to all foreigners now living illegally inside the country	33	23	15	16	7	2	4

Do you want to become a permanent resident of SA?	
Yes	53
No	38
Don't know (DO NOT READ)	9

Do you want to become a citizen of SA?	
Yes	24
No	66
Don't know (DO NOT READ)	9

78c. Do you want to live in when you retire?	
Yes	18
No	68
Don't know (DO NOT READ)	14

Do you want to be buried in SA?	
Yes	9
No	80
Don't know (DO NOT READ)	11

Would you want your children to think of themselves as South African citizens?	
Yes	17
No	6
Don't know (DO NOT READ)	20

How about people from other countries coming to SA? Which one of the following do you think the South African government should do? SINGLE MENTION.	
Let anyone in who wants to enter	25
Let people in as long as there are jobs available	42
Place strict limits on the number of foreigners who can enter SA	28
Prohibit people from entering from other countries	1
Don't know (DO NOT READ)	5

How about people from other countries who are presently living in SA? Who do you think the government should send back to their own countries? READ OUT. SINGLE MENTION.	
All of these people	2
Only those who are not contributing to the economy	13
Only those who are here without the permission of the South African government	19
The government should not send back any people to their own countries	10
Only those who have committed crimes	53
Don't know (DO NOT READ)	2

With regard to letting people into SA and returning to their own country, should the government give any special preferences to:	Yes	No	Don't know (DO NOT READ)
People from neighbouring countries in southern Africa	77	19	5
People from elsewhere in Africa	67	24	10
People from Europe or North America	40	45	15
Refugees escaping war and famine in other countries	91	7	2
Those with skills needed by SA	90	8	2
Those with contracts to work on the mines	87	9	4
People marrying South Africans	85	10	5
People from other parts of the world	46	35	18
Descendants of South Africans	91	6	3

Survey results of African migrants living in South Africa

Here is one more statement. Please state whether you agree or disagree with it. People in all the countries in southern Africa should be able to more freely between those countries. PROBE FOR STRENGTH OF OPINION.	
Strongly agree	63
Agree	24
Neither agree nor disagree	3
Disagree	5
Strongly disagree	6
Don't know (DO NOT READ)	–

How many years of formal education have you completed?	
Minimum	1
Maximum	24
Mean	11
Median	12

What is your highest educational qualification?	
No schooling	1
Some primary schooling	15
Primary school completed	11
Some secondary schooling	17
Secondary school completed	18
Some tertiary/non-university	2
Tertiary/non-university completed	1
Some tertiary/university	16
University completed	13
Postgraduate	3
Other	4

Do you know what the South African equivalent is?	
No schooling	1
Some primary school completed	16
Primary school completed	11
Some secondary schooling	17
Secondary school completed	17
Some tertiary/university	16
University completed	13
Postgraduate	4
Some tertiary/non-university	2
Tertiary/non-university completed	1
Other	3

How many rooms are there in the dwelling that you live, in total?	
Minimum	0
Maximum	17
Mean	2
Median	2

How many people who are family members usually sleep in your household/dwelling?	
Minimum	0
Maximum	10
Mean	1
Median	0

How many other people usually sleep in your household/dwelling?	
Minimum	0
Maximum	17
Mean	2
Median	1

What is the total number of people sleeping in your household/dwelling?	
Minimum	0
Maximum	17
Mean	4
Median	3

What about your marital status? Are you:	
Married	45
Cohabiting/living together	4
Separated	2
Divorced	2
Abandoned	–
Widowed	2
Unmarried	46

How many children do you have?	
Minimum	0
Maximum	13
Mean	1
Median	1

How many are *totally* dependent on the head of household?	
Minimum	0
Maximum	15
Mean	2
Median	1

How many people are *partially* dependent on the head of household?	
Minimum	0
Maximum	30
Mean	2
Median	0

Purely for statistical purposes, we would like to know the total MONTHLY income of your household, in SA, counting all wages, salaries, pensions and other incomes that come in. You need only give me the number of the group in which your income falls. If income is irregular, please provide an average for six months.	
A. No income	15
B. R1–R99	2
C. R100–R199	2
D. R200–R499	3
E. R500–R699	6
F. R700–R899	6
G. R900–R999	5
H. R1 000–R1 299	9
I. R1 300–R1 499	10
J. R1 500–R1 799	7
K. R1 800–R1 999	5
L. R2 000–R2 999	8
M. R3 000–R3 999	4
N. R4 000–R4 999	2
O. R5 000–R5 999	1
P. R6 000–R6 999	1
Q. R7 000–R7 999	1
R. R8 000–R8 999	–
S. R9 000–R9 999	–
T. R10 000+	1
Don't know	4
Refused	7

Is this income regular or irregular?	
Regular	51
Irregular	36
Student/unemployed (not applicable)	13

Survey results of African migrants living in South Africa

Approximately how much money do you send back to [respondent's country of citizenship] ENTER AMOUNT PER MONTH (in rands). SPECIFY IF NONE. IF NO MONEY SENT BACK, SKIP NEXT TWO QUESTIONS.	
Minimum	0
Maximum	800
Mean	345
Median	300
Note: N = 236.	

How is this money sent back?	
Post	19
Other people	62
Self	12
Bank transfers	6
Note: N = 494.	

If yes, who do you send this money to? (DO NOT READ) OPTIONS	
Parents	56
Grandparents	3
Spouse	26
Children	10
Sister, brother	3
Other family	1
Other non-family	1
Note: N = 484.	

Approximately what value of goods do you send back? IF NOT APPLICABLE, PLEASE INDICATE.	
Not applicable/no amount given	97
R0–R100	2
R101–R500	1
>R500	–
Note: N = 313.	

If yes, whom do you send these goods to? (In order of importance)	1st choice*	2nd choice**	3rd choice***
Parents	1	24	4
Grandparents	45	1	28
Spouse	3	20	17
Children	31	37	30
Sister, brother	12	15	9
Other family	8	3	11
Notes: N = 183. N = 87. N = 46.			

How do you send these goods back?	
Freight	7
Formal transport by land	27
Formal transport by rail	2
Private transporter	62
Other	2
Note: N = 170.	

INDEX

A

African migrants 5, 18-20, 168-95
    attitudes to South Africa 177-84
    future plans of 188-90
    immigration policy and 188-9, 190-3
    profile of 171-7
    surveys 268-91
    see also migrants; immigrants; non-citizens
age 226
    African migrants 172-3, 269
    Lesotho 38, 39
    long-term migration and 154
    Namibia 113
    Zimbabwe 78
agricultural workers 17
    Mozambique 51
Aliens Control Act (1991) 2, 196
amnesty, for undocumented migrants 202-3, 254
    (1995) 16
    (1996) 21
    Namibia 96
anti-immigrant action, attitudes towards (South Africa) 204-6
apartheid 1, 19, 20, 21, 87, 88, 177
asylum seekers 175
attitudes 57-9, 60-2, 102-12
    African migrants 178-82, 184-8
    international 201
    Lesotho 36-44
    Mozambique 62-4
    Namibia 112-16
    South Africa 6, 9-10, 178-82, 197-219

B

borders 8, 31-2, 106-108, 229-30
    African migrants 189, 273
    colonial 25
    Lesotho 25-6, 42-3
    Mozambique 62-4

Namibia 116-117

C

census figures 17, 18
citizenship 102-6, 153, 252, 254, 270, 288
    African migrants 172, 270, 288
    Lesotho 43
colonial borders 25
Commonwealth 72
community 226
    impact of migration on 139-41
conditions (in South Africa)
    African migrants 282, 283, 284, 285, 286
    overall 282-3
contract migration 13-16
    amnesty and 202
    figures for gold mines 15
    Mozambique 46, 50-1, 67-8
cost of living 237
crime 59, 74, 180, 181, 191, 227, 238
cross-border migration *see* migration
cross-border trade 73-4

D

dependents 289
deportation 96, 286
    African migrants 175-6, 188
    attitudes towards (South Africa) 200-2
    Mozambique 52
destination 29, 233, 250-1
    African migrants 268, 270
    gender and 126, 131-2, 142
    Lesotho 39
    Namibia 114-115
diseases 59-60, 75, 229, 239
documentation 233, 243, 259
    African migrants 175-6, 275, 276, 287
    illegal 50-1
    Mozambique 55-6, 66
    Namibia 95-6
Draft Green Paper on International Migration (1997) 3, 143, 145-9, 191
Draft Protocol on the Facilitation of Movement of Persons in the SADC 3

dwelling 263-4
    African migrants 268, 288

E

Economic Structural Adjustment Programme 72-3
education 261
    African migrants 172-3, 289
    by gender 126-7
    Lesotho 39
    long-term migration and 155-6
    Namibia 114
    Zimbabwe 78-9
Employment 29-30, 56-7, 95, 159-61, 229, 233-4, 237, 244, 250, 253, 262
    African migrants 173-4, 270, 274, 278-80
    Lesotho 39-40, 43-4
    Mozambique 66
    Zimbabwe 79

F

family 28, 164-6, 226, 233
    African migrants 276, 277
    attitudes to migration 241
    impact of migration on 139-41
    Lesotho 38
food 236
free movement 112
    African migrants 289
freedom 239
Freedom Charter 32
Frelimo 47
friends 28, 164-6, 226, 233
    gender and 139-40
Froneman Commission of Inquiry into Foreign Bantu 18

G

gender 269
    African migrants 269
    long-term migration and 154-5
    Namibia 116
    see also women migrants

grandparents 226, 275
Greater Lesotho 32-3, 44
Gun War 32

H

health care 238, 253
home country
    attitudes to migration to 255-6
    impact of migration on 139-41
    links with (African migrants) 177-8
    perceptions of 257-9
    reason for return to 31, 40-1, 94-5, 235
    return to 273, 278, 282
home ownership, Namibia 115
household status 261, 273, 290
    by gender 125-6
    Lesotho 38, 39
household status, Namibia 116
housing 237, 253
human rights 191
Human Sciences Research Council (HSRC) 6

I

illegal immigrants, 244-5, *see also* undocumented migrants
illegal legals (Mozambique) 51-2
IMF 48, 72
immigrants
    attitudes towards (South Africa) 9-10, 206-8
    South African policy on 147
    see also African migrants; migrants; non-citizens
immigration legislation 76, 196
immigration policy 3, 8, 101-11, 287-9
    African migrants and 184-89, 190-3, 288
    apartheid 1, 2
    education and 153
    gender and 141-8
    international 201
    Lesotho 44-5
    long-term migration and 166-7
    Mozambique 62-4, 66-9
    Namibia 105-7
    South Africa 9-10, 75-6, 198-206

South African attitudes and 213-16
selective 203
Zimbabwe 83-4
impact of migration 227-8
African migrants 184-5, 284
gender and 139-41, 142
South African attitudes to 208-9
income 263
African migrants 174, 290
Namibia 113
source of 279-80
incorporation 112, 230-1
informal crossing points 82
informal migration 17-19
interviews *see* methodology

J

job preferences 161
gender and 137-8
jobs *see* employment

L

labour exploitation (Mozambique) 68-9
land 236
language 28-9, 226
African migrants 269
legal status 268, *see also* documentation; illegal migrants
Lesotho 8, 25-45, 191
compared with South Africa 158-62
family history of migration 12-13
field workers for research 220
research strategy for 221
living conditions 237
location *see* destination

M

Maputo Corridor 68
marital status 260
African migrants 290

    by gender 124-5
    Lesotho 43
    long-term migration and 156
    Namibia 116
    Zimbabwe 78
media 2, 217, 260
methodology 3-5, 6-7, 123, 197-8, 219-24
    African migrants 170-1
    challenges to 168-9
    communications 223-4
    data analysis 223
    field workers 220
    Lesotho 26-7
    Mozambique 53
    Namibia 89
    number of interviews 225
    number of (African migrants) 268
    planning workshop 219
    primary sampling units 197-8
    questionnaires 219-21
    sampling strategy 220-3
    snowball sampling 171-2
    Zimbabwe 76-7
migrant labour *see* contract migration
migrants
    action against 204-6
    African 5, 18-19
    numbers of 18, 19, 74
    perceptions of 2
    professionals 74
    profile of (African migrants) 2-3, 77-9, 90-3, 116-17, 153-6, 171-8
    South African policy on 146-7
    unskilled 74
    see also African migrants; immigrants; non-citizens
migration 7-8
    attitudes to (African migrants) 57-9, 102-12, 184-8
    behaviour and gender 129-34
    by gender 124-7
    circular nature of 8
    concerns about 59
    decision-making and 61, 96-8, 165-6, 241-41, 276-7
    degree of permanence of 35-6, 43-4
    difficulties 275
    factors discouraging 245-7
    family history of 12-13
    from South Africa to 34

future 5, 64-6, 98-102, 151-67
gender and 142
historical overview 3, 12-24
internal (Namibia) 116-17
likelihood of 65, 98-102, 103-4
long-term 152-3
pan-African 8
patterns of 121
perceived impact of 58, 98, 99
permanence of (Mozambique) 64-5, 66, 67
reasons for (African migrants) 94-6, 96-8, 184-8; (gender and) 141-2
socio-economic indicators 124-7
to other SADC countries 93-4, 232
to other countries 270
see also contract migration; informal migration; refugee migration; white settler migration
migration networks 177, 176, 235
migration typologies (Mozambique) 50-3
mine migrancy, *see* contract migration
miners (Lesotho) 38, *see also* contract migration
modes of entry *see* transport
Mozambique 46-70
    amnesty for undocumented migrants 202
    compared with South Africa 158-62
    demography 49-50
    economy of 47-9
    family history of migration 12-13
    field workers for research 220
    methodology 53
    research strategy for 221
    surveys 54-64

N

Namibia 86-118
    attitudes to migration and immigration policy 102-16
    economic activity 115-16
    field workers for research 220
    historical background to migration in 87-9
    likelihood of people moving to South Africa from 98-102, 103-4
    methodology 89
    migration to South Africa 90-3
    migration to SADC countries 93-4
    research strategy for 222-3
Namibian War of Liberation 88

Napier Boundary (1843) 25
non-citizens
    attitudes to 206-8
    contact with 209-10
    number of in South Africa 168
    rights of 33-4, 64, 108-12, 185-8, 204, 252-4, 287
    see also African migrants; migrants; immigrants
NRC 14

P

parents 176, 226, 275
pass laws 1
passports 28, 37, *see also* documentation
peace 238
perceptions of South Africa 236-41
    gender and 138, 142
permanent residency 153, 242, 252, 254, 288
    application for 1995 amnesty 16
PLAN 88
population, profile of sample
    Lesotho 27
    Mozambique 54
    Namibia 90
    Zimbabwe 77
population, statistics (Mozambique) 49-50
Portuguese settlers 47
public education 9-10, 214-16
public opinion 7, 196, 200

R

race 106, 113
    and attitudes to migrants 199, 212-14
Refugee Act (1998) 3, 53, 175
refugee migration 20-1, 175, 180
    Mozambique 52-3
    South African policy on 147
remittances 29-30, 234, 251
    African migrants 178, 291
    gender and 137, 138
Renamo 47
rights, for non-citizens *see under* non-citizens

S

SADC 72, 82, 83
    amnesty for undocumented migrants 202
    attitudes to (Namibia) 116-17
    migration to 93-4
    visitors to South Africa 2
SADF 88
safety 238
schooling 238, 253
sexual abuse 181-2
shopping 38, 239
snowball sampling 170-1
South Africa
    attitude to anti-immigrant action 204-6
    attitudes of African migrants to 178-84
    attitudes to foreigners 180-1, 206-12
    attitudes to deportation 200-2
    attitudes to immigrants and immigration policy 6, 9-10, 198-208
    attitudes to legalising undocumented migrants 201-2
    attitudes to right for non-citizens 203
    attitudes to selective immigration policy 202
    compared with home country 157-61
    expected treatment in 248-9
    impressions of 274, 278
    information on 274
    knowledge of 243-4
    overall conditions in 282-3
    special treatment expected from 153-4
    satisfaction with (African migrants) 182-3
    treatment in 280-1
Southern African Development Community *see* SADC
Southern African Migration Project (SAMP) 3
sovereignty (Lesotho) 32-3
status in South Africa, African migrants 267
stereotypes
    of African migrants 2-3
    of migrants 7, 9, 74-5, 83
    of migration 7, 8
    of perceived impact of migrants 209
    of potential migrant 123, 153, 156-8
    women migrants and 135
surveys 225-66
    African migrants 267-91
    Human Sciences Research Council (HSRC) 6-7
    interviewer's questions 264-6

Lesotho 26
Mozambique 54-64
public opinion 7
Zimbabwe 77-83
see also methodology
SWAPO 88
SWATF 88

T

TEBA 14, 38
transport/travel 28-9, 95, 232, 243-4
    African migrants 174-5, 275
    gender and 136
    Lesotho 37
    Mozambique 55-6
    Zimbabwe 80-2

U

undocumented migrants
    action against 206
    attitudes to 200-8
    attitudes to legalising (South Africa) 202-3
    gender and 135
    Mozambique 51-52, 68-9
    Namibia 96, 117
    numbers of 52, 75, 96, 168
    Zimbabwe 75
Union of South Africa 32

V

violence 2, 74, 204-5, 217
visits to South Africa
    demographic breakdown (Mozambique) 54-5
    factors related to (Lesotho) 36-7
visits, frequency of 27-8, 93, 131-2, 231, 251
    African migrants 176, 275, 286
    Zimbabwe 80-2
visits, length of 35-6, 93, 131-3, 231, 251
    African migrants 176-7, 271, 286
    Zimbabwe 80, 81, 82

visits, reasons for 30-1, 57, 135-6, 232
    African migrants 277, 284-6
    Lesotho 37-9
    Zimbabwe 82-3
voluntary refugee repatriation programme 21
voting rights 253

W

wage labour (Mozambique) 48-9
water 236
white flight 19-20
White Paper on International Migration (1999) 3, 7, 216
white settler migration 19-20
WNLA 14
women migrants 5, 17-18, 19, 119-50, 192
    African migrants 171-2, 185
    economic and social aspects of 135-9
    factors influencing 127-9
    friends in South Africa 138-9
    harassment of 181-2
    immigration policy and 141-8
    impact of migration on 139-41, 142, 185
    international context 120-2
    job preferences 137-8
    Lesotho 38, 40
    logistics of 133-5
    marginalisation of 122
    migration experience of 141-3
    obstacles for 133
    patterns of movement 129-33
    perception of South Africa 138, 142
    profile of 141
    remittances 137, 138
    Zimbabwe 71-85
    see also gender
work, *see* employment
World Bank 48, 72

X

xenophobia 2, 9, 74, 179, 210-12

Z

Zimbabwe 71-85
    compared with South Africa 158-62
    economy of 72-6
    family history of migration 12-13
    field workers for research 220
    methodology 76-7
    research strategy for 221
    surveys 77-83

⑤ 26, 31, 32, 33, 35, 39

T.C. 39